John Updike's
Human Comedy

MODERN
AMERICAN
LITERATURE
New Approaches

Yoshinobu Hakutani
General Editor

Vol. 43

PETER LANG
New York • Washington, D.C./Baltimore • Bern
Frankfurt am Main • Berlin • Brussels • Vienna • Oxford

Brian Keener

John Updike's
Human Comedy

Comic Morality in *The Centaur*
and the Rabbit Novels

PETER LANG
New York • Washington, D.C./Baltimore • Bern
Frankfurt am Main • Berlin • Brussels • Vienna • Oxford

Library of Congress Cataloging-in-Publication Data

Keener, Brian.
John Updike's human comedy: comic morality in the centaur
and the rabbit novels / Brian Keener.
p. cm. — (Modern American literature: new approaches; v. 43)
Includes bibliographical references and index.
1. Updike, John—Humor. 2. Humorous stories, American—History and criticism.
3. Updike, John—Characters—Harry Angstrom. 4. Angstrom, Harry (Fictitious character)
5. Middle class men in literature. 6. Comic, The, in literature. 7. Updike, John. Centaur.
8. Mythology in literature. 9. Updike, John—Ethics. 10. Ethics in literature.
I. Title. II. Series: Modern American literature (New York, N.Y.); v. 43.
PS3571.P4Z744   813'.54—dc22   2004006665
ISBN 0-8204-7090-2
ISSN 1078-0521

Bibliographic information published by **Die Deutsche Bibliothek**.
Die Deutsche Bibliothek lists this publication in the "Deutsche
Nationalbibliografie"; detailed bibliographic data is available
on the Internet at http://dnb.ddb.de/.

© 2005 Peter Lang Publishing, Inc., New York
275 Seventh Avenue, 28th Floor, New York, NY 10001
www.peterlangusa.com

Printed in Germany

To my mother,
Anne M. Keener,
also a lover of literature and laughter

CONTENTS

ACKNOWLEDGMENTS

I want to thank three scholars for their guidance and encouragement, particularly in the early stages of this project: Joan Richardson and N. John Hall of the City University of New York Graduate Center and my brother, Frederick M. Keener. Thanks to Lowell Scheiner for proofreading the final version of this book, to Bob Cermele for his computer expertise, and to Lily Lam for assisting me in myriad ways. Thanks to the City University of New York and to the Professional Staff Congress for a grant to help support the preparation of this manuscript, and to two colleagues from the English Department at New York City College of Technology, Juanita But and George Guida, for encouraging me to apply for this grant. Finally, thanks to my family, especially Tonya, for their moral support.

I would also like to thank the following for their permission to reprint from the following works:

From THE CENTAUR by John Updike, copyright ©1962, 1963 by John Updike. Used by permission of Alfred A. Knopf, a division of Random House, Inc.

From THE CENTAUR by John Updike (Penguin Books 1966) Copyright © John Updike, 1966.

From RABBIT, RUN by John Updike, copyright © 1960 and renewed 1988 by John Updike. Used by permission of Alfred A. Knopf, a division of Random House, Inc.

From RABBIT, RUN by John Updike (Penguin Books, 1964) copyright © John Updike, 1960, 1964.

From RABBIT REDUX by John Updike, copyright © 1971 by John Updike. Copyright renewed 1999 by John Updike. Used by permission of Alfred A. Knopf, a division of Random House, Inc.

Also, I want to note that my introduction's epigraph, quoting Updike, is from an interview by Jane Howard entitled "Can a Nice Novelist Finish First?" in *Life* magazine, November 4, 1966, page 82.

· INTRODUCTION ·

UPDIKE'S COMIC WORLD

"The comical is always the mark of maturity."
— KIERKEGAARD, *Concluding Unscientific Postscript*

"It seems to me that critics get increasingly querulous and impatient for madder music and stronger wine, when what we need is a greater respect for reality, its secrecy, its music. Too many people are studying maps and not enough are visiting places."
— UPDIKE

The comedy in John Updike's most important fiction—*The Centaur; Rabbit, Run; Rabbit Redux; Rabbit Is Rich; Rabbit at Rest,* and "Rabbit Remembered"—depicts a comic world and its morality. Critics, however, have not recognized the extent and importance of this comedy, viewing it as peripheral or mere comic relief. In this introduction, I briefly survey this criticism, provide a taxonomy of Updike's comedy, and review the themes and concerns of traditional comedy. Then, after explaining my focus on *The Centaur* and the *Rabbit* novels as Updike's richest works, I devote a chapter to each novel to show that an awareness of the importance of the comedy in these works results in a better understanding of them and resolves a number of problems. Finally, I locate Updike's comic morality within traditional American literature by linking it to Emersonian transcendentalism.

Essentially, critics have seen Updike primarily as a writer of high seriousness, concentrating on exploring, for example, theological and philosophical aspects of his work. Alice and Kenneth Hamilton, in *The Elements of John Updike* (1970), the first book-length critical study, view Updike as a "teller of parables" (248). William R. Macnaughton, in his "Introduction" to *Critical Essays on John Updike* (1982), describes "the learned, humorless study by the Hamiltons" as "both illuminating and irritating. Consciously setting out to prove that

Updike has 'something to say' they emphasize their Christian quasi-allegorist theory until one sometimes forgets that Updike is a maker of fiction" (13). In *John Updike: Yea Sayings* (1971), Rachel C. Burchard notes comedy in Updike's novels but slights its importance: "There are hilarious moments [. . .] but the undercurrent of meaning is anything but comic. The bulk of Updike's work is earnest portrayal of people whose business is the serious business of life" (6).

Larry Taylor's *Pastoral and Anti-Pastoral Patterns in John Updike's Fiction* (1971) sees Updike's central theme as the depiction of "the pastoral and anti-pastoral in our time" and describes *Rabbit, Run* as "a type of fable with satiric overtones" (87). Robert Detweiler's *John Updike* (1972), focusing on Updike's technique and its relationship to his themes, states that "Updike had limited his use of humor to his poetry and *Assorted Prose*," reserving "for his fiction a certain wit often more cynical than comic" (1). Joyce Markle, in *Fighters and Lovers* (1973), detects humor in *The Centaur; Rabbit, Run; Rabbit Redux; The Poorhouse Fair; Of the Farm*, and *Couples*, but she considers this comedy as antithetical to Updike's serious vision: "The comic and the serious often seem to coexist dialectically in Updike's work; the major characters often struggle against insignificance, against perhaps the acceptance of a comic rather than a serious world" (169).

Edward Vargo, in *Rainstorms and Fire* (1973), views Updike's novels as demonstrating the need for ritual in contemporary life and the realization of the "sacral" universe but argues that because of "a failure of vision" the "material clutter overwhelms the transcendent"(102). George Hunt, in *John Updike and the Three Great Secret Things: Sex, Religion, and Art* (1980), briefly notes Updike's humor: "Several of Updike's novels are funny indeed, and humorous incidents are found even in his most sober fiction" (6). Hunt, however, does not pursue this observation further except for noting the depiction of the Kierkegaardian "humorist" in the short story "The Astronomer." Suzanne Henning Uphaus, in *John Updike*(1980), observes, "The common theme behind Updike's writing is the profound religious searching that grows from this despair, a quest in which doubt fights desperately with faith" (5).

Donald J. Greiner, in *John Updike's Novels* (1984), offers a detailed analysis of *The Centaur* and the first three *Rabbit* books but does not touch upon Updike's comedy. Judie Newman, in *John Updike* (1988), calls attention to the responsiveness of Updike's fiction to social developments in modern America. In *The Fiction of Philip Roth and John Updike* (1985), George J. Searles contrasts Roth's comedy with Updike's: "While Roth is completely at ease with—and remarkably skilled at—broad, burlesque farce and roisterous slapstick, Updike's humor runs more to witty repartee and intellectualized parody, the type of humor that characterizes his light verse. But low comedy is not his forte" (159). Ralph C. Wood, in *The Comedy of Redemption: Christian Faith and*

Comic Vision in Four American Novelists (1988), includes Updike as "a parabler of comic redemption" despite the fact that Updike is "the hardest case to make" (283). Although he makes some pertinent points regarding Updike's comedy, Wood's perspective is essentially theological.

As their titles indicate, three critical studies focus on aspects of Updike's work other than his comedy: Dilvo I. Ristoff's *Updike's America: The Presence of Contemporary American History in John Updike's Rabbit Trilogy* (1988); *Rabbit Tales: Poetry and Politics in John Updike's Rabbit Novels*, edited by Lawrence R. Broer (1998); and *John Updike and Religion*, edited by James Yerkes (1999). *Rabbit Tales*, however, does contain essays by Charles Berryman and James J. Waldmeir that perceive comedy in *Rabbit Is Rich*. Both James A. Schiff, in *Updike Revisited* (1998), and William H. Pritchard, in *John Updike: America's Man of Letters* (2000), in providing overviews of Updike's work, note comic scenes in the series, with Pritchard mentioning that Rabbit's viewpoint "becomes increasingly humorous and ironic" (54). Marshall Boswell, in *John Updike's Rabbit Tetralogy* (2001), exploring the writer's "mastered irony," asserts that the tetralogy "paints a two-sided, ambiguous vision of America" that confounds critics looking for "a unified, coherent critique" (236–37). Finally, in a stimulating 1975 essay, "Updike's American Comedies," Joyce Carol Oates points out Updike's "basic clownishness, that seems to go largely unnoticed in his writing, but which gives it its energy, its high worth" (67). Defending Updike as a writer of substance, Oates says that "it is far more difficult to do what Updike does. Like Caldwell/ Chiron, he accepts the comic ironies and inadequacies of ordinary life" (68).

Updike's comedy may be classified as farce, burlesque, and irony. In his essay "Comedy and the Comic Spirit," Robert W. Corrigan quotes Samuel Johnson's observation that "comedy has been particularly unpropitious to definers" (4). Nevertheless, definitions in *The Princeton Encyclopedia of Poetry and Poetics* offer a starting point for classifying Updike's comedy. *The Princeton Encyclopedia* defines farce as that which "exploits the surprise of sudden appearance or disclosure, the mechanism suggested by many physical actions, repetition, gross exaggeration of character, and so on." Farce "may pursue its laughter into a world of fantasy, where the unpredictable, even the impossible is commonplace" (271). In *The Centaur*, farce is evident in the surrealistic description of the bizarre classroom episode in the first chapter and in the carnivalesque scene with the Dionysian beggar. In "Rabbit Remembered," Nelson recalls how the family unceremoniously left the urn with Rabbit's ashes in a motel on their return to Pennsylvania after the funeral.

The Princeton Encyclopedia describes burlesque as "incongruous imitation and deflationary treatment of serious themes for satiric purposes" (88). Updike's burlesque, however, is not distancing as satire is; rather, it is sympathetic to humanity, undercutting pretension and vanity to establish a person's proper place in the world. Updike has vigorously maintained that he does not write satire in his novels: "You cannot be satirical at the expense of fictional characters because they're your creatures. You must only love them" ("One Big Interview" [519]). V.C. Clinton-Baddeley observes: "Caricature and burlesque exhibit all distortions and exaggerations whatever but under this discipline—that they purpose that way to get closer to essential truth" (5). Venus' burlesque of the gods (Zeus becomes a "lecherous muddler" [25]) and Caldwell's disdain for the local "aristocrats" ("*Make Nero look tame*" [189]) reveal the truth beneath the pretense. Caldwell, however, burlesques himself as well by means of his mismatched clothes and comic behavior. His son, Peter, points out, "He was always bringing junk like this home as if burlesquing his role of provider" (48). Caldwell caricatures the incompetent dentist as "Dr. Yankem," but as his former teacher he accepts the blame for the man's deficiencies. In *Rabbit Is Rich*, Rabbit burlesques Brewer's business and political leaders: "How can you respect the world when you see it's being run by a bunch of kids turned old?" (275).

The Princeton Encyclopedia defines irony as a device by which a writer expresses a meaning contradictory to the stated or ostensible one. Both verbal and dramatic irony are evident in Updike's fiction. In *The Centaur*, Zimmerman/Zeus warns his mistress: "You overestimate my omnipotence" (163). In *Rabbit Is Rich*, after Rabbit finds himself unexpectedly paired with the plain Thelma rather than the glamorous Cindy, he learns a great deal from the experience. In regard to Updike's comedy, W. H. Auden's distinction in the essay "Don Juan" is pertinent: "Satire would arouse in readers the desire to act so that the contradictions disappear; comedy would persuade them to accept the contradictions with good humor as facts of life against which it is useless to rebel" (388).

From my research in the criticism and theory of comedy, I have drawn upon a number of sources. Especially useful in describing comedy's general nature and concerns have been William F. Lynch's *Christ and Apollo*, Edward L. Galligan's *The Comic Vision in Literature*, Joseph Meeker's *The Comedy of Survival*, George McFadden's *Discovering the Comic*, Northrop Frye's *The Anatomy of Criticism*, Wylie Sypher's "The Meanings of Comedy," Robert Bernard Martin's "Notes Toward a Comic Fiction," and James Feibleman's *In Praise of Comedy*. In each Updike novel, I have found subtle depictions of Frye's idyllic "green world" as well as of the pharmakos figure mentioned by a number of critics. Robert W. Corrigan's anthology, *Comedy: Meaning and Form*, contains a wealth of pertinent criticism: Corrigan's own essays, "Comedy and the Comic Spirit" and "Aristophanic Comedy: The Conscience of a Conservative"; Susanne K. Langer's "The Comic Rhythm"; Nathan A. Scott's

"The Bias of Comedy and the Narrow Escape Into Faith"; Martin Grotjahn's "Beyond Laughter"; and L.J. Potts' "The Subject Matter of Comedy." I have drawn upon Edith Kern's *The Absolute Comic*, with its explication of Bakhtin, for an understanding of carnivalization. In Freud's *Jokes and Their Relation to the Unconscious*, Soren Kierkegaard's *Concluding Unscientific Postscript*, and F.M. Cornford's *The Origin of Attic Comedy*, I have discovered valuable information regarding the importance of comedy in Updike. In particular, Kierkegaard's morphology of the spheres of human existence has helped frame my study.

In comedy, life appears absurd, uncertain, contradictory, and frustrating: "We have, in short, been forced to admit that the absurd is more than ever inherent in human existence: that is, the irrational, the inexplicable, the surprising, the nonsensical—in other words, the comic" (Sypher 195). Kierkegaard writes: "The comical is present in every stage of life [. . .] for wherever there is life, there is contradiction, and wherever there is contradiction, the comical is present" (459). According to Martin, "Prudence then becomes irrelevant because man's essential existence is not led in a prudential world" (80). Comedy focuses on the everyday and the commonplace: "Lynch argues that the comic mode is the most finite, most concrete, least magical, least univocal of the modes of the literary imagination" (Galligan 24). Moreover, "Tragedy deals with the past, and by inference with the future, with a timelessness. But comedy's concern is with the present" (Feibleman 28).

For Galligan, "time and change" are seen "as cyclical and unthreatening. Progressions—of seasons and generations—matter in comedy; progress does not" (34). William McCollom indicates the importance of society as the setting for comedy: "In contrast to tragedy, comedy directs itself toward those levels of mind and feeling concerned not with perilous moral choices made in isolation from others but with the steps or leaps taken, the adjustments made, the routines rehearsed, and the chance encounters in an endless variety of social settings from family to committee room to carnival" (VII). Frye observes that "the theme of the comic is the integration into society which usually takes the form of incorporating a central character into it" (*Anatomy* 43). The comic hero accepts his role in time and society; in contrast, the anti-comic "meticulous man" attempts to isolate himself from everyday reality (Lynch 108). According to Lynch, "The one offense, therefore, which comedy cannot endure is that a man should forget he is a man, or should substitute a phony faith for faith in the power of the vulgar and limited finite" (105).

The Princeton Encyclopedia describes the central values of comedy as "the ability to adjust, common sense, and humility, or a clear-eyed sense of one's relationship to others" (145). Martin describes comedy as "that genuine quality embracing sympathy, tolerance, acceptance, even celebration of the human condition, imperfect as it is" (78). McFadden finds that comedy "encourages us to face commonplace reality and live with it" (166). Meeker, discussing Dante's *The Divine Comedy*, avows that the poet is presenting "an image of human adaptation to the world and acceptance of the given conditions without escape, rebellion, or egotistic insistence upon human centrality" (187). Meeting his familial and societal responsibilities requires that the comic hero sacrifice himself. McFadden alludes to Coleridge's insight that within the comic character there tends to be "an absence of effective self-interest" (35). For McFadden, this negation of self-interest "presents a vision of the hollowness of mere selfishness, of calculating motives, and of their disproportion to 'the godlike within us'" (35). By accepting his obligations, the comic hero matures. As Kierkegaard points out, "The comical is always the mark of maturity" (250).

The comic hero is a developing character. According to Kenneth Burke, comedy "considers human life as a project in 'composition,' where the poet works with the material of social relationships" (173). Langer underscores the comic hero's vitality: "This human life-feeling is the essence of comedy. It is at once religious and ribald, knowing and defiant, social and freakishly individual" (123). Skeptical of orthodoxy and authority, the comic hero learns from experience that is often bewildering and humiliating. Martin Gurewitch elaborates: "Humor seeks, not to expunge folly, but to condone and even bless it, for humor views folly as endearing, humanizing, indispensable" (9). The univocal—whether expressed by pretension, habit, or pedantry—is ridiculed: "unincremental repetition, the literary imitation of ritual bondage, is funny" (*Anatomy* 168). To which Frye adds, "one feels that the social judgment against the absurd is closer to the comic norm than the moral judgment against the wicked" (163). Sypher notes the ubiquity of doubleness throughout comedy: "comedy is built upon double occasions, double premises, double values" (213). Doubleness characterizes the comic hero as well. According to Frye, the comic hero is "ordinary in his virtues, but socially attractive" (44); essentially passive, he, nevertheless, proceeds uninhibited by decorum or conventionality. The comic hero develops double vision: "the comic perception comes only when we take a double view—that is, a human view—of ourselves, a perspective by incongruity" (Sypher 255). His experience reflects the survival of the species: "the truest and the most accurate form of comedy and laughter: this song of indestructibility, the song of the indestructibility of the people" (Lynch 107).

Essentially, comedy reveals truth. By challenging conventionality and the status quo, comedy reveals a deeper, more human reality: "On the surface, comedy, with its antipathy to the order of things, seems anarchic. [. . .] But it is not at all anarchic: it is only a defender of another and more human order (more muddy, more actual, more free). Metaphysically, it is a defender of being against the pure concept of category" (Lynch 114). A number of theorists mention a device called the comic discussion. McFadden describes its function: "The essence of the discussion is that it tests and sorts things out but changes nothing radically; it shows up situations and characters for what they are" (35).The alazons, or impostors of traditional comedy, are liars, though as Frye points out, "it is more frequently a lack of self-knowledge than simple hypocrisy that characterizes them" (172). The reasonable eiron enlightens them: "In the course of the comic debate (between the alazon and the eiron), the supposed wisdom of the alazon is reduced to absurdity and the alazon himself becomes a clown" (Sypher 228).

By disclosing truth, comedy reaches Martin's congruity beneath the incongruity (86) and Lynch's "power of rock-bottom being" (108). The happy ending of comedy reflects this faith and hope: "The function of comedy is to sustain hope" (Galligan 28). Still present in modern comedy are its ritual origins "that we celebrate in reverence for the vital generative forces that enable us to survive and be happy" (McFadden 159). According to Galligan, "comedy plunges in to discover that when we wholly submit to it the finite itself generates the insight we need" (26). For the Christian Updike, the transcendent exists within the quotidian. Lynch refers to "the centrality of the *finite concrete* as the only healthy and effective path to whatever has always traditionally been regarded as the goal of the human imagination or, for that matter, of the total human personality. It does not matter whether we call that the infinite or peace or insight or maturity" (99–100).

Why would a writer as artful as Updike include so much comedy if it were not significant? Updike has stated that in all of his books the essential question is: "What is a good man?" or "What is goodness?" ("One Big Interview" [502]). I think that his comedy illustrates the limitations of existence and elucidates how human beings can come to a mature apprehension of themselves and others. McFadden, in *Discovering the Comic* (1982), cites Charles Mauron's *Psychocritique du genre comique:* "To Mauron, comedy is one of the defenses against anxiety, one of the most important in the whole sphere of play and the arts; and these, he believes, constitute the chief aids (along with love and procreation) in our maturation" (153). Reflecting the link that exists among comedy and love and procreation, Updike's eponymous hero, Rabbit Angstrom, defines the purpose of life: "'Have a few laughs,' he offers. 'Have a few babies'" (*Redux* 194). In Updike's fiction, characters are mature when they recognize the comic nature of the human condition and yet accept their own place in it. They do not distance themselves from humanity's follies by retreating or escaping into egotism, fantasy, or pedantry. Updike's characters are most fully human when exhibiting a conscious willingness to cross back and forth over the boundaries between rationality and irrationality, conventionality and outrageousness. George Caldwell, in *The Centaur,* is Updike's paragon, but the shrewd Charlie Stavros, in *Rabbit Is Rich*, expresses this perspective succinctly: "Being crazy's what keeps us alive" (90). In maturing, the individual advances from the isolation of Kierkegaard's aesthetic sphere to the ethical, where one lives for others.

An understanding of the function of comedy in expressing Updike's morality will help answer two related critical questions: does Updike have anything of substance to say and why, as critics such as Vargo have wondered, does the everyday world dominate his fiction to the exclusion of the transcendent? In regard to the latter criticism, Richard Duprey's comment is pertinent: "Great comedy is the result of keen observation of the world" (244). Perceiving the extent of Updike's use of comic elements and understanding them in the context of their connection to questions about goodness also help explain one of the most conspicuous features of Updike's work: his almost constant preoccupation with religion. In a mid- and late-twentieth century world view, a comic attitude seems perhaps the most appropriate stance. Sypher states that "The modern hero lives amid irreconcilables which, as Dostoevsky suggests, can be encompassed only by religious faith—or comedy" (196). Finally, Updike has claimed that "I cannot imagine being a writer without wanting somehow to play [. . .] to insert [. . .] secrets into my books" ("One Big Interview" [499]), and this study will disclose a number of these secrets.

Analyzing Updike's comic morality, I focus first on *The Centaur*. Many critics regard this novel, winner of the National Book Award in 1964, as Updike's outstanding work. This novel, with its merging of the mythic and the realistic, its disjunctive narration, and its surrealism, is Updike's most puzzling; at the same time, with its emphasis on tradition and learning, its focus on art and religion, and its breadth of vision encompassing evolution and the pagan and Christian worlds, it is also his most profound. In "One Big Interview," Updike describes this autobiographical novel as his "gayest and truest book" (500). Given its extraordinary scope and variety, *The Centaur* provides the underpinning for the other novels, and that, as I have suggested, its comedy expresses its profundity.

Next, I analyze how comedy expresses the morality in the *Rabbit* novels. Updike's devoting four full-length novels to chronicling the life of Rabbit Angstrom (as well as a postmortem novella) indicates the centrality of this series in his work. Nor does Rabbit's ordinariness diminish the series' importance. Updike has stated: "Today either everyone is a hero or no one is. I vote for everyone" ("One Big Interview" [518]). The books depict the America of, respectively, the conformist 1950's, the turbulent 1960's, the complacent 1970's, and the problematic 1980's and thus provide a social history of these decades following the post-war 1940's of *The Centaur*. Finally, "Rabbit Remembered" takes the series through the high-tech 1990's and into the new century as Rabbit's son, Nelson, illustrating the succession of the generations, replaces his father as comic hero. Overall, through an analysis of Updike's comedy, my study will reveal a dimension of this writer's fiction that is essential to understanding his work. In doing so, I hope that my work will contribute to a greater awareness of the significance of comedy as a dominant and informing genre.

· 1 ·

THE COMIC PARAGON AND
THE METICULOUS MAN
IN *THE CENTAUR*

*"The mortals have the joy of struggle, the satisfaction of com-
passion, the triumph of courage; but the gods are perfect."*

*"And the man that has anything bountifully laughable about him, be sure there is
more in that man than you perhaps think for."* — MELVILLE, *Moby Dick*

*T*he Centaur chronicles three days in the lives of George Caldwell, a
public school science teacher, and his fifteen-year-old son, Peter, in
1947 Pennsylvania. Updike, in the manner of Joyce limning 1904
Dublin in *Ulysses*, details the experiences of father and son in their rural home,
the Olinger high school, and a variety of other locales, including the luncheonette after-school hangout, Doc Appleton's office, and a seedy downtown
hotel. At the same time, the novel transcends realism. As in *Ulysses*, all of the
characters have mythic correspondences: Caldwell is Chiron, "noblest of all
the centaurs"; the proud Peter, with his "fiery" red shirt, Prometheus; a raving
drunk clad in motley, Dionysos; the lecherous, domineering principal Zimmerman, Zeus; Deifendorf, an unruly student and member of the swimming team,
at different times appears as a centaur, a merman, and even Hercules; and so
forth. Throughout, *The Centaur* alternates realistic passages with surrealistic
ones, which likely represent Peter's dreams ("In that way we have in dreams,
where we are both author and character, God and Adam" [159]).

The disjunctive narration also contributes to the novel's complexity. Peter
narrates four of the nine chapters, with the others told in the omniscient third

person. Moreover, the use of the synchronic blurs the distinction among the past, present, and future. Partly because of the incongruous effect of merging the mythic, realistic, and surrealistic as well as because of the antics of Caldwell, the undercutting of authority figures, and the bizarreness of characters and situations, the novel's mood is zany. Yet the plights of father and son remain serious. Plagued by poverty, numerous physical ailments, disruptive students, the overbearing "gods" of the town, worries that he will lose his job and be unable to support his family, and the fear that he has cancer, Caldwell is a modern-day Job; for his part, the adult Peter despairs over his unfulfilled life.

In the opening chapter, an apparent nightmare of Peter's dramatizes Caldwell's trying existence. As the teacher lectures in front of the class, a student wounds him with an arrow. Overwhelmed by pain, the centaur flees the boisterous classroom, taking refuge at Al Hummel's (Hephaestus) nearby garage. Upon returning to his classroom, he finds to his dismay that one of the local gods, the principal (Zimmerman/Zeus), has chosen this day for an unannounced "visitation." While Caldwell struggles to finish his lesson, rowdy students disrupt the class with scuffles and antics. The second chapter, as a counterpoint to the previous chapter's depiction of Caldwell at work, portrays his home life. Inside the Caldwells' dilapidated farmhouse, both the love and the tensions within the family are apparent. Peter overhears his parents discussing Caldwell's concerns about his health and job; the family's poverty and hardships frustrate Cassie (Ceres), planted in the isolation of the countryside; Caldwell teases his sententious father-in-law, Pop Kramer (Kronos); Peter rues his psoriasis, daydreams of a glorious future as a successful artist, and competes with his father for his mother's attention. Nevertheless, as the adult Peter avers, all in all their life "was good" (57). On the way to school, however, after a loathsome hitchhiker (Hermes) steals the elder Caldwell's new gloves, Peter senses his father's death as "a grave and dreadful threat" (73). Abruptly, the idyllic third chapter provides a contrast with the raucous first chapter by presenting Chiron teaching the respectful "princely children of Olympus" the Greek mythic version of the creation: "And Love set the universe in motion" (78).

The fourth chapter relates Caldwell's after-school travails: counseling dull students, suffering the torment of Zimmerman's ambiguous official observation report, visiting the patronizing Doc Appleton for a physical examination, and coaching the inept swimming team in a losing meet at the YMCA. Peter, after spending the afternoon at Minor's (Minos) luncheonette ("It was a maze, Minor's place" [91]) with his girlfriend, Penny, and the "tall criminals" who frequent this teenage lair, and passing the early evening at a downtown movie, meets his father for the journey home. The breakdown of their aged car, however, thwarts their plans. Aimlessly wandering the frigid streets of the nearby city of Alton, they chance upon a raving drunk. From this bizarre episode,

Caldwell recognizes the urgency of immediately locating shelter for Peter and leads him to a hotel. Without explanation, Chapter Five consists entirely of an honorific newspaper obituary for Caldwell. The sixth chapter depicts Peter, Prometheus-like on his rock, tortured by a hallucinatory collage of threatening images, including the exposure of his humiliating psoriasis and a future when his father is forgotten by the local community.

In Chapter Seven, Caldwell, remaining after school to grade exams and to investigate the mystery of missing basketball tickets entrusted to him, surprises the officious school board member, Mrs. Herzog (Hera), leaving Zimmerman's office after a tryst with the principal. Scorned by the haughty woman, the dejected teacher fears that this unlucky encounter will result in his dismissal from the faculty. That night, however, at the high school game, after Peter discloses to Zimmerman his father's apprehensions, the principal astounds Caldwell by assuring him that his job is safe. Afterwards, Caldwell questions the arrogant Reverend March (Mars) about faith, but the clergyman, more interested in the charms of Vera Hummel, rebuffs him. Later, on the Caldwells' way home, fate changes their plans again. This time their ancient Buick becomes stuck in a blizzard when they are unable to fasten snow chains to the tires. The chapter ends with their trudging to the shelter of the Hummels' house, Caldwell shielding his son from the storm.

Chapter Eight depicts Peter awakening in the cozy Hummel home to find school closed and his father already out gathering information about the snowstorm. After Hummel attaches the chains to their car, father and son arrive home to a hero's welcome and the joyful news that Caldwell's x-rays are negative. A relieved Peter, weakened by the three-day ordeal, gratefully retires to his bed with a fever. The next morning, from his bedroom window, he watches his restless father make his way through the snow toward their car. The final chapter depicts Chiron/Caldwell readying himself for a merciful death, which will end his suffering. Gradually, however, he recognizes that a "change" is not in store for him: "There would be none" (221). Instead, his fate is to continue living in order to sustain his family. In an epilogue, Zeus rewards the centaur by setting him among the stars as the constellation Sagittarius.

The Centaur portrays a good man in a comic world. Describing his own father as the inspiration for this novel, Updike writes, "For fifteen years I'd watched a normal, good-doing Protestant man suffering in a kind of comic but real way" ("One Big Interview" [500]). With clowning and joking, George Caldwell acknowledges life's absurdity and uncertainty; at the same time, he accepts his place within the human comedy as family man, teacher, and dutiful member of the community. Unlike his dreamy son, Peter, who lives in a glorified past and a vaguely grandiose future, Caldwell inhabits the problematic present. Although beset by doubts, he personifies the humble Christian, who lives his faith daily. In the morphology of Kierkegaard, Caldwell represents the "humorist" poised on the final boundary between the "ethical" and "religious" spheres of existence. The epigraph from Karl Barth reflects Caldwell's position: "Heaven is the creation inconceivable to man, earth the creation conceivable to him. He himself is the creature on the boundary between heaven and earth." George Hunt (although he does not apply Kierkegaard's morphology to *The Centaur*) characterizes the "humorist":

> Each of these spheres has a boundary-line which can be crossed only by a "leap," i.e., a decision to renounce the former sphere and embrace the next; it is the "leap of faith," the decision to entrust one's life to God in faith, that bridges the boundary between the ethical and the religious. The "humorist," then, is one who stands before this final boundary but does not cross it. He is sympathetic with the follies of the human comedy (Aesthetic) and aware of the limits of moral effort (Ethical) and, though he is attracted to religious commitment (Religious), he seeks a way out of it. He is called a humorist because in his situation he is very cognizant of the contradictions of life, the basis of all humor; as a result he retreats to the shared laughter and acknowledged foibles of common humanity rather than confront the highly individual demands that faith requires. (25)

Within this context, Caldwell's unconventional behavior becomes fathomable. His humor stems from his awareness "of the contradictions of life"; his tolerance for outcasts like the drunk and the thieving hobo reflects his sympathy "with the follies of the human comedy"; his humility and self-deprecation result from his recognition "of the limits of moral effort." While the adult Peter remains ensnared within the aesthetic sphere, where the individual limits himself to personal satisfaction, Caldwell has attained the next level of existence, the ethical, where the individual lives for the benefit of others. Within the quotidian, the resilient and resourceful comic hero learns the value of self-sacrifice: "he discovered that in giving his life to others he entered a total freedom" (220). In the novel, Caldwell never attains the religious sphere of existence (although the Epilogue hints that he does so afterwards); instead, as the humorist, he "retreats to the shared laughter and acknowledged foibles of common humanity."

Throughout, *The Centaur* associates humor and laughter with the acceptance of one's "common humanity." Caldwell recalls his first meeting with the principal Zimmerman fondly because of their "shared laughter": "He had liked Zimmerman and had felt liked in return. They had shared a joke about Pop Kramer. He cannot remember the joke but smiles to remember that one was made, fifteen years ago" (151). With heaven "inconceivable," the comic hero Caldwell discovers meaning in the mundane: "Only goodness lives. But it does live" (220). His experience reflects the insight that comedy "descends dramatically through the varieties of the concrete to reach a rock-bottom reality and there discovers that life is good" (Galligan 24).

Nevertheless, although Caldwell dominates this novel as well as his son's imagination, finally this is Peter's book. He is the unfinished character trying to make sense of his unhappy life. An allusion to the Cumaen Sibyl (during one of Peter's dreams, in a jar he hears an ominous voice "saying with microscopic distinctness, 'I want to die. I want to die'" [128]) links Peter to *The Waste Land*. In *T.S. Eliot*, Frye notes: "Another story about the Cumaen Sibyl hanging in a jar between heaven and earth and waiting only to die, a most vivid image of the 'nightmare life in death,' which is Eliot's theme, is told by Petronius, and forms the motto of the poem" (66). Moreover, Updike subtly identifies Peter with Tiresias. Mythologically, Peter is both male and female (Prometheus and Ocyrhoe) and in both the realistic and mythic worlds possesses the gift of prophecy (also, Prometheus means "foresight"). Frye continues, "*The Waste Land*, we are told in the notes, is a reverie of Tiresias," whose "hermaphroditic shadow-mind contains all the men and women who appear in it" (67).

Similarly, Peter is the sensibility of *The Centaur*. Vargo notes, "The entire novel is a fusion of the dreams and reveries and actual narration of Peter" (85). Like the inhabitants of *The Waste Land*, Peter, trapped within his own egotism ("that atrocious ego Peter Caldwell" [152]), despairs and contrasts his life with an idealized earlier time. In fact, however, Peter's memories reveal the past as problematic also. The comic world prevails no less in 1947 Olinger than in 1961 New York City. Even the teenage Peter's feelings toward his beloved father are ambivalent. Illustrating the rivalry between the generations, the young man competes with the older for love and attention. Essentially, the difference between Peter's unfulfilled adult life and George Caldwell's meaningful one is the son's failure to assimilate his father's morality. Years later, Peter seeks to comprehend the elder Caldwell's double vision: "My father for all his mourning moved in the atmosphere of such laughter. He would have puzzled you. He puzzled me" (201). Like Saint Peter, he requires an exemplar of faith. From his father's everyday heroism, Peter, like the inhabitants of *The Waste Land*, ultimately discovers the hope that exists within the quotidian.

The human comedy of *The Centaur* resembles Dante's *The Divine Comedy* not only in its range of style, which includes the colloquial and humorous as well as the loftiness of the idyllic Chapter Three, but also in its depiction of a journey that starts in misery and ends in happiness. Peter's mental odyssey, which begins in despair, concludes with the possibility of rebirth. His future after the novel's conclusion, however, remains uncertain. It remains to be seen whether Peter will ever mature or negotiate, in Kierkegaard's terms, the boundary between the aesthetic and ethical spheres of existence. Such an open-ended conclusion fits the nature of comedy. Distinguishing between tragedy and comedy, Susanne Langer describes the former as "a fulfillment, and its form therefore closed, final"; on the other hand, "Comedy is essentially contingent, episodic" (126).

Continually, *The Centaur* alludes to the problematic modern world: Caldwell's wry comment on the environmental havoc inflicted by war ("Then to win World War ll, we gouged all those battleships and tanks and Jeeps and Coke machines out of it" [36]); Peter's nightmare of Hitler as a "white-haired crazy man with a protruding tongue" (40) alive in Argentina; the clichéd cold-war rhetoric of Minor Kretz ("The Russkies'll be in France and Italy before the year's over" [153]); and the juvenile delinquent Johnny Dedman's rapture over the atom bomb ("I love that mushroom-shaped cloud" [154]). The novel's setting, post-World War II during the after-Christmas letdown when school resumes in January, contributes to the sense that, as Caldwell soberly remarks, "It's no Golden Age, that's for sure" (19). According to the younger Caldwell, Kretz's "black Republican stupidity and stubborn animal vigor embodies everything in the world that is killing Peter's father" (154). The teenager Dedman (Daedalus), with his police record and his talent for "all the meaningless deeds of coordination, jitterbugging and playing pinball" (96), personifies the rebellious adolescent subculture of the period.

The mechanic Hummel's plight during the transition between war and peace reflects the individual's economic precariousness. With "everything mass-produced" and "Mobilgas moving in and now the rumor was Texaco too" (19), the squeezed independent small businessman finds himself an anachronism. Intellectually and spiritually as well, the individual experiences alienation. Serious for once, Caldwell admits his desperation: "Everything. The works. I can't make it add up" (188). When the science teacher washes the blackboard, his "long rhythmic swipes shaped like sideways 8's" (87) suggest the Einsteinian universe. Feibleman observes, "The pursuit of comedy always flourishes during periods of excessive unrest and change, troubling times" (30). Characteristically, however, Caldwell jokes about these troubling times: "When do you think the Russians will reach Olinger? They're probably getting on the trolley up at Ely now" (158).

Yet, *The Centaur,* contrary to the critical consensus, does not neatly contrast a glorious past with a grim present. Caldwell's reductive lecture on evolution describes man's origin as less than heroic: "'There are over two billion people in the world right now,' he said, 'and it all began around a million years ago when some dumb ape swung down out of a tree and looked around and wondered what he was doing here'" (32). Synchronically, the past repeats itself in the present: the student Deifendorf "began to scratch his scalp and armpit and make monkey chatter" (32). Lynch points out, "Comedy is perpetually reminding the uprooted great man that in some important sense he was once, and still is, a bit of a monkey" (104). In effect, modern man is no less confused than his simian ancestors. The mythic correspondences also emphasize that the world remains essentially the same. Venus philosophizes, "We all flow from Chaos" (28). Caldwell's identification with Chiron is pertinent: the centaur, not fully a god, must navigate among the capricious Olympians just as Caldwell does among the small-town gods of Olinger. In "One Big Interview," Updike explains, "It is part of Chiron's plight that he is living in a town full of gods, and he's not quite a god himself, hence this failure of communication all the time" (499).

Venus' lampooning of the gods brings them down to earth: "Your gods, listen to them—a prating bluestocking, a filthy crone smelling of corn, a thieving tramp, a drunken queer, a despicable, sad, grimy, grizzled, crippled, cuckolded tinker—" (26). Caldwell's harsh fate parallels Chiron's. Updike includes a passage from Josephine Preston Peabody's *Old Greek Folk Stories Told Anew:* "in the general confusion, Chiron, blameless as he was, had been wounded by a poisonous arrow." As with Chiron (also a teacher) at the wedding feast, Caldwell suffers his injury in an unlikely setting. Moreover, it is Peter who perceives the mythic within the mundane; Caldwell lives in the present, the everyday, and the finite—the domain of comedy. Updike has explained the use of the mythology as, among other things, a representation of "prototypes" in life as well as a source of humor ("One Big Interview" [500]). Mythic or mundane, the "gods" of the novel are characterized as pretentious, pedantic, and vain. *The Centaur* continually equates the past with the present. When Johnny Dedman, whining about his lack of opportunities, cites his "police record," Caldwell rejoins, "So did Bing Crosby. So did St. Paul" (156).

At once, *The Centaur* plunges the reader into the confusion, frustration, and absurdity of its world. Without explanation, an arrow pierces the teacher's ankle and the students revert to beasts, "leering and baying at the teacher" (9). "The confusion became unbearable" amid the carnivalesque "festal noise" (9). On Caldwell's flight down the corridor, he overhears "children's voices chanting French, singing anthems, discussing problems of Social Science" (9). In his panic, the words blur: "*Avez-vous une maison jolie? Oui, j'ai une maison tres jolie* for amber waves of grain, for purple mountain majesties above the fruited plain throughout our history boys and girls (this was the voice of Pholos), the federal government has grown in prestige, power, and authority" (9–10). Apparently now four-footed, he defecates like a beast in front of the school trophy case; at the garage, the mechanic Hummel/Hephaestus, as if repairing a machine, uses a blowtorch to remove the projectile from Caldwell's ankle. Characters change back and forth from mythic and realistic identities. Taking a shortcut through the basement on his return to class, suddenly Caldwell turns into Chiron recalling an embarrassing chance encounter with a naked Venus (the gym teacher Vera Hummel) emerging from the swimming pool. Saucily, the goddess entices him: "'Horse,' she breathed, 'ride me. I'm a mare. Plough me.'" When the transfixed centaur hesitates, "Venus vanished into the underwood" (29).

Back in the classroom, chaos reigns. "Slyly pussyfooting" and with a "pantomime of whispers," Zimmerman, a carnivalesque trickster figure, incites the class to riot. Outrageously, the principal fondles "the milky" Iris Osgood (Io). Disruptive students release live extinct trilobites, which wear "partially unrolled condoms, like rubber party hats" (38); a student metamorphoses into a parrot and nonchalantly chews one of the insects; acne leaps from a face and blisters the wall paint; scuffles ensue; the din rises. When a student erroneously names "Venus" as the only star in the solar system, the class puns: "Venus, venereal, V.D. Someone clapped" (32). Ironically, as Caldwell lectures on evolution, the students regress to primitivism. Eventually, Caldwell loses patience and beats Deifendorf with the bloody arrow shaft, the alliteration of "bastard beast's bare back" (40) evoking the regression to an earlier period. In the midst of the uproar, the immense numbers that Caldwell writes on the board, such as "1,998,000,000,000,000,000, 000,000, 000" (33), have a dizzying effect. Afterwards, the alternation of realistic chapters with unexplained passages like the idyllic chapter depicting Chiron teaching, the premature obituary, and the nightmare-like sixth chapter keeps the reader off balance. Throughout, the novel's episodic structure creates a mercurial mood that suggests anything is possible.

Mysteries abound. Caldwell identifies the first evidence of life as "Corycium enigmaticum." He continues: "As the name suggests, this primitive form of life remains enigmatic"(36). In a school lavatory, Caldwell is "puzzled" by the transforming of a scribbled "FUCK" on the wall into "BOOK"; fearful that Peter has done this, "The mystery depresses him" (185). Not all of the missing basketball tickets are accounted for. After his medical examination, Caldwell informs Peter of the rumor that Zimmerman has fathered Doc Appleton's son, Skippy. When Peter inquires about Mrs. Appleton, Caldwell replies portentously, "Nobody knows where she went. She's either alive or dead." In turn, Peter finds his father "rich with mystery" (105).

Most perplexing are the mysterious "seeds" that possess a significance never made explicit. The janitor, Heller, shows Caldwell seeds found in his cleaning: "'One goddam more mystery,' my father said, and he seemed to shy, and we went out into the weather" (89). In fact, their unobtrusive presence among the janitor's sweepings indicates the cyclic nature of life. These humble seeds recall the mythic pomegranate seeds of Persephone, Ceres' daughter and Hades' (Heller) reluctant wife, that symbolize the cycle of death (causing the centaur's mortal equine nature to "shy" in fear) and resurrection. Despite his forebodings, however, Caldwell continues on "into the weather." Near the end of the novel, as the dejected Caldwell agonizes over his life, he ponders the fundamental human mystery of one's own particular fate: "how could his father's seed, exploding into an infinitude of possibilities, have been funnelled into this, this paralyzed patch of thankless alien land, these few cryptic faces, those certain four walls of Room 204?" (221). At the same time, he remembers his responsibility for his own child, "his one seedling" (219). His mood brightens, however, when he acknowledges the paradox of life evolving from death: "Yet even in the dead of winter the sere twigs prepare their small dull buds. In the pit of the year a king was born. Not a leaf falls but leaves an amber root, a dainty hoof, a fleck of baggage to be unpacked in future time" (219). Scattered about the comic landscape, these ubiquitous seeds, like the buried seeds of *The Waste Land*, imply the promise of rebirth.

Nevertheless, daily life remains unsettling. Caldwell laments, "Things never fail to fail" (149). On successive nights, the family car strands Caldwell and Peter. Their chaotic household, exemplified by its two clocks keeping different time, depresses Peter: "I wondered why some people could solve at least the mechanical problems of living while others, my people, seemed destined for lifetimes of malfunctioning cars and underheated toiletless homes" (203). Their poverty gnaws at him. When he irritably demands of his father, "Why *don't* we have any money?" Caldwell confesses, "I've been asking myself that for fifty years" (125).

During a blizzard, when Peter strains to attach chains to the mired car's tires, "a tiny gap" defeats him: "He prays; and is appalled to discover that, even when a microscopic concession would involve no apparent sacrifice of principle, matter is obdurate. The catch does not close. He squeals in agony, 'No!'" (195) These chains are as limiting as those of Prometheus. A fountain in the Alton Museum dismays the young Peter, for within it an "eternally expectant" statue of a woman thirsts for water that falls an "enduring inch" from her mouth. Peter insists that when the museum is deserted at night, the figure would somehow "reach the spray" (200). Peter's inability to bear life's frustrations reveals his callowness: instead, he daydreams about a life as a rich, glamorous New York painter ("my skin as smooth as milk as I painted, to the tune of great wealth and fame, pictures heavenly and cool, like those of Vermeer" [63]). Caldwell harbors no such illusions: "I don't know why the damned car doesn't move. Same reason the swimming team doesn't win, I suppose" (115).

Caldwell has learned to accept absurdities such as Zimmerman's assigning him, a nonswimmer, to coach the swimming team as well as discouragements like the team's lengthy losing streak. Sadly, "Cruelness is clever where goodness is imbecile" (105). At the same time, Caldwell knows that, when least expected, the sublime—tantalizingly—may suddenly appear. During another losing meet, one of the Olinger divers inexplicably executes an almost perfect dive, which produces startled cheers from both teams. On his next attempt, however, with the crowd expecting a repeat performance, the boy tenses and flops entering the water: "And when Danny surfaced this time, my father, and only my father, clapped" (110). Like the inhabitants of *The Waste Land*, Peter finds glimmers of hope depressing. Reading two articles in *Reader's Digest*, "Miracle Cure for Cancer?" and "Ten Proofs That There Is a God," he is "disappointed, more than disappointed, overwhelmed—for the pang of hope roused fears that had been lulled" (206).

The science teacher Caldwell, however, recognizes that fact is often stranger than fiction: "Leptothrix [. . .] a microscopic fleck of life [. . .] fantastic as it seems, existed in such numbers that it laid down all the deposits of iron ore which man presently mines" (36). Caldwell, though he characteristically rants ("'I wouldn't mind plugging ahead at something I wasn't any good at,' my father said, 'if I knew what the hell the point of it all was. I ask, and nobody'll tell me'" [102]), nevertheless continues "plugging ahead" anyway. Synchronically, his experience in the chaotic classroom during his lecture on evolution reenacts early man's precarious survival: "'One minute ago, flint-chipping, fire-kindling, death-foreseeing, a tragic animal appeared—'The buzzer rasped; halls rumbled throughout the vast building; faintness swooped at Caldwell but he held himself upright, having vowed to finish.'—called Man'" (40). Earlier, Caldwell's chalk had "chipped" (33); during the class "the kids were catching fire" (34) (the image alluding to Prometheus as well); as a centaur, his bottom half is animal; and throughout he remains acutely conscious of death. Just barely, he keeps himself "upright" in a way that resembles early man's achievement in standing erect. The chapter's triumphant final words, "called Man," evoke his surname: "Caldwell."

In such a world, nothing may be taken for granted. Ironically, as the prescient Peter foresees, the rambunctious Deifendorf eventually becomes a teacher like Caldwell. When Peter encounters him on an Alton side street fourteen years later, Deifendorf wears "a saggy brown suit from whose breast pocket the pencils and pens thrust as from my father's pocket in the old forgotten days" (81). The succession of gods depicted—Kronos, Zeus, Dionysos, Christ—suggests the inherent flux of life. Even within the idyllic Chapter Three, life does not remain static. Chiron's daughter, Ocyrhoe, "claimed to foresee a day when Zeus would be taken by men as a poor toy they had themselves invented, and be terribly taunted, be banished from Olympus, sent scrambling down the shingle, and branded a criminal" (77). Moreover, Chiron perceives an ominous sign when a black eagle appears ("But on *his* left" [77]). Yet, while death hovers over Caldwell, there are only two deaths in the novel

(McFadden observes that "there cannot be much peril or toilsome adventure in great comedy" [41]). One is a reference to a former student who, as a flight instructor, is killed in a training accident. This young man (Achilles), returned safely from World War II, "bright and respectful and athletic and handsome,"dies unexpectedly while the weary Caldwell, desirous of death, lives on. Caldwell underscores the paradox: "Isn't that funny? To go all through war without a scratch and then get nailed in peacetime" (167).

The other death depicted also emphasizes the uncertainty of life. Kierkegaard's *Concluding Unscientific Postscript* contains a passage describing an illustrative incident whose similarity to an occurrence in *The Centaur* is uncannily revealing. Kierkegaard is describing the "subjective existing thinker" who with his "double reflection is as sensitive to the comic as to the pathetic" (81). He then cites an incident from Lucian in which Charon recounts a story of a man invited to dinner who accepts "definitely." Thereupon, the guest is killed by a falling tile. "And Charon comments, 'Is not that something to laugh yourself to death over?'" (80). *The Centaur* contains a corresponding scene. When father and son are forced to stay at a hotel in town, the night clerk, Charlie, identified with Charon, allows them to pay in the morning: "I guess we'll all still be here" (124). During the night, Charlie dies: "'It's a funny thing,' the new clerk said, without smiling at all. 'Charlie died last night'" (129). For Lucian, Kierkegaard, and Updike, life's uncertainty is comic.

While the Promethean Peter represents the tragic rebel straining against human limitations, his father personifies the comic hero who accepts his humanity. Caldwell appears ordinary, flawed, and foolish; at the same time, he is attractive, resilient, resourceful, playful, open to experience, and blessed with double vision. *The Centaur* identifies the fifty-year-old Caldwell with the middle ground of comedy: by nature, he is half man, half beast and both human and divine; the Barth epigraph situates man on "the boundary between heaven and earth"; mythologically, "it was rumored that Zeus thought centaurs a dangerous middle ground" (26); Zimmerman describes Caldwell as "a teacher in the middle of his career" (186); Caldwell loves the cities "of the great Middle Atlantic civilization" (112); at novel's end, Caldwell estimates his chances of freeing his Buick from a snow bank as "fifty-fifty" (220). These odds refer to his own survival, for throughout he is identified with his car as, for example, in Peter's insight that "Now it occurred to me he had an 'attack' and the inexplicable behavior of the car was in fact an illusionistic reflection of some breakage in himself" (115). Within Kierkegaard's morphology, Caldwell inhabits the ethical state midway between the aesthetic and the religious.

A scientist, Caldwell understands the individual's humble place in the universe. The current geological era, the Cenozoic, "began seventy million years ago" (84). Caldwell's self-deprecating humor reveals his humility: "One nice thing about having a simple mind, you can only think of one pain at a time" (106); "He could read at terrific speed, and claimed never to learn or remember a thing" (49). To Peter's shame, his father looks ridiculous: "He had on his overcoat, a tattered checkered castoff with mismatching buttons, which he had rescued from a church sale, though it was too small and barely reached his knees. On his head he wore a hideous blue knitted cap that he had plucked out of a trash barrel at school. Pulled down over his ears, it made him look like an over grown dimwit in a comic strip" (53).

Caldwell at times behaves foolishly as well. Peter recalls a long-anticipated trip to New York City, where they had planned to visit the Metropolitan Museum of Art, but "My father's blundering blocked it. [. . .] The strangers my father stopped on the street resisted entanglement in his earnest, circular questioning" (68). When the vile hitchhiker names short-order cook as his "profession" (Hermes had roasted cattle stolen from Apollo and the cook was one of the lowest stock alazon figures), Caldwell fulsomely praises him: "You *cook*! That's a wonderful accomplishment" (66). Insensitively, Caldwell blurts out to this coarse stranger the secret of Peter's embarrassing psoriasis: "He has a terrible skin problem" (71). Caldwell is flawed in other ways as well. His wife hints at a lack of passion in their marriage: "'If there's anything I hate,' my mother said, half to me, half to the ceiling, while my father bent forward and touched her cheek with one of his rare kisses, 'it's a man who hates sex'" (56). The repeated use of the word "half" indicates her double vision. Nor is Caldwell above self-pity: when the family learns that he does not have cancer, Cassie observes wryly, "Now he'll have to think up some new way of getting sympathy" (215).

Despite shortcomings, however, Caldwell personifies Frye's "socially attractive" (44) comic figure. Two female colleagues, Vera Hummel and Hester Appleton, are drawn to him. Even his rambunctious students celebrate Caldwell's charisma. In the terminology of McFadden, Caldwell's antics in the classroom achieve "anecdotal permanence" in which "what is funny may be grasped with enough directness to be recalled or retold" (11). At Minor's luncheonette, the teenagers congregated there relate "sweetly cruel memories" of the teacher:

"He used to lie down in the aisle and holler, 'Come on, walk all over me, you will anyway'. . ."
". . . about six of us filled our pockets up with horse chestnuts . . ."
". . . seven minutes to the hour everybody stood up and stared as if his fly was open . . ."
"Christ, I'll never forget . . ."
". . . this girl in the back of the class said she couldn't see the decimal point . . .

he went to the window and scooped some snow off the sill and made a ball . . . hard as hell at the fucking blackboard . . ."

"'Now can you see it?' he said."

"Christ, what a character."

"You got a great father there, Peter." (95)

By their mythologizing of a popular teacher (the horse chestnuts, an allusion to the centaur's equine nature), the students reveal their affection and respect for him. Subconsciously, their irreverent expletives associate the self-sacrificing Caldwell with Christ.

As the students' banter indicates, Caldwell has learned how to cope with adversity. Both in his mythic and realistic guises, the teacher is a survivor. The tumultuous classroom scene in Chapter One illustrates Caldwell's resiliency. In pain, he returns to the classroom; undercut by the mischievous Zimmerman ("Please behave, boys and girls, as if I were not present" [31]) and tormented by the students, he nevertheless manages to complete his lecture. When the cut-up Deifendorf responds curtly, "Caldwell disarmed his impudence by agreeing. He had been teaching long enough to keep a step or two ahead of the bastards occasionally" (34). Although not a disciplinarian, the resourceful Caldwell knows how to hold the attention of restive students: describing "These first cells who got tired of sitting around forever in a blue-green scum" as "the first altruists," the beleaguered teacher announces: "'If I had a hat on, I'd take it off to 'em.' He pantomimed doffing his cap and the class screamed" (37).

Caldwell expends himself for the sake of his family. Facetiously, he threatens Deifendorf: "I'll strangle you with my bare hands if I have to. I'm up here fighting for my life. I have a wife and a kid and an old man to feed" (79). Dealing with the Greek gods or the Olinger aristocrats, he has learned the art of diplomacy: "Politic, he had long ago made it his policy to ask of the gods only what he believed they could not help giving" (219). In his compromising meeting with Venus at the pool, the centaur recognizes his danger: "His position was difficult; he knew that the indulgent Zeus would never harm his young aunt. But he might, in annoyance, toss his bolt at her innocent auditor, whose Olympian position was precarious and ambiguous" (26). When the cruel goddess gratuitously insults him, he responds ambiguously: "a deferential rebuke if she chose to accept it; otherwise a harmless medical truth. His long survival had not been attained without a courtier's tact" (23–24).

The centaur's resourcefulness is evident in Olinger as well. The school board member Mrs. Herzog urges Zimmerman to fire the teacher, but the pragmatic principal defends Caldwell: "He stays in the room with them, which is the most important thing" (163). His colleague Phillips (and fellow centaur Pholos), although regarding himself as Caldwell's "guide," acknowledges his friend's superior ingenuity: "At the same time he cannot rid himself of an obscure expectation that Caldwell out of his more chaotic and mischievous resources would produce a marvel, or at least say the strange thing that had to be said" (167). When the blizzard at the end of the novel effectively shuts everything down, Caldwell lets Peter sleep while he makes his way around Alton to gather the latest news. Peter cannot help admiring his father: "I marvelled at all this information and imagined him gathering it, wading through snow banks, halting snowplows to question the drivers, running up and down raggedly heaped mounds in his too-small overcoat like an overgrown urchin." Impishly, Caldwell delights in this game: "He clenched and unclenched his hands happily as he gazed into this vision of confusion" (208).

Caldwell draws his strength from the quotidian. He prefers the company of the cafeteria workers and the janitor to that of the town's aristocrats: "A modest man, Caldwell was most comfortable in the under reaches of the high school. It was warmest there; the steam pipes sang; the talk made sense" (21). In the spirit of comic inclusiveness, he accepts everyone: dull students, bores like Doc Appleton, the mean-spirited Minor Kretz ("He's just fascinated by that kind of man, isn't he?" [160]), and even society's outcasts like the thieving hitchhiker and the drunken beggar. Essentially passive, he takes life as it comes. After he learns that he does not have cancer, Caldwell proclaims his faith: "I've always been lucky. God takes care of you if you let Him" (217). At the same time Caldwell remains alert to life's subtle revelations. His interaction with the drunk illustrates Caldwell's openness to experience and willingness to cross boundaries.

This scene is carnivalesque. The drunk is one of the trickster figures who, as Kern describes, "are the instigators of carnivalesque activities, whether Lords of Misrule, jesters, clowns, devils or saintly prophets" (117). Each of these guises fits him: in preposterously accusing the noble Caldwell of soliciting Peter for sex, he is a Lord of Misrule ("Shall we call the cops, kid? Let's kill this old nance, huh?" [121]); in his slap-stick buffoonery, he plays the jester and clown ("He waved his finger back and forth in front of his nose and peered at us roguishly through this wind-shield wiper action" [120]); his hypocritical willingness to abet pederasty ("I'll even tell you a hotel where they don't ask any questions" [122]), as well as his "sulphurous" breath, reveals his devilishness; and the revelation the drunk provides Caldwell indicates that finally he is a prophet. With his chameleonic nature, the drunk recalls that "Originally, Trickster was the name given to a clownish figure of mercurial unpredictability and changeability" (Kern 117). On first sight, Peter confuses him with the hobo Hermes: "For an instant I thought he was the hitchhiker, but this man was smaller and further gone in degeneracy" (120). Kern notes that "the trickster seems to be a direct descendent of Hermes the thief" (206).

The drunk's mythic correspondence is apt. Citing Huizinga, Kern notes that attic comedy developed from the "licentious *komos* at the feast of Diony-sus" (33–34). The drunk's "hair was wild like the mane of a muddy lion" (120), recalling Dionysos' disguising himself as a lion on one occasion. Furthermore, "God of wine and all reproductive forces in nature, Dionysos was also revered as the god of creative imagination and of theater in particular" (Kern 16–17). To hold their attention, the drunk stages a theatrical performance on the de-serted street: "his empty arms waved and bobbled around him as he pirouet-ted"; he "exercised an elaborate, pleased control over his intonation, like an actor marveling at his own performance" (120).

The drunk ("His face under the blue streetlight seemed splashed with pur-ple" [120]) is like all tricksters who "belong to the realm of fantasy and imagi-nation and are far from being mimetic" (Kern 207). His identification with the cycle of death and rebirth is indicated by his association with the ubiquitous "seeds" ("his teeth were set in his grin like a row of small seeds" [120]) and Caldwell's joke about a hotel named the Osiris (the Egyptian god whose death and resurrection symbolize the self-renewing vitality and fertility of nature): "The bedbugs got to be as big as the prostitutes so the customers couldn't tell them apart. I guess the Osiris was before your time" (122). Finally, the drunk's union of hardship and revelry depicts the duality of the god: "For all his rag-gedness on this bitter night there was much that was merry about him" (120). Kern observes: "In his ambivalence, the trickster seems to be of the very es-sence of the absolute comic and of farce, personifying in his own person the genre's proximity to laughter and tears" (205). This figure, according to Kern, is "almost always, in some form, a scapegoat" (206). Like Dionysos, the youth-ful drunk knows pain as well as pleasure. Alternating between mania and de-pression, tricksters like the drunk reflect the cyclic nature of life.

Predictably, the drunk's antics repel the Apollonian Peter; Caldwell, how-ever, perceives method amid the madness. Unlike Peter, who wishes to dis-tance himself from such lost souls, Caldwell recognizes his shared humanity with this pathetic figure. The drunk's insulting and coarse language ("Doesn't the old bastard feed you?" [121]) does not deter Caldwell. Within the carniva-lesque, "Speech and gesture were those of the market place: frank and free and disallowing any and all distance between those who came into contact with one another" (Kern 9). In the spirit of the absolute comic, the drunk's outra-geous behavior stems from "a conception of man's place in the universe quite different from that of so-called realism" (Kern 7). Thus, the drunk represents a deeper reality: "the trickster makes apparent the frailty of human existence and the proximity of laughter and tears" (Kern 208).

The drunk's carnivalization presents "a vision of man *sub specie aeternitatis*— quite in contrast to bourgeois notions of the individual's importance and his obligations to standards of propriety" (Kern 8). When father and son attempt to brush past him, the drunk almost takes a pratfall: "'Knock me down when I want to save your soul. Are you ready to die?' This made my father jerk still like a halted movie. The drunk, seeing his triumph, repeated, *'Are you ready to die?'*" (121). Although his breath, "both sulphurous and sweet" (reflecting his dual nature), repels Peter, the unexpected question arrests Caldwell: "'I wonder now if a ninety-nine-year-old Chinaman with tuberculosis, gonorrhea, syphilis, and toothache is ready to die. [. . .] No, Peter,' my father said, 'this gentleman is talking sense. Are *you* ready to die?' he asked the drunk. 'What do *you* think the answer is?'" (121). Like Elijah in *Moby Dick* warning Ishmael and Queequeg, the drunk's question *"Are you ready to die?"* resounds ominously. As usual, Caldwell, with the analogy of the "ninety-nine-year-old Chinaman," expresses himself jestingly, although the inclusion of a "toothache"—one of his own ailments—makes clear the identification with his own plight. Soberly, Caldwell recognizes how ordinary concerns pale in the light of mortality.

Kern notes, "Carnival was the true feast of time, the feast of becoming, change and renewal. [. . .] It laughed at rigidity and at the individual's exaggerated notion of his own importance, considering him but a link in the great chain of death" (11). Bizarrely, the pathetic drunk symbolizes man's place in eternity:

> He inflated his chest as if to shout, but the street dwindled northward toward infinity without upholding another visible soul—just the painted brick fronts with the little railed porches characteristic of Alton, the stone stoops now and then bearing an ornamented cement flower-pot, the leafless curbside trees alternating and in the end mixing with the telephone poles. Parked cars lined this street but few passed down it because it met a dead end at the Essick's factory wall two blocks away. (121–22)

Set against this stark background, the drunk looms as an existential figure. Like him, all human beings ultimately arrive at dead ends. Caldwell gives the beggar his last thirty-five cents and thanks him: "'You've clarified my thinking,' he told the drunk." The wretched state of the drunk (Peter is shocked to discover that "he was virtually a boy like me" [122]) reinforces Caldwell's sense of his son's vulnerability. Now he knows his destination: "That man brought me to my senses. We gotta get you into where it's warm. You're my pride and joy, kid; we gotta guard the silver. You need sleep" (123). From this comic discussion, sense emerges from nonsense: the older generation, before it passes away, must provide for its successor.

With his myriad obligations, Caldwell continually feels the pressure of time. Kern, distinguishing the comic from the tragic, cites Girard that "in the comic mode, the sovereignty of the individual is minimized to an extent that makes us aware of a hidden clockwork which controls him" (20). After the arrow is removed, the centaur hastens back to his classroom: "A clock in his head was ticking on; the school called to him urgently" (18). During the class, he races against time: "Caldwell looked at the clock. Five minutes left, and the main part of the story all before him" (37). At home, he hurries Peter to get ready for school: "I got to be there at eight. Zimmerman'll have my neck" (43). After Peter falls asleep at the hotel in Alton, his father, instead of resting, leaves the room to call Cassie, contact Hummel about the broken-down car, and even chat with a traveling salesman in the lobby because he thinks that the man might be helpful for Peter's career. Even within the pastoral Chapter Three, "Chiron hurried, a little late" (74).

Like Benjamin Franklin and Gatsby, Caldwell, driven to accomplish as much as he can in a limited period, organizes his time carefully:

> Nevertheless, among disintegrating surfaces he tries to hold his steadfast course.
> Hummel
> Call Cassie
> Go to the dentist   This is his program.
> Be here for game by 6:15
> Get in the car and take Peter home (149)

This ceaseless restlessness exasperates his wife and son. Peter reflects "that our family's central member, my father, had never rid himself of the idea that he might soon be moving on" (203). Caldwell's sense that time is running out emboldens him. Peter observes that reaching the age of fifty has made his father willing to cross boundaries: "Breaking the barrier had unbridled his tongue, as if, being in mathematical fact dead, nothing he said mattered. His ghostly freedom at times did frighten me" (46). In time, the comic hero recognizes that prudence is irrelevant in such a world.

Unlike the rigid and smug local gods, Caldwell retains a youthful open-mindedness and flexibility. Kierkegaard proclaims that the subjective thinker "is therefore never a teacher but a learner; and since he is always just as negative as he is positive, he is always striving" (78). Recalling Mr. Deasy's advice to Stephen Daedalus in *Ulysses*, Doc Appleton (Apollo), diagnosing Caldwell, informs him, "You're not a teacher. [. . .] You're a learner" (101–02). Charon, on his way to teach Achilles, Jason, and the others, distinguishes various herbs with "His student's eyes—for what is a teacher but a student grown old?" (74). During his theological discussion with Reverend March at the basketball game, Caldwell implores, "I'm trying to learn" (189). In Peter's eyes, his middle-aged father, despite the ravages of his harsh life, appears youthful.

When the car fails, Caldwell "looked up with a smile of sorts on his bumpy and battered urchin's face" (115).

The many dualities in the novel reflect the comic hero's double vision: approaching the mechanic, the wounded Caldwell experiences "a mocking sensation of walking toward a mirror, for Hummel also limped" (12); Doc Appleton and his sister, Hester, are twins; in Peter's eyes, his father and Deifendorf make a "sickening duet" (79); Peter at first mistakes the drunk for the hobo; because of his psoriasis, Peter takes care to dress in order that "my disguise as a normal human being was good" (45); Caldwell announces, "So when you say 'Pennsylvanian,' you can mean either a dumb Dutchman or a stretch of Paleozoic time" (38). According to Frye, "ambivalence is apparently the main reason for the curious feature of doubled characters which runs all through the history of comedy" (*Anatomy* 181). To Peter, Caldwell "seemed both tender and brutal, wise and unseeing" (53).

Settings in the novel convey life's dualism. At the farmhouse, "The downstairs was two long rooms, the kitchen and the living-room, connected by two doorways side by side" (48); two clocks keep divergent time; and there are two doors that to Peter appear a "double curtain" (49). Symbolically, an advertisement in Hummel's garage, picturing two eyes, warns of the need to guard one's sight. In town, Minor's Luncheonette "shared a brick building with the Olinger Post Office":

> There were two plate-glass windows side by side: behind one of them fat Mrs. Passify, the postmistress, surrounded by Wanted posters and lists of postal regulations, doled out stamps and money-orders; behind the other, wreathed in adolescent smoke and laughter, Minor Kretz, also fat, scooped ice cream and concocted lemon Pepsis. The two establishments were symmetrically set up. Minor's butterscotch-marble counter mirrored, through the dividing wall, Mrs. Passify's barred windows and linoleum weighing-counter. [. . .] The pinball machine and the cancellation machine were twins of noise [. . .] the symmetry, carried right through to the worn spots of the two floors and the heating pipes running along the opposing walls, was so perfect that as a child I had imagined Mrs. Passify and Minor Kretz were secretly married. At night, and on Sunday mornings, when their windows were dark, the mirroring membrane between them dissolved and, filling the unified brick shell with one fat shopworn sigh, they meshed. (89–90)

Peter's "mythy" imagination posits a relationship between Kretz and Mrs. Passify (King Minos' wife Pasiphae) because he cannot yet reconcile life's duality.

The experienced Caldwell, however, utilizes his double vision daily. Peter notes his father's dual nature: "My father for all his talk was at heart a man of silence" (112). When the manager of a garage cannot spare a mechanic to fix his car, the teacher nevertheless thanks the man profusely. Once out of earshot, however, Caldwell changes his tune: "I've been a bluffer all my life so I can spot another. He was what they call talking through your hat. [. . .] He acted just the way I feel half the time" (119). The phrase "half the time" indicates the doubleness of his perspective; the verb "acted" reflects his playfulness. When his inept dentist, clumsily pulling a sore tooth, blithely surmises, "This must have been giving you a great deal of pain," the suffering Caldwell deadpans, "Only when I noticed it" (165). Nevertheless, the teacher takes responsibility for "Dr. Yankem's" callousness because the dentist had once been a student of his: "Caldwell recognizes the pain branching in his head as a consequence of some failing in his own teaching, a failure somewhere to inculcate in this struggling soul consideration and patience; and accepts it as such" (164). According to Galligan, "The comic vision forces those who are faithful to it to acknowledge that they are themselves part of what they laugh at" (XII). Making light of his pain, Caldwell parodies, "Another day, another molar" (165).

Caldwell's double vision is especially apparent in his professional life. He refers to Olinger High as "the hate factory" and announces his departure for school by declaring, "The monsters are ready to learn" (217). He insists, "I love lies. I tell 'em all day. I'm paid to tell 'em" (42). His actions, however, belie his words. Despite the students' misbehavior and the stifling bureaucracy (Zimmerman's report faults Caldwell because "The humanistic values implicit in the physical sciences were not elicited" [86]), Caldwell remains a dedicated teacher. His lecture on evolution is erudite and inspired, he participates in extracurricular activities, and after school he willingly spends his free time tutoring the same students who torment him in the classroom. Coaching the grade-conscious but dull Judy Lengel for an exam, Caldwell presents the subject humorously: "It may interest you for your own information that the brontops looked a lot like William Howard Taft, who was President when I was your age" (85). When she fails to grasp the material, he reductively consoles her, "After Wednesday you can forget all about it and in no time you'll be married with six kids." Meanwhile, Peter realizes, to his "indignation," that before she leaves, "my father had hinted away to her the entire quiz" (85). Caldwell views education as "a jungle, an unholy mess" (151); at the same time, he gets to school early to be ready for class: "I left a whole mess of papers to correct" (43).

Caldwell's theatricality reveals a sense of life as play. When Hummel helps Caldwell dig out his car, "the two men enacted a pantomime with a wallet" (210); after school, "At the front entrance, Mr. Caldwell and Mr. Phillips meet on the steps and enact, one tall and one short, an Alphonse and Gaston routine" (166). This element is especially evident in Chapter Two. As Peter awakes, he overhears his parents' conversation: "He had a way of not speaking to her, but performing in front of her, as if there were an invisible audience at her side" (42). Afterwards, Caldwell teases Pop Kramer until his exasperated wife exclaims, "You can stop the performance any time" (46). Galligan observes that the image of play in comedy evokes "the possibility of treating even the most ordinary and serious of activities as though it were like play, free of worldly purpose, simply the utterly absorbing occasion for fun" (5). Caldwell even jokes about his greatest responsibility. Inside the house are numerous combs that Caldwell "had scavenged from the high school Lost and Found department. He was always bringing junk like this home, as if he were burlesquing his role of provider" (48). According to Clinton-Baddeley, "Burlesque serves truth, not with the bitterness of its tongue, but with the irreverence and deliberate impropriety of its laughter" (2). In truth, on his meager salary, Caldwell barely supports his family. His supplying the household with an abundance of "junk" underscores his difficulty in providing the basic necessities in "his role" as the family breadwinner.

Caldwell's playfulness is infectious. At times even Cassie cannot resist taking a part in the "familiar opacities of clownish quarreling" (41). Repeatedly, the self-deprecating Caldwell calls attention to his wife's theatricality: "If I'd been any kind of man I would have put her on the burlesque stage when she was young" (58). Pop Kramer performs a "trick" of tucking an entire piece of bread into his mouth. Staging this routine, "He moved with a pronounced and elaborate air of being inconspicuous that made us all watch him" (56). At home, even the self-conscious Peter, inspired by his father, enjoys playacting: "I was like my father in performing for an unseen audience, but his was far off and needed to be shouted at, whereas mine was just over the footlights. *Boy, clutching stomach comically crosses stage left*" (53). The members of the Caldwell family nourish and sustain one another with playfulness and humor. As an adult, looking back, Peter explains to his mistress: "And yet, love, do not think that our life together, for all its natural frustrations, was not good. It was good. We moved, somehow, on a firm stage, resonant with metaphor. [. . .] Yes. We lived in God's sight" (57).

Galligan, citing Lynch, elaborates on the significance of playfulness:

Absorption in the concrete and trust in the generative finite lead directly to full, innocent acceptance of the present moment, which is the essence of play. Hostility toward the univocal and celebration of the analogical mind and imagination compel one to respect witty, playful ways of thinking. Above all, an argument that the course of comedy is a descent below all the categories to rock-bottom reality, "which is profoundly and funnily unbreakable" is an argument that comedy is a call to play, an imitation to dance. (37)

At the end of the novel, when Peter and his father finally reach their farmhouse after their odyssey, the image of the "fire dancing" (213) in the hearth reinforces the sense of the Caldwells' home life as warm, vibrant, and good. According to Corrigan, "Comedy always ends in fusion and with a sense of social union" ("Aristophanic Comedy" [354]). The sense that life is fundamentally playful is evident in the antics of ordinary people like the drunk, the pinball wizard Johnny Dedman ("He played the machines as if he invented them," [96]), and the janitor, Heller, who makes sweeping the corridor a performance: "Here comes Heller down the annex hall! Twiddle, piddle; piddle, pat!! How the man does love his own broad broom!!!" (165). Within humble Olinger, nature and the cityscape create a theatrical effect: "The streetlights strung along the pike made a forestage of brightness where the snowfall, compressed and expanded, by the faintest of winds, like an actor postures" (179). This image of streetlights and snowfall combining to form a theater evokes the Shakespearean notion in *As You Like It* that "All the world's a stage" (2.7.141). Caldwell tells his colleague Phillips, "Phil, I don't know any other way to act. I'll have to act childish until they put the half-dollars over my eyes" (167).

In comedy, characters are most fully human when they recognize their inherent foolishness and refuse to take themselves too seriously. The clown Touchstone's paradoxical distinction in *As You Like It* applies: "The fool doth think he is wise, but the wise man knows himself to be a fool" (5.2.34–36). Humorless figures like Doc Appleton, Mrs. Herzog, and Reverend March are the true fools; unlike the gregarious Caldwell, these self-centered characters distance themselves from common humanity. Henri Bergson observes, "Any individual is comic who automatically goes his own way without troubling himself about getting into touch with the rest of his fellow beings" (147). Doc Appleton, as "the learned doctor," and March, a war hero and mythologically Mars, the god of war, as "the swaggering soldier," resemble stock alazon figures whom Cornford characterizes as "touched with some form of pretentiousness, swagger, conceit, which makes them ridiculous and incurs the irony of the hero-buffoon" (134). Venus describes Appleton/Apollo as an "unctuous prig" (25); Caldwell resists visiting the physician's office: "All he does, Pop, when I go to him, is brag about himself" (54); he and his twin, Hester ("She spoke of the gods with a certain authority, Miss Appleton did" [140]), are known for their "ill-humor" (146). Excluding himself, Appleton declares, "People are foolish" (104). Reflecting his single vision, Appleton exemplifies "that strange way monologuists have of ending a conversation as if *their* time had been wasted" (104).

In his obliviousness, Appleton resembles the aged Pop Kramer, another creature of habit, whose rigidity inspires Caldwell to sport with the old man: "'Yeah but Pop,' my father said, 'did you ever stop to think, does any man wait for time and tide?'" (52). Arthur Koestler describes creativity as "an act of liberation—the defeat of habit by originality"(96). Nevertheless, Doc Appleton, a conscientious general practitioner, remains a benign figure compared with the cold Reverend March and the haughty school board member Mrs. Herzog. Despite Updike's protestations, satire is evident in the depiction of these minor characters. Reflecting the limitations of her single vision, the pompous Herzog remains blind to her own foolishness. When Caldwell surprises her emerging from a tryst with Zimmerman, "her eyes widen behind her cockeyed butterscotch hornrims" (151). The adjective "cockeyed" indicates that her perspective is askew. After the embarrassed Caldwell blurts a joke to make light of this awkward encounter, the unamused woman's face "freezes the harder at this greeting." In a novel that celebrates humor (Vera claims, "In laughter her girlhood, her virginity is reborn" [178]), Mrs. Herzog is defined by her humorlessness: "She is customarily slow to see her own humor" (163). By contrast, her lover is witty. After she asks whether they should feel "guilty," the principal cynically replies, "Absolutely. Afterwards" (163).

Reverend March, however, lacks any sense of his place in life. He postures heroically: "Life is a hell but a glorious hell" (176). Like another clergyman in Updike's fiction, the sardonic Roger Lambert in *Roger's Version*, March represents the anti-comic meticulous figure who wishes to distance himself from an imperfect world: "This minister is a tall and handsome man with a bony brown face and a crisp black mustache fastidiously shaped" (175). In order to curry favor with the alluring Vera Hummel, March paints himself as the helpless victim of deluded parishioners:

> Her wet lips are framed to release laughter even before his jokes, indignant questions, are out. "Why does anything like this happen to me?" he sternly asks, slightly pop-eyed. "Why do all the ladies of my parish bake cupcakes once a month and sell them to each other? Why does the town drunk keep calling me on the telephone? Why do these people keep showing up in fancy hats on Sunday morning to hear me prattle about an old book?" (178)

March's self-serving satire excludes himself from life's comedy; the ludicrous reference to his sight ("pop-eyed"), however, reveals that, like Mim Herzog, his perspective is distorted.

A comic discussion between March and Caldwell illustrates the distinction between the meticulous man and the comic hero. When, during a basketball game, the despairing Caldwell urgently seeks the minister's counsel, March is appalled by "this preposterous interruption" of his flirtation with Vera. Irked, March attempts to flee "this tall tousled maniac" (189). When Caldwell persists, the clergyman loses patience and dismisses him: "'This is burlesque!' he shouts. 'A basketball game is no place to discuss such matters'" (189). Caldwell's burlesque, however, exposes March. Soon, the minister terminates the interview: "He firmly restores his attention to Vera, presenting to Caldwell a profile as handsome and final as if stamped onto an imperial coin" (189). As in all comic discussions, the truth emerges. The behavior of alazon-like March ("*Make Nero look tame, small town aristocrats*, Caldwell thinks" [189]) reveals that "Though his faith is intact and infrangible as metal, it is also like metal dead. He mocks it" (178). With all his doubts, Caldwell's faith is vital; in contrast, the smug clergyman's is lifeless. March's association with imperial Rome (the comparison with Nero, the allusion to his World War II battlefield exploits "in the hills above Rome," and "a profile as handsome and final as if stamped onto an imperial coin" [189]) suggests his paganism. His cynicism evokes the Roman soldiers' derision at the crucifixion. Paradoxically, it is the minister March who lacks faith: "He mocks it" (189).

Ultimately, however, the central dramatization of the dichotomy between the comic hero and the meticulous figure exists in the relationship between Caldwell and Peter. According to Frye, fiction contains a "comic" tendency to integrate the hero with his society and a "tragic" tendency that isolates him (*Anatomy* 54). As a child and as an adult, the son envies his father's vitality and gaiety. Langer identifies vitality with comedy: "The pure sense of life is the underlying feeling of comedy" (120); Galligan describes "that spirit of gaiety which permeates all comedy" (37). What the older Peter misses most from his childhood is his family's "white laughter that like heat lightning bursts in an atmosphere where souls are trying to serve the impossible" (201). The single-vision son, however, lacks his father's faith grounded in everyday life.

Repeatedly, Peter reveals his distaste for everyday reality. His propensity for dreaming is telling. Freud observes that dreams and jokes are related; the former, however, are private and the latter social. Peter dreams and his father jokes. Freud observes: "A dream is a completely asocial mental product; it has nothing to communicate to anyone else. A joke, on the other hand, is the most social of all the mental functions that aim at a yield of pleasure" (179). Symbolically, the teenage Peter's psoriasis (a condition he shares with the pedantic Doc Appleton) is "allergic, in fact, to life itself" (44). At the same time that his family's poverty shames him, he feels superior to "his fellow members" of the 4-H Club: "The dull innocence of some and the viciously detailed knowingness of others struck me as equally savage and remote from my highly civilized aspirations"(60). His snobbishness is apparent in his exasperation with the hobo: "I vividly resented that he should even speak of me to this man, that he should dip the shadow of my personality into this reservoir of slime. That my existence at one extremity should be tangent to Vermeer and at the other to the hitchhiker seemed an unendurable strain" (67). As an adult, Peter behaves like one of the local gods. Encountering the school teacher Deifendorf, now overweight and balding, Peter is disdainful: "He asked me, dared in all seriousness to ask me, an authentic second-rate abstract expressionist living in an East Twenty-third Street loft with a Negro mistress, *me*, if I was ever going to teach" (81).

Despite his bravado, however, Peter remains troubled. He thinks of his clergyman-grandfather and father and reflects, "Priest, teacher, artist: the classic degeneration." In bed with his mistress, "at the hour in the afternoon when my father and I would be heading home in the car" (201), he assesses his art and his life:

> I glance around at the nest we have made, at the floorboards polished by our bare feet, at the continents of stain on the ceiling like an old and all-wrong explorer's map, at the earnestly bloated canvases I conscientiously cover with great streaks straining to say what I am beginning to suspect is the unsayable thing, and I grow frightened. I consider the life we have made together, with its days spent without relation to the days the sun keeps and its baroque arabesques of increasingly attenuated emotion and its furnishings like a smattering of worn-out Braques and its rather wistful half-Freudian half-Oriental sex-mysticism, and I wonder, *Was it for this that my father gave up his life?* (201)

Peter's uneasiness stems from his estrangement from the quotidian ("life we have made together, with its days spent without relation to the days the sun keeps"). Unlike his father, whose life is ruled by time, Peter yearns to escape the limitations of the finite. Lynch stresses the importance of accepting one's place in time: "The withdrawal from the flow of time is such an escape from experience; the attempt to reject or to ignore any part of the temporal movement, to hold on too tightly to any part of it, produces not freedom, and not inviolability but a kind of slavery" (52). The cerebral Peter's art reveals his wish to stop "the flow of time." As a child, Peter had been attracted to art by what he perceived as its power to suspend flux: "It was this firmness, I think, this potential fixing of a few passing seconds, that attracted me, at the age of five, to art" (51). Such a viewpoint is anti-comic: "For it is simply not true to say that the function of all art is to immobilize time, to freeze into permanence some instant of peace or illumination so that we may have it forever and thus share in that quality of eternity that does not move but simply is" (Lynch 57).

Near the conclusion of the novel, the adolescent Peter vows "that I must go to Nature disarmed of perspective and stretch myself like a large transparent canvas upon her in the hope that, my submission being perfect, the imprint of a beautiful and useful truth would be taken" (218). In "Laughter," Bergson observes: "By organizing laughter comedy accepts social life as a natural environment—and in this respect it turns its back upon art which is a breaking away from society and a return to pure nature" (170–71). In contrast, Caldwell passionately rejects Cassie's suggestion that he retire from teaching and work their farm: "I hate Nature. It reminds me of death. All Nature means to me is garbage and confusion and the stink of skunk—*brroo!*" (216) Ultimately, Peter becomes "an authentic second-rate abstract expressionist." In *Just Looking: Essays on Art*, Updike observes, "Abstract Expressionism has the effect of glamorizing the painter, of making him, rather than the sitter or the landscape or the Virgin, the star" (115). According to Newman, "Peter uses art as an escape route from the ugly realities of the present, into the timeless" (83). The novel's use of the synchronic reflects Peter's predilection for what Lynch terms anticomic "simultaneity": "The term covers the impulse to pack the past and the future, indeed the whole of scattered being, into the present moment—thus to possess all things in a single instant and to demolish the narrow gates of both space and time" (48).

Peter's personal life is equally unfulfilling. His egotism isolates him. Peter's girlfriend, Penny, charges, "You're just so wrapped up in your own skin you have no idea what other people feel" (139). Like Reverend March ("Their value is not present to themselves, but is given to them by men" [177]), Peter uses women for ego gratification. As a teenager, Peter relishes Penny's willingness "to sacrifice" for him: "This was a fresh patch of paint in my life" (44). Significantly, Peter's black mistress remains unnamed and without individuality. He speaks at her, not with her; his recollections are for his own benefit, not hers. Asleep throughout, she functions as an objective correlative for Peter's unconvincing bohemianism. He loves her "mouth whose corners compress morally"; making love with her, he feels "radically confirmed." The references to "morally" and "confirmed" suggest that Peter is using his black lover to fabricate a morality for himself. Inevitably, he fails: "But I cannot quite make that scene. A final membrane restrains me. I am my father's son" (201). The self-conscious slang ("make that scene") betrays Peter's inauthenticity. In desperation, Peter looks not to the fabled glory of Greek mythology but to the comic reality of 1947 small-town Pennsylvania.

Caldwell's humble life serves as a model for Peter. Caldwell endures the pain of the social world in order to provide for his family: "My father provided; he gathered things to himself and let them fall upon the world; my clothes, my food, my luxurious hopes had fallen to me from him" (73). Caldwell's self-sacrifice ("*Was it for this that my father gave up his life?*" [201]) is illustrated by Updike's subtle depiction of the ritualistic humiliation of the comic scapegoat. C.L. Barber observes, "The pattern of all clowning involves, moment by moment, the same movement from participation to rejection that appears at large in scapegoat ritual. The artist gives the ritual pattern aesthetic actuality by discovering expressions of it in the fragmentary and incomplete gestures of daily life" (376).

The scapegoat is the pharmakos, the word a cognate of pharmacist, the profession of Chiron and the unrealized ambition of Caldwell. The father's empathy with the drunken beggar indicates his identification with this scape-goat figure. Dreaming, Peter imagines his father: "Face ashen, his father, clad in only a cardboard grocery box beneath which his naked legs showed spindly and yellowish, staggered down the steps of the town hall while a crowd of Olingerites cursed and laughed and threw pulpy dark objects that struck the box with a deadened thump" (159). McFadden states that "the characters of comedy became the successors of the pharmakoi, victims of humiliation, pun-ishment, and ridicule but happy in the assurance that they were helping to give continued fertility to the tribe" (158).

Upon learning that his painful life will continue, Caldwell nevertheless re-joices: "He thought of his wife's joy in the land and Pop Kramer's joy in the newspaper and his son's joy in the future and was glad, grateful, that he was able to sustain these for yet a space more" (220). Frye elaborates on the pharmakos' dual nature: "The pharmakos is neither innocent nor guilty. He is innocent in the sense that what happens to him is far greater than anything he has done provokes, like the mountaineer whose shout brings down an ava-lanche. He is guilty in the sense that he is a member of a guilty society, or liv-ing in a world where such injustices are an inescapable part of existence. These two facts do not come together; they remain ironically apart. The pharmakos, in short, is in the situation of Job" (41). In his nightmare,

> Peter understood that inside the town hall there had been a trial. His father had been found guilty, stripped of everything he owned, flogged, and sent forth into the world lower than the hoboes. [. . .] He tried to explain aloud to the angry townspeople how innocent his father was, how overworked, worried, conscien-tious, and anxious; but the legs of the crowd shoved and smothered him and he could not make his voice heard. He woke with nothing explained. (159)

Within this context, the perplexing last chapter may be seen as a dream of Peter's dramatizing the sacrifice of the pharmakos. Sypher describes the an-cient ritualistic "purging or catharsis" of "the scapegoat," who "was often the divine man or animal": "Behind tragedy and comedy is a prehistoric death-and-resurrection ceremonial, the rite of killing the old year (the aged king) and bringing in a new season (the resurrection or initiation of the adolescent king)" (216).

The "aged king," Caldwell, representing the older generation, dies for Peter, the "adolescent king." Kern notes, "But the punishment of the guilty son is usually death and the result tragedy, whereas the punishment of the guilty father is degradation and laughter—hence comedy" (25). Daily, Caldwell suffers his pharmakos "punishment" in the form of the "degradation" he endures amid the students' derisive laughter and the local gods' haughtiness. Rather than escaping to what Hester Appleton calls the "luxury" of death, Caldwell resigns himself to continue living: "Atropos had opened her shears, thought twice, smiled, and permitted the thread to continue spinning" (221). Reflecting comedy's double perspective, fate "thought twice" and "smiled." For years Caldwell has sublimated his own desires for the sake of his family. During the scene with the hobo, Caldwell fleetingly reveals a Rabbit Angstrom-like desire to "Bum around from place to place" (66) that he has never acted upon.

Sypher elaborates, "The rites may take the form of an initiation or testing of the strength of the hero or his fertility, perhaps in the form of a 'questioning' or catechism, after which there comes to him a 'discovery' or 'recognition'—an *anagnorisis* or new knowledge" (217). For Caldwell, the questions include "*Why do we worship Zeus?*" and "*What is a hero?*" with the answer, "A hero is a king sacrificed to Hera" (221). Caldwell learns that he will continue to be tested by having "again to maneuver among Zimmerman and Mrs. Herzog and all that overbearing unfathomable Olinger gang" (221). As the centaur agonizes, he has a revelation: "he discovered that in giving his life to others he entered a total freedom" (220). According to Sypher, linked to this ceremony "lies the myth of the primal union between the earth-mother and the heaven-father" (217). In *The Centaur*, "Mt. Ide and Mt. Dikte from opposite blue distances rushed toward him like clapping waves and in the upright of his body Sky and Gaia mated again" (220). Sypher continues: "Comedy, however, kept in the foreground the erotic action, together with the disorderly rejoicing at the rebirth or resurrection of the god-hero who survives his agon" (217).

Peter enjoys no such transcendence. Just as *The Waste Land*'s apparent fragmentation represents the confusion of its inhabitants, *The Centaur*'s disjunctive narration conveys Peter's ambivalence. The first-person narration indicates a desire to integrate himself into the quotidian, while the use of the omniscient third person reflects his proclivity for distancing himself from it. In his own terms, Peter cannot decide whether to be Adam or God. Like the inhabitants of *The Waste Land*, who must learn to give, sympathize, and control in order to live, Peter must transcend his own egotism in order to live a meaningful life. The union of sky and earth represents the fulfillment missing from Peter's life.

At the end of the novel, the "cliff edge" that Caldwell/Chiron approaches symbolizes the boundary line that separates Kierkegaard's spheres of existence. Before making the leap of faith, he "uttered the final word, *Now*" (222). For Peter to make a similar leap, he too must learn to live in the present. A quotation in Greek from Apollodorus' *The Library* follows: "But the hurt proving incurable, Chiron retired to the cave and there he wished to die but he could not for he was immortal. However, Prometheus offered himself to Zeus to be immortal in his stead and so Chiron died." The novel concludes with Chiron accepting death. This "death" of the pharmakos symbolizes the sacrifice on behalf of the younger generation that the older generation accepts as its responsibility.

The scapegoat's guilt reflects the imperfect nature of man, symbolized in Christianity by original sin. One of Caldwell's colorful images conveys this recognition. Worried about his father's health, Peter has resolved to protect him from manipulative students and overbearing townspeople. Instead, Caldwell suggests that Peter "kill time" with his friends. Peter feels guilty because in fact he is drawn to the teen-age society of the local luncheonette, described as "criminal," where his girlfriend awaits him. Caldwell insists, "Take your time. [. . .] You got lots of time to kill. At your age I had so much time to kill that my hands are still bloody" (91). In *Self-Consciousness*, discussing his ambivalent attitude toward the Vietnam War, Updike uses the same imagery when criticizing anti-war protestors: "pretending that our great nation hadn't had bloody hands from the start, that every generation didn't have its war, that bloody hands didn't go with having hands at all. A plea, in short, for the doctrine of Original Sin and its obscure consolations" (136). The repeated references to killing time, by alluding to the overthrow of Kronus (Caldwell's father-in-law, Pop Kramer, and—mythically—Chiron's father), suggest the inevitable overthrow of the old by the young, the comic emphasis on the natural succession of generations.

This theme manifests itself in the teen-age Peter's oedipal feelings. As Corrigan notes in "Comedy and the Comic Spirit," a traditional theme of comedy is an "inverted oedipal pattern" (3). In *The Centaur*, father and son reverse roles with the former playful and the latter grave: "They had been too poor to afford a baby carriage; the kid had learned to steer, too early?" (15). At home Peter competes with Caldwell for his mother's attention and sulks when she rebuffs him: "'I can't,' I told her. 'I'm too upset. My stomach hurts.' I wanted revenge for her snub of my flirting overture: It dismayed me that my father, that silly sad man whom I thought our romance had long since excluded, had this morning stolen the chief place in her mind" (52). Staying at the Hummels' house, Peter, after fantasizing that the glamorous Vera is his "wife," resents his father's intrusion: "The snow on his coat and pants and shoes, testimony of adventure, made me jealous. Mrs. Hummel's attention had shifted all to him; she was laughing without his even saying anything" (207).

Upon reaching home, Peter admits, "I tried to get back into the little intricate world my mother and I had made, where my father was a strange joke" (215). Cassie's barb—"'I think it's so sad,' my mother said, 'that they don't allow men to marry their mothers'" (47)—is aimed at her husband but applies to her son as well. Throughout, the continual references to Caldwell's death—especially the obituary composed by an unidentified former student (likely Peter)—suggest Peter's subconscious rivalry with his charismatic father. Rather than competing with his son, Caldwell sacrifices himself to protect him: "using his body as a shield against the wind for his son, [he] pulls down upon Peter's freezing head the knitted woolen cap he has taken from his own head" (198). Like Chiron atoning for Prometheus, Caldwell suffers for Peter. The gift of the ridiculed cap, a symbol of Caldwell's foolishness, represents the succession of the generations.

The frequent references to "humiliation" in the novel underscore the reality that social intercourse can be painful for the individual. In "One Big Interview," Updike avers that "The general social contract—living with other people, driving cars on highways—all this is difficult, it's painful. It's a kind of agony really" (509). Juxtaposing "agony" with "really" fits: reality can be painful. Caldwell's reaction to the students' derision illustrates the agony of the individual in society: "The laughter of the class, graduating from the first shrill bark of surprise into a deliberately aimed hooting, seemed to crowd against him, to crush the privacy that he so much desired, a privacy in which he could be alone with his pain" (9). Yet it is by meeting his obligations that the individual attains maturity. This theme is evident in Caldwell's farcical account of the origin of life during his classroom lecture:

> "the volvox, of these early citizens in the kingdom of life, interests us because he invented death. There is no reason intrinsic in the plasmic substance why life should ever end. Amoebas never die; and those male sperm cells which enjoy success become the cornerstone of new life that continues beyond the father. But the volvox, a rolling sphere of flagellating algae organized into somatic and reproductive cells, neither plant nor animal—under a microscope it looks like a Christmas ball—by pioneering this new idea of *cooperation*, rolled life into the kingdom of certain—as opposed to accidental—death. For—hold tight kids, just seven more minutes of torture—while each cell is potentially immortal, by volunteering for a specialized function within an organized society of cells, it enters a compromised environment. The strain eventually wears it out and kills it. It dies sacrificially for the good of the whole." (37)

Caldwell identifies the volvox as one of the "early citizens" who enter into a social contract with "an organized society." By "volunteering" to do so, the volvox subjects itself to "a compromised environment." The volvox's altruism reflects the survival instinct. Langer points out, "It takes life to produce further life. Every organism, therefore, is historically linked with other organisms" (122).

Eons later Caldwell repeats this sacrifice on a daily basis ("just seven more minutes of torture"). Unnoticed is the similarity between Langer's remarks in "The Comic Rhythm" and Caldwell's lecture. She explains: "death, which is an accident in amoeboid existence, becomes the lot of every individual—no accident, but a phase of the life pattern itself" (122). Nevertheless, as Updike insists, Caldwell does not literally die at the end of the novel: "he dies in the sense of living, of going back to work, of being a shelter for his son ("One Big Interview" [498]). Peter acknowledges "my father's teaching was what sheltered us and let us live" (87). Like the humble but heroic volvox, Caldwell sacrifices himself for others. His compromised environment is the society of Olinger, which, with its overbearing "aristocrats" and demanding students, over the years wears him out. In the epigraph, Chiron dies "like any wearied man" for Prometheus. When Peter recognizes with horror, "*I'm killing my father*" (193), he is expressing not only his subconscious oedipal feelings, but also the reality that the younger generation inevitably supplants the older.

Yet, comedy sustains hope. At the conclusion of the dream-like Chapter Six, Peter informs his father that he has gained hope "From *you*" (144). When Caldwell is dubious, Peter musters the courage to imagine a Kierkegaardian "leap of faith": "I closed my eyes; between the voiceless 'I' inside my head and the trembling plane of darkness also there, there was a gap, of indeterminate distance but certainly not more than an inch. With a little lie I leaped it. 'Yes,' I said" (144). Unlike Peter's fruitless attempts to overcome the tiny gap that prevents him from attaching the chains to the tires or his fantasy that the museum statue at night would at last reach the water that falls an inch from her lips, hope can be achieved with the "little lie" of faith. Its inclusion within a dream, however, reveals that Peter's waking life yet lacks faith. According to Freud, "the wish which creates the dream shall be one that is alien to conscious thinking—a repressed wish" (161).

In comedy, however, hope does have a basis in reality. Frye describes comedy's inclusion of "the green world [. . .] as visualizing the world of desire, not as an escape from 'reality,' but as the genuine form of the world that human life tries to imitate" (*Anatomy* 184). Peter at first locates the green world in the statue of the "naked green lady" (199) with "her verdigrant hair" (199) thirsting for "pearlish green" (200) water that continuously eludes her, and later he finds it briefly in Penny's green eyes. Ultimately, however, the green world manifests itself in the cyclic nature of life. When Caldwell represents death in the form of an equation on the blackboard, Peter asks, "But can't the process ever be reversed?" (142). His father responds: "Yes. Read the equation backwards and you have photosynthesis, the life of green plants. They take in moisture and the carbon monoxide we breathe out and the energy of the sunlight, and they produce sugar and oxygen, and then we eat the plants and get the sugar back and that's the way the world goes round" (142–43).

Caldwell's "Yes" counters his son's nay-saying. The fundamental process of photosynthesis, "the life of green plants," drives "the way the world goes round" (143). Galligan identifies the cyclical nature of time and change as "one of the five major recurring images in comic literature" (30). For Frye, "The green world charges the comedies with the symbolism of the victory of summer over winter" (*Anatomy* 183); it also reflects "the triumph of life and love over the waste land" (*Anatomy* 182). Recurrently, *The Centaur* links life's cyclical nature with rebirth: the seeds identified with Persephone; Caldwell's description of the school calendar ("'The long haul' he called the stretch between Christmas and Easter" [41]); and the seasonal nature of Peter's psoriasis: "God, to make me a man, had blessed me with a rhythmic curse that breathed in and out with His seasons. [. . .] The curse reached its climax of flower in the spring; but then the strengthening sun promised cure" (45).

A key passage in the novel reflects the comic insight that everyday life is the path to the transcendent (Lynch 104). In the final chapter, the despairing Caldwell recalls walking with his minister father "down a dangerous street in Passaic":

> From within the double doors of a saloon there welled a poisonous laughter that seemed to distill all the cruelty and blasphemy in the world, and he wondered how such a noise could have a place under the sky of his father's God. In those days he customarily kept silent about what troubled him, but his worry must have made itself felt, for he remembered his father turning and listening in his backward collar to the laughter from the saloon and then smiling down to his son, "All joy belongs to the Lord." It was half a joke but the boy took it to heart. All joy belongs to the Lord. Wherever in the filth and confusion and misery, a soul felt joy, there the Lord came and claimed it as his own; into barrooms and brothels and classrooms and alleys slippery with spittle, no matter how dark and scabbed and remote, in China or Africa or Brazil, wherever a moment of joy was felt, there the Lord stole and added to His enduring domain. And all the rest, all that was not joy, fell away, precipitated, dross that had never been. He thought of his wife's joy in the land and Pop Kramer's joy in the newspaper and his son's joy in the future and was glad, grateful that he was able to sustain these for yet a space more. The X-rays were clear. A white width of days stretched ahead. The time left him possessed a skyey breadth in which he swam like a grandchild of Oceanus; he discovered that in giving his life to others he entered a total freedom. [. . .] Only goodness lives. But it does live. (220)

Scott suggests the nature of the relationship between comedy and Christianity: "the Christian imagination is enabled to rejoice in the quiddities and hecceities of existence in a way that accords very closely with the path that is taken by the comic vision. And though this world of ours has been injured by man's sin, it is, despite his distinctness from God, essentially good, because it proceeds from Him and exists by His design" (108). The "double doors" of the raucous saloon indicate Caldwell's father's double vision. Unlike Reverend March, this clergyman does not distance himself from the quotidian; instead, he rejoices in life's "quiddities and hecceities." That this insight is expressed as "half a joke" reflects his comic perspective. Amid the "poisonous laughter that seemed to distill all the cruelty and blasphemy in the world," Caldwell discovers that "All joy belongs to the Lord." This passage echoes the 100th Psalm: "For the Lord is good and his love is everlasting, / His constancy endures to all generations," with the final clause expressing comedy's emphasis on the succession of generations.

Aptly, this revelation occurs not in a church but outside a rough working man's bar; moreover, Updike does not quote the 100th Psalm but paraphrases its imagery and rhythm in the vernacular. Although Caldwell identifies himself as a Christian ("I was a minister's son. I was brought up to believe, and I still believe it, that God made man as the last best thing in His Creation" [52]), establishment Christianity fails to address spiritual needs. Caldwell's clergyman father loses his faith on his deathbed; the teacher is plagued by doubts ("What I could never ram through my thick skull was why the ones that don't have it [faith] were created in the first place" [189]) that March dismisses; Peter never attends church or finds consolation in religion.

Symbolically, when Caldwell gazes at the heavens, "The clear blue of the towering sky seemed forceful yet enigmatic," echoing "this dividing and indifferent blue" (line 45) of Wallace Stevens' "Sunday Morning." Vargo asserts, "Yet the effect of *The Centaur* is to leave us unconvinced of this other world [. . .]. God is still a vague, bloodless being" (102). Caldwell, however, has not attained the Kierkegaardian religious sphere marked by a personal relationship with God; instead, he remains in the earthly ethical sphere. Divinity can be understood only in terms of this world. As James A. Schiff notes, "God is beyond the finite world yet reveals himself within it" ("Updike's Domestic God" [52]). When the aesthete Hester Appleton describes God as "Very fine, very elegant, *very* slender, *very* exquisite," Caldwell responds reductively, "He's a wonderful old gentleman. I don't know where the hell we'd be without Him" (147). This characteristic reductiveness is comic in its undercutting of pretentiousness.

Thereupon, he recites a poem from his youth, "'Song of the Passaic' By John Alleyne MacNab":

> "The great Jehovah wisely planned
> All things of Earth, divinely grand;

And, in His way, all nature tends
To laws divine, to serve His ends.

The rivers run, and none shall know
How long their waters yet shall flow;
We read the record of the past,
While time withholds the future cast."(148)

When Hester comments that "It's not a very happy poem," Caldwell replies, "It is for me, isn't that funny?" (148). His comic perspective finds a joyful faith in the natural world's reflection of the divine. For Caldwell, the divine is evident both in the graceful Passaic River and in the rowdy Passaic bar. Unlike Peter's abstract paintings, which take him away from the world, this uncelebrated poem leads Caldwell deeper into life. Peter's true canvas is *The Centaur* itself. During a snowstorm, "Olinger under the vast violet dome of the storm-struck night sky becomes yet one more Bethlehem. Behind a glowing window the infant God squalls. Out of zero all has come to birth. The panes, tinted by the straw of the crib within, hush its cries" (179).

Recurrently, the birth of a new generation redeems the world. Yet, life continually reenacts the crucifixion. This is evident even at the most fundamental level. The lowly volvox is identified with Christ: it "looks just like a Christmas ball"; the description "flagellating" evokes Jesus' agony; like Christ, "It died sacrificially for the good of the whole" (37). Similarly, Caldwell sacrifices himself. The students' behavior during Caldwell's lecture represents society's response to Christ: "Mute faces marvelled and mocked" (33). This dual reaction reflects Frye's contention that the comic "emotions" are "sympathy and ridicule" (*Anatomy* 43). Undeterred, Caldwell continues to meet his responsibilities. As a father, he does not want to die at an early age, as his own father did: "I didn't want to doublecross my own kid like that" (169), the infinitive subtly linking his sacrifice to Christ's.

The quotidian contains the hope of resurrection. During his lecture, Caldwell shrinks the history of the universe into "our scale of three days," beginning with darkness and concluding with the emergence of man. When the Caldwells' ancient car stalls in the morning, "The resurrection felt impossible" (58). Nevertheless, Caldwell succeeds in starting the engine:

We listened so intently that a common picture seemed crystallized between our heads, of the dutiful brown rod straining forward in its mysterious brown cavern, skidding past the zenith of its revolution, and retreating, rejected. There was not even a ghost of a spark. I closed my eyes to make a quick prayer and heard my father say, "Jesus kid, we're in trouble." He got out and frantically scraped at the windshield frost with his fingernails until he had cleared a patch for the driver's vision. I got out on my side and, heaving together on opposite doorframes, we pushed. Once. Twice. An immense third time.

With a faint rending noise the tires came loose from the frozen earth of the barn ramp. (58)

The allusions to "mysterious brown cavern," "ghost," "prayer," and "Jesus" evoke the resurrection. Upon his return home, Peter reflects: "As I resettled myself in bed I relaxed into the comfortable foreknowledge of the familiar cycle of a cold: the loosening cough, the clogging nose, the subsiding fever, the sure three days in bed" (217). Just as the car starts on the third try and Caldwell learns over the three-day period that he does not have cancer, Peter will recover after three days in bed. When they reach home, Caldwell apologizes to Peter: "I gave you a rough three days" (217); but it is this period that furnishes Peter with the hope of renewal.

In *T.S. Eliot*, Frye notes that "Dante's journey through hell begins on Good Friday evening [. . .]. Thus his journey fits inside the three-day rhythm of the redemption" (65). Through a number of allusions, *The Centaur* associates Peter's mental journey with a Dantean descent into the underworld: Mr. Rhodes, the service-station manager, is mythologically Rhadamanthus, one of the judges of the dead; in the obituary, Caldwell's nickname is "Sticks" (Styx); the traditional Olinger High School cheer is "Hell" (171); the hotel desk clerk is identified with Charon; the school janitor is Heller. Peter's identification with the Cumaen Sibyl also is pertinent. Frye adds, "Apart from Easter, the idea of a descent into hell came to Dante from the sixth book of the *Aeneid*, where Aeneas enters the lower world with the aid of a 'golden bough' and the Cumaen Sibyl" (*T. S. Eliot* 66). Moreover, the many references to death in the novel suggest the need for the old Peter to die in order that the new may be born: "Easter represents the end of a long period of religious symbolism in which a 'dying god,' a spirit representing the fertility of nature, was thought to die and rise again, usually in a three-day festival" (*T.S. Eliot* 65). Seeds must be buried to bring forth life. Frye's depiction of *The Waste Land* applies to Peter's predicament: "Human beings, who live like seeds, egocentrically, cannot form a community but only an aggregate where 'Each man fixed his eyes before his feet,' imprisoned in a spiritual solitude" (*T.S. Eliot* 64).

In "The Varieties of Religious Experience," William James quotes Leuba: "The love of life, at any and every level of development, is the religious impulse" (455). Despite his travails, Caldwell loves life. Peter remembers his parents' voices as "full of life" (40). The pagan Chiron preaches, "And Love set the Universe in motion. All things that exist are her children—sun, moon, stars, the earth with its mountains and rivers, its trees, herbs, and living creatures" (78). The Christian Caldwell expresses his faith in his love of ordinary life: "Think about the earth. Don't you love her?" (84). In *The Centaur*, "All joy belongs to the Lord" (220). Peter will free himself from his Promethean chains when he lives his father's comic morality and loves life.

· 2 ·

THE COMIC HERO'S PLACE IN THE GENERATIONS IN *RABBIT, RUN*

"Today either everyone is a hero or no one is.
I vote for everyone."

UPDIKE, "ONE BIG INTERVIEW"

"he runs. Ah: runs. Runs."

Rabbit, Run covers three months in the troubled and confused life of Harold "Rabbit" (a childhood nickname) Angstrom. In 1959 Rabbit, 26 years old, lives with his pregnant wife, Janice, and three-year- old son, Nelson, in Mt. Judge, a suburb of Brewer, Pennsylvania. Once a high school basketball star, Rabbit now is employed demonstrating a kitchen gadget in department stores. Within the first few pages of the novel, Rabbit makes clear his dissatisfaction with his home life. Janice, who "Just yesterday [. . .] stopped being pretty" (13), drinks during the day. Their home with its clutter of toys and uncollected dirty glasses, dismays Rabbit. Viewing his home life as "a tightening net" (19), he "senses he is in a trap" (20). One afternoon after work, instead of picking up Nelson at his parents' home, where Janice had left the child while shopping, Rabbit impulsively flees this "muddle" and drives south toward Florida. He expresses his goal romantically: "He wants to go south, down, down the map into orange groves and smoking rivers and bare-foot women" (29). Driving at night on unfamiliar roads, Rabbit loses his way and ends up on a country lane in West Virginia: "Indeed the net seems thicker now" (37). His plight recalls Peter Rabbit's ensnarement in the gooseberry net. In *Just Looking*, Updike recalls as a child being greatly affected by the "pathos" of the accompanying drawing in Beatrix Potter's *Peter Rabbit*, showing Peter *"upside down"* (36). Like his namesake, Rabbit Angstrom panics. Trying to find his way, he studies "the map whole, a net, all those red lines and blue lines and stars, a net he is somewhere caught in" (39). Chagrined, he rips up the map and "turns instinctually north" (40).

The next morning, Rabbit, unwilling to return home, seeks out his former high school coach, Marty Tothero, for assistance: "Next to his mother Tothero had had the most *force*" (21). Now, however, Rabbit finds him down on his luck, dismissed from the high school and, estranged from his wife, living in the shabby Sunshine Athletic Club. Tothero can do little for Rabbit except arrange a blind date for him with Ruth Leonard, a prostitute. After spending the night together, Rabbit moves in with Ruth. Later, he encounters his in-laws' Episcopalian pastor, Jack Eccles, who, in order to counsel Rabbit, arranges a golf date. During their golf game, Eccles berates Rabbit for his fecklessness: "you're monstrously selfish. You're a coward. You don't care about right or wrong; you worship nothing except your own worst instincts" (125–26).

In the novel's second half, Rabbit begins a temporary gardening job at the estate of Mrs. Smith, an elderly widow. This work—natural and physical—renews Rabbit. Meanwhile, Ruth, uncertain of Rabbit's commitment, does not divulge to him that she is pregnant with his child. On a date at a Brewer nightclub, Rabbit and Ruth run into Ronnie Harrison, Rabbit's ex-high school teammate and nemesis. During the evening, it becomes apparent that Ruth has had sexual relations with Harrison. Afterwards, as retribution, the jealous Rabbit pressures the reluctant Ruth into humiliating sex. Later that night, he receives a phone call from Eccles informing him that Janice has given birth. Leaving Ruth desolate, Rabbit rushes to the hospital, where he and Janice reconcile. With no thought of Ruth, Rabbit moves back home.

One night, however, when the exhausted Janice resists his advances, Rabbit storms from the apartment. When he fails to return by the following day, the despairing Janice gets drunk and accidentally drowns the baby in the bathtub. During the mourning period, Rabbit is repentant, but at the grave he loses his composure and, to the horror of those assembled, blames Janice for their loss. Rabbit then flees, finally arriving at Ruth's apartment. There he is overjoyed to learn of her pregnancy and begs her not to have an abortion. The resentful Ruth demands that if he wants her and the baby he must divorce Janice and marry her. Rabbit vaguely promises "to work it out," but soon "he runs. Ah: runs. Runs" (284).

Rabbit, Run depicts a young man's incipient comprehension of his role in time and society. Rabbit Angstrom embodies the comic hero: ordinary but attractive, passive, resilient, playful and, above all else, vital. Quintessentially, he is a developing character who, in Kierkegaard's morphology, inhabits the aesthetic sphere where individuals focus on personal satisfaction. By the end of the series, Rabbit will grasp Eccles' insight that "God rules reality" (140), but here he resembles the vain Peter Caldwell rather than the mature George Caldwell. Both young men prefer a nostalgized past and a fantasized future to the problematic present. Tellingly, Rabbit, like Peter, is too self-absorbed to appreciate the comedy around him: "*He* is the Dalai Lama" (52). Yet, though the humor is muted, *Run* does contain irony, farce, and burlesque. Eccles chides the smug Rabbit, "It's the strange thing about you mystics, how often your little ecstasies wear skirts" (121). Encountering Lucy Eccles in the rectory, Rabbit outrageously "slaps! her sassy ass. Not hard; a cupping hit, rebuke and fond pat both, well-placed on the pocket." In response, "Her leaping blood bleaches her skin, and her rigidly cold stare is so incongruous with the lazy condescending warmth he feels toward her, that he pushes his upper lip over his lower in a burlesque expression of penitence" (112–13). After the ex-coach Tothero sermonizes, "A boy who has his heart enlarged by an inspiring coach [. . .] can never become, in the deepest sense, a failure in the greater game of life" (62), Rabbit answers Ruth's inquiry about his occupation, "I uh, it's kind of hard to describe. I demonstrate something called the MagiPeel Kitchen Peeler" (62).

Mauron's linking of comedy with maturity is as pertinent for the *Rabbit* series as for *The Centaur*. Rabbit's inability to accept his place in the human comedy ensures that he must continue to run, that is, gain experience in order to mature. The title of this first *Rabbit* novel indicates the link between running and experience: it alludes to a line in Wallace Stevens' poem "The Comedian as the Letter 'C'": "Let the rabbit run, the cock declaim" (377).[1] Joan Richardson observes that in this poem "Not God but experience itself would be celebrated" (521). Updike's inclusion of a comma in *Rabbit, Run*, thereby emphasizing the imperative mood, indicates the indispensability of experience in maturation. Stevens' poem also links this novel to *The Centaur*, for as Richardson points out, the "Letter 'C'" refers to the 100th Psalm (521), paraphrased in the passage describing the noise from a bar that frightens Caldwell as a youth.

Robert Detweiler emphasizes Updike's achievement in making such an ordinary character compelling: "Updike gives himself practically nothing to create from: not a colorful setting but just a common, conventional, slightly squalid Pennsylvanian suburban town; not even an anti-hero but just a non-hero with still less potential for tragedy than Arthur Miller's salesman" (46). Rabbit's surname suggests his place in life. Angstrom means a unit of wavelength of light equal to one ten-billionth of a meter, the ratio reflective of an individual's standing in a crowded world. Rabbit's humble status, recalling

---

1. Joan Richardson has suggested the source of *Rabbit, Run*'s title.

Stephen Daedalus' location of his position within the Christian hierarchy in *Portrait of the Artist as a Young Man*, is indicated by his address: "Wilbur Street in the town of Mt. Judge, suburb of the city of Brewer, fifth largest city in Pennsylvania" (10). Rabbit lives in a tacky apartment development, earns a modest living (Ruth refers to his jobs as "a joke" [281]), and by his own admission has a lackluster marriage.

Not a reader, he gains his information about the larger world from television and radio. With only a high school education, Rabbit's lack of sophistication is evident. During a conversation with Lucy, it is apparent that he has never heard of Freud. Except for his military service spent isolated on a post in rural Texas, Rabbit has never been away from home. Updike's intention is neither satirical nor condescending; rather, it is to delineate the provincial background that circumscribes the ordinary person. Rabbit feels his ordinariness all the more because for a brief period in his life, as a high school basketball star, he had known what it was like to stand out from the crowd. Fondly, Rabbit remembers that for one fan, "he had been a hero of sorts" (40). When Rabbit attempts to explain to Eccles his "second-rate" marriage, he contrasts it with "playing first-rate basketball" (101). The novel at once emphasizes Rabbit's fall from glory. In the opening scene, Rabbit joins a street basketball game with some youngsters. Despite flashes of skill, he fails to impress most of the boys: "They've not forgotten him; worse, they never heard of him" (11). The depiction of Rabbit as a local celebrity quickly forgotten emphasizes the fickleness of life.

Nevertheless, other characters, including Ruth, Eccles, Mrs. Smith, and Lucy Eccles, find themselves attracted to Rabbit. Tothero vouches for Rabbit's resiliency: "I know you well enough to know you always land on your feet, Harry" (45). Ruth acknowledges Rabbit's perseverance with a backhanded compliment: "'Cause you haven't given up. 'Cause in your stupid way you're still fighting" (89). Rabbit's interest in basketball and golf reveals his playfulness. Eccles' account of golfing with Rabbit captures the comic experience: "only Harry gives the game a desperate gaiety, as if they are together engaged in an impossible, startling, bottomless quest set by a benevolent but absurd lord, a quest whose humiliations sting them almost to tears but one that is renewed at each tee, in a fresh flood of green" (157). According to Galligan, "Absorption in the concrete and trust in the generative finite lead directly to full, innocent acceptance of the present moment, which is the essence of play" (37).

Within the series, the primacy of the present is indicated, formally, by the use of the present tense; thematically, by the undercutting of nostalgia; and, imagistically, by the vivid rendering of the concrete and quotidian. When Rabbit experiences a moment of transcendence, it occurs during a round of golf. He makes a perfect shot when he, for a moment, forgets his ego and embraces immediate experience: "That's *it*" (126). In addition, as Galligan notes, the comic hero "loves to speculate about the world, to play with metaphors, and to toy with analogies" (89). When Eccles parks on the wrong side of the street, Rabbit muses, "Funny how ministers ignore small laws" (86). Langer views the comic figure as "the personified élan vital" (133). Mrs. Smith gushes: "You kept me alive [. . .]. That's what you have, Harry: life. It's a strange gift and I don't know how we're supposed to use it but I know it's the only gift we get and it's a good one" (207). Rabbit's vitality indicates his Caldwell-like love of life. Discussing their wayward son with the senior Angstroms, Eccles sheepishly confesses, "When I'm with him—it's rather unfortunate really—I feel so cheerful I quite forget what the point of my seeing him is" (153).

Rabbit's nickname fits. Feibleman observes, "The use of comparisons between animals and humans, often to the detriment of the latter, has been a characteristic of comedy from earliest times to the present" (23). According to Langer, the comic figure "is neither a good man nor a bad one, but is generally amoral—now triumphant, now worsted and rueful, but in his ruefulness and dismay he is funny, because his energy is really unimpaired and each failure prepares the situation for a new fantastic mood" (133). The comic hero's ups and downs reflect the cyclic nature of life; his rolling with the punches illustrates his resiliency and determination to survive. His vitality overrides his faults. Rabbit is flawed, but this is the human condition. Meeker avers, "Comedy is concerned with muddling through, not with progress or perfection" (26). Like Peter Caldwell, Rabbit must learn to accept the "muddle" that is life. The death of the infant Rebecca dramatizes not only life's precariousness but also the devastating effect on the family. Since the novel does not portray the baby as an individual, the focus remains on the survivors. The comic hero's energy provides him with the strength—and inspires others, like Mrs. Smith—to endure life.

A developing character, Rabbit struggles to find his way. The novel underscores Rabbit's confusion by continually depicting him misinterpreting statements and events. In one such instance, the venerable Mrs. Smith, after meeting the three-year-old Nelson, warns Rabbit: "You have a proud son; take care" (207). The narration hints at Rabbit's failure to comprehend her meaning: "She must mean he should be proud of his son and take care of him" (207). His error is understandable because the widow's warning is cryptic; nevertheless, in light of his earlier dismissal of the oedipal syndrome as explained by Lucy Eccles and his subsequent bitter conflicts with Nelson, depicted in the following novels, it is revealing. The presumption of Rabbit's explanation ("must mean") betrays his callowness, for comedy undercuts certitude and exposes the superficiality of pat assumptions. From social relationships that are frequently humiliating, Rabbit, over the course of the series, learns what it means to be a human being. McFadden notes that "comedy in general, encourages us to face commonplace reality and to live with it. This ability has much to do with our being able to transform it; survival is a more practical program than revival" (166). The novel's brief opening scenes establish how reality frustrates the inexperienced Rabbit as well as how comedy locates meaning within the mundane.

The novel opens with boys playing a pick-up basketball game. As this scene delineates the boundary between Rabbit's past and his present, it quickly becomes apparent that Rabbit has difficulty accepting his place in time. The unorganized street game with a backboard attached to a telephone pole belongs to the domain of boyhood. Rabbit immediately feels the pressure of the new generation: "He stands there thinking, The kids keep coming, they keep crowding you up" (9). Once a standout in this world, he now is an outsider: "in a business suit, [he] stops and watches, though he's twenty-six and six three." The "real boys" are wary of him: "It seems funny to them" (9). They perceive an adversarial relationship between this "adult" and themselves, but, despite his size, they know that the generational odds are in their favor ("there are six of them and one of him" [9]). The youths resent his presence ("They're doing this for themselves, not as a show for some adult" [9]). During the game, save for one "natural," who identifies with Rabbit (and who with his "knitted cap with a green pompom well down over his ears and level with his eyebrows, giving his head a cretinous look" [11], recalls George Caldwell), they attack him ("As the game goes on he can feel them at his legs, getting hot and mad, trying to trip him" [10]).

This episode adumbrates the inevitable generational conflict that becomes the main theme of the series: the emergence of the new signals the demise of the old. Rabbit, although only twenty-six, is an adult: after "a kid he accidentally knocks down gets up with a blurred face and walks away, Rabbit quits readily. 'O.K.,' he says. 'The old man's going'" (11). His sense of being supplanted by the younger generation, especially his son, Nelson, will contribute to his subsequent panic and flight. The boys' antagonism parallels the opening of *The Centaur* with its depiction of unruly adolescents tormenting the middle-aged Caldwell. This scene underscores as well the importance of living in the present. Instead of recognizing that everyday adult life, with its cares and responsibilities, cannot match the glory of his basketball youth, Rabbit exacerbates his current dissatisfaction by contrasting his problematic life today with his romanticized yesterday. Yet the scene also suggests the value of crossing boundaries even at the price of rejection and humiliation. Essentially passive, Rabbit "likes things to happen of themselves" (281). After risking his adult dignity in play, "He feels liberated from long gloom" (11). In his essay "Dingley

Dell & The Fleet," W.H. Auden cites Nietzsche: "To become mature is to recover that sense of seriousness which one had as a child at play" (407).

Passing "stalks of dead flowers," Rabbit longs for a fresh start. It is spring and "Things start anew" (11). Winded from his exercise, he vows to quit smoking and tosses away his cigarettes. As a symbol of his rebirth, Rabbit notices a toy clown left in his yard all winter and identifies himself with it by explaining his lateness to Janice as "clowning around" (17). Once home, however, he confronts the usual disorder: "The clutter behind him in the rooms [. . .] clings to his back like a tightening net" (19). Disgusted, Rabbit reacts by distancing himself from this "mess": "It seems to him he's the only person around here who cares about neatness" (19). Limited by his single vision, Rabbit ignores the images of doubleness, symbolic of comedy, contained within this ordinary housing development: "each double house" with "two wan windows" and "two doors" (12). Her husband's anti-comic fastidiousness exasperates the pregnant, weary Janice: "You don't drink, now you don't smoke. What are you doing, becoming a saint?" (14). When she asks him to pick up a pack of cigarettes for her, Rabbit "senses he is in a trap. It seems certain" (20).

As he trudges to his parents' home to retrieve Nelson, the familiar locale evokes powerful memories. Telephone poles—associated with youth in the basketball opening—remind Rabbit of his climbing them as a boy and "Listening to the wires as if you could hear what people were saying, what all that secret adult world was about. The insulators giant blue eggs in a windy nest" (20). The reference to insulators applies to his memories as well. Overwhelmed by his problems, Rabbit retreats to the safety of an idealized past. He remembers as a child hiking up Mt. Judge and from its pinnacle viewing the city of Brewer below: "unlike the color of any other city in the world yet to the children of the county is the only color of cities, the color all cities are" (22). This striking image evokes the certitude of childhood, when life makes profound sense. Contrasting his own childhood in small-town Pennsylvania with his subsequent life, Updike concludes the essay "A Soft Spring Night in Shillington": "But it had all, from the age of thirteen on, felt not quite my idea. Shillington, its idle alleys and darkened foursquare houses, had been my idea" (41). In *Jokes and Their Relation to the Unconscious*, Freud describes "the mood of our childhood, when we were ignorant of the comic, when we were incapable of jokes and when we had no need of humor to make us feel happy in our life" (236). In the following scene, however, Updike subtly undercuts his hero's nostalgia. The past, though helpful in understanding the present, cannot replace it.

Approaching his parents' home, Rabbit recalls another episode from his youth. At one point new neighbors, "strict Methodists," had moved in next door and, when mowing their half of the strip of grass between the two houses, had failed to continue their predecessors' practice of doing the Angstroms' side as well. This change so infuriated Mrs. Angstrom that in retaliation she obstinately forbade Rabbit or his father to mow their portion. With no communication between the neighbors, a stalemate ensued. Before long, the Angstroms' side became so overgrown that a town official arrived to threaten them with a summons. This impasse embarrassed the teenage Rabbit, but he never questioned his mother's stance, although there was no reason for her to expect the new neighbors to mow the Angstroms' grass. In this absurdly overblown comic dispute, the rigid Mrs. Angstrom (as well as the Methodists) displayed the univocal vision that is antithetical to comedy. Finally, Rabbit's father pragmatically resolved the problem. One afternoon, while his wife was away, he enlisted Rabbit's help and cut the grass. Anticlimactically, their side now "looked as trim as the Methodists' half, though browner" (24).

On his mother's return, Rabbit felt "guilty" and feared a quarrel between his parents, but his father deftly avoided any unpleasantness by coolly claiming that the Methodists had capitulated: "His father shocked him by simply lying and doubled the shock by winking as he did it" (25). Together, this wink and the verb "doubled" suggest a capacity for double vision, an indication of the father's ability to perceive both sides of an issue and mediate between them. In the spirit of compromise, the father recognized that survival is paramount. Meeker notes a crucial distinction between tragedy and comedy: "Tragedy demands that choices be made among alternatives; comedy assumes that all choice is likely to be in error and that survival depends upon finding accommodations that will permit all parties to endure" (33). Unfortunately, years later the son has not yet assimilated his father's comic maturity: still resentful of the Methodists, Rabbit continues to sympathize with his single-vision mother. This shortsightedness will distort Rabbit's current perspective.

Rabbit, instead of entering the house, conceals himself and peers, undetected, through the kitchen window at the tableau of his parents, sister Mim, and, in his former place, his son, Nelson, seated, eating dinner: "He sees himself sitting in a high chair, and a quick strange jealousy comes and passes. It is his son" (25). The image reveals Rabbit's fear of Nelson's usurping him. Again distancing himself—on the outside looking in—Rabbit misreads what is before him: "Rabbit, with the intervening glass and the rustle of blood in his head, can't hear what they say" (25). Envying the Caldwellian warm domestic scene with his father laughing, his mother spooning the beans, and his sister grinning as she feeds Nelson, Rabbit concludes ruefully that "this home is happier than his" (26). Despite memories of the bitterness with the Methodists and his parents' recurrent ugly quarrels, he romanticizes this scene at the expense of his own family life. Updike hints at Rabbit's misinterpretation.

When Nelson drops his spoon, "The kid cries, 'Peel! Peel!': this Rabbit can hear, and understand. It means 'spill'" (26). Given the flatness of the description of Rabbit's assumption, his conclusion appears dubious; it seems much more likely that the boy's cry is a reference to Rabbit's "MagiPeel Peeler," and thus an appeal to his absent father. Elsewhere, Eccles assures Rabbit that he "is needed" at home (251). Nelson's grandparents cannot replace his father: Rabbit's place is with his family.

In Rabbit's current state, however, he feels unable to cope with his domestic problems. Like Peter Caldwell, Rabbit, as indicated by his expectation of seeing his boyish self seated in his old place, is guilty of Lynch's "simultaneity" (48), the anti-comic blurring of the past and the present. Given his frustration with the present, he panics: "His acts take on decisive haste" (26). As he starts out, he stops at a garage and the attendant gives Rabbit disconcerting advice, "The only way to get somewhere, you know, is to figure out where you're going before you go there" (32). The enigmatic nature of this counsel is indicated by the ambiguous description of the speaker: he looks like "a scholar," but, as with Tothero, the image is undercut when Rabbit smells whiskey on his breath. This "farmer," with his "two shirts" symbolizing his double vision, recalls the scholarly-looking janitor, Heller, who, in *The Centaur*, is associated with rebirth. Although disregarded, the advice haunts Rabbit: "It missed the whole point and yet there is always the chance that, little as it is, it says everything" (39). Thirty years later, the seasoned Rabbit will finally grasp the wisdom of the man's words. Now, however, the advice is merely unsettling because the comic hero learns more from experience than from authorities.

From the outset, Rabbit confronts a world marked by unpredictability, frustration, uncertainty, absurdity, and apparent arbitrariness. Attempting to reach paradise, he repeatedly gets lost, becomes unnerved (an Amish buggy unaccountably disappears in the rear-view mirror), and feels menaced by strangers and the countryside, which "grows wilder," until he realizes that, paradoxically, the "road of horror is a lovers' lane" (38). During the hours of driving, Rabbit listens to the radio and what he hears—a hodge-podge of popular music, advertisements, and news—depicts the jumble of American culture that surrounds him. Popular songs, baseball scores and golf-tournament results, commercials ("New Formula Barbasol Presto-Lather, the daily cleansing action tends to prevent skin blemishes and emulsifies something") mix with news of world events ("Tibetans battle Chinese Communists in Lhasa, the whereabouts of the Dalai Lama, spiritual ruler of this remote and backward land, are unknown" [33–34]).

The effect of the radio is bewildering—as indicated by his increasing inability to make sense of what he hears. The repeated references to the missing Dalai Lama indicate life's uncertainty. One image, "Saxes doing the same figure

8 over and over again" (36), with the symbol of eternity suggesting the Ein-steinian universe, recalls a similar description in *The Centaur* of the teacher Caldwell washing the blackboard "With long rhythmic swipes shaped like sideways 8's" (87). Eventually, Rabbit switches off the radio: "its music no longer seems a river he is riding down but instead speaks with the voice of the cities and brushes his head with slippery hands" (37). Unlike Huck Finn's raft ride down the Mississippi, Rabbit's flight provides no idyllic respites; instead, the threatening image of "slippery hands" foreshadows the drowning of the infant Becky. Finally, Rabbit prefers silence—for dreaming, not reflection—to the problematic and ubiquitous voice of society.

On Rabbit's return to Brewer, he encounters the unexpected. His old coach, Marty Tothero, once revered by Rabbit, is "stranger than Rabbit had ex-pected. He looks like a big tired dwarf" (44). Tothero's fellow members of the Sunshine Athletic Club regard him as "a fool" (53). When Rabbit blames Janice's drinking as a major cause of his departure, Tothero paradoxically sug-gests that he should have drunk with her. Far from offering the reassurance that Rabbit seeks, Tothero behaves bizarrely: " 'Janice! Let's not talk about lit-tle mutts like Janice Springer, Harry boy. This is the night. This is no time for pity. The real women are dropping down out of the trees.' With his hands he imitates things falling out of trees. 'Plip, plip, plippity' " (55). In his carniva-lesque ravings, Tothero (dead hero) echoes the bizarre Dionysos in *The Cen-taur*; and Rabbit's response, "discounting the man as a maniac" (55), matches Peter's disdain rather than George Caldwell's empathy. Even the local Chinese restaurant, where Rabbit and Tothero take their dates, presents incongruities: an American girl in a kimono sits beyond the counter, scenes of Paris adorn the walls, and the Chinese waiter lapses into hipster slang: " '—and then this other cat says, 'But man, mine was helium!' " (71). Throughout, Rabbit's expe-rience, such as his inability to determine whether Lucy Eccles is flirting with him or not ("The woman winks. Quick as light: maybe he imagined it" [196]) is confusing and unsettling.

In response, Rabbit attempts to escape from reality. Daniel Fuchs, discuss-ing the poem "The Comedian as the Letter 'C,' " asserts, "The central incon-gruity and source of comedy in the poem is precisely the juxtaposition of the everyday and our, alas, archaic, abortive attempt to rise above it" (33). Person-ifying the anti-comic meticulous figure, Rabbit likes Chinese food because it contains no "disgusting proof of slain animals" (62). His father comments spitefully that after Rabbit's military service, "He didn't want to get dirty" (152). The earthy Ronnie Harrison recalls that as the star scorer on the high school basketball team, Rabbit had left the work of defense to others: "You were too much of a queen to dirty your hands" (164). Against Ruth's wishes, Rabbit insists on washing the make-up off her face before they make love (80).

Despite his lustiness, "There's that in women repels him; handle themselves like an old envelope. Tubes into tubes, wash away men's dirt, insulting, really" (84). The juxtaposition of "insulting" and "really" reflects his discomfort with reality. Even Rabbit's religion is marked by squeamishness: "Harry has no taste for the dark, tangled, visceral aspect of Christianity, the *going through* quality of it" (219).

He masks his uneasiness with arrogance. When Ruth asks him, "Don't you ever think you're going to have to pay a price?" (136) Rabbit responds in a "cocksure voice" with "an idle remote smugness" that makes her cry: "'If you have the guts to be yourself,' he says, 'other people'll pay your price'" (140). Lynch observes that "the action of 'paying the price' is central to all creation, and to all real knowledge" (54–55). Human beings pay for their mistakes and delusions. Rabbit's attempt to distance himself from the muddle of everyday life will indirectly lead to the sadness of his daughter's death. In another eerie premonition of the infant's death, Rabbit early in the novel recalls that "One time Janice, who is especially clumsy when pregnant or drunk," had almost pulled over the television set, but "Luckily he got to it while it was still rocking in the metal cradle" (13).

Later, however, because of his irresponsibility, he will not be present to rescue Rebecca. After the baby's death, Rabbit is dismayed that he is not held legally responsible for what happened: "It disgusts him to feel the net of law slither from him. They just won't do it for you, they just won't take you off the hook" (264). His wish that society relieve him of the pain of confronting his guilt parallels Caldwell's yearning for death to relieve his misery. Both learn better. Debating the minister Eccles, Rabbit identifies maturity with death: "If you're telling me I'm not mature, that's one thing I don't cry over since as far as I can make out it's the same thing as being dead" (102). Unconsciously, Rabbit's identification of maturity with death is accurate, for in fulfilling its responsibilities the older generation does sacrifice itself for the younger. Responding to Rabbit's petulance, Eccles defines maturity with reductive succinctness: "[God] wants a little tree to become a big tree" (102).

Through example more than precept, Eccles serves as a model for Rabbit in a way that parallels the relationship between father and son in *The Centaur.* Eccles, a secondary character, does not equal Caldwell in stature. Yet, he resembles the centaur in a number of important ways (symbolizing the link between them are the Buicks each drives): his humility ("I'm immature myself" [102]); his clowning, such as his foolishly alienating an elderly member of his congregation by referring to him as "Happy Beans" (193); his flawed human nature, evident, as with George Caldwell, in an imperfect marriage ("You couldn't bear to love anyone who might return it" [245]); his wrestling with faith; and, most of all, his acceptance of his role in society despite frustration and humiliation. Each man's occupation—public school teacher and parish minister—serves the community. A fleeting image subtly depicts Eccles, like Caldwell, as a comic scapegoat sacrificing himself for others. Eccles remembers being "humiliated" (141) by his inability to assemble a swing-slide-and-sandbox set for his daughters. The set had arrived in "a long cardboard box" and this detail links it to Peter's nightmare of his father stark naked in "a grocery cardboard box," being ostracized by the townspeople. Although the incident itself is minor, it illustrates that Eccles suffers for the sake of his children just as Caldwell endures his difficult life for his family.

Eccles, as the Lutheran minister Kruppenbach charges, lacks spirituality, and, as his wife points out, he is often ineffectual; nevertheless, despite his failures and admitted shortcomings, like Caldwell, he continually strives, amid frustrations, to help others. "Making awkward calls is agony for Eccles"(140), but he makes them nonetheless. In his efforts to reunite Rabbit and Janice, he visits, in turn, her parents, Rabbit's parents, and, seeking consolation himself, the senior minister Kruppenbach. These scenes, following in swift succession, depict the humiliation, comic in its repetition and unexpectedness, that a good man endures fulfilling his obligations in society. In the comic universe, no good deed goes unpunished. First, he suffers the barbs of Mrs. Springer ("Well if the world is going to be full of Harry Angstroms how much longer do you think they'll need your church?" [144]); next, the bitterness of Rabbit's parents; and, finally, a scathing denunciation of his efforts by the farmer-clergyman Kruppenbach: "All the rest, all this decency and business, is nothing. It is Devil's work" (159). Although Eccles had anticipated that the first two visits might be uncomfortable for him, he is unprepared for the condemnation from a fellow clergyman. The shattering effect of Kruppenbach's tirade indicates the gap in comic maturity between Eccles and George Caldwell: the latter, older and more experienced, possesses a deeper understanding of his Job-like existence.

Nevertheless, Eccles personifies the Kierkegaardian "humorist," who with his moral commitment and sense of duty belongs to the ethical sphere of existence. Eccles is sympathetic to the plight of those, like Rabbit, trapped within the aesthetic sphere and, unlike the overbearing Reverend March in *The Centaur*, he is aware of his own shortcomings. Moreover, Kruppenbach correctly perceives Eccles' lack of spirituality. Eccles acknowledges that his own unresolved oedipal conflict has caused him to enter the ministry: "He commits fraud with every schooled cadence of the service, mouthing Our Father when his heart knows the real father he is trying to please, has been trying to please all his life, the God who smokes cigars" (144). These self-recriminations are appropriate for a Christian comic hero. Auden, in his essay "The Globe," notes that comedy in a Christian society "is based upon a belief that all men are sinners" and that "the more virtuous, in the Greek sense, a man is, the more he realizes that he deserves to be exposed" (177).

Even Rabbit notices the minister's doubts: "Underneath all this I-know-more-about-it-than-you-heresies-of-the-early-Church business he really wants to be told about it, wants to be told that it is there, that he's not lying to all these people every Sunday" (125). Eccles' faith is more evident in his ministry in society—shepherding his youth-group softball team, visiting his parishioners, counseling Rabbit on the golf course—than it is in church. His sermon "is an unpleasant and strained performance, contorted, somehow; he drives his car with an easier piety" (219). The distinction is apt. Like Caldwell, Eccles' faith is grounded in everyday life. Kruppenbach speaks with authority if not charity, but he (Kruppenbach means "horse's ass" in German) fails to appreciate the comic nature of Eccles' faith. As a humorist, Eccles exists on the boundary between the ethical and the religious but does not cross it. Contrary to Kruppenbach's censure, Eccles' position within the ethical sphere does involve him with "all this decency and busyness" (159).

When he accepts the blame his wife assigns him for the death of the Angstrom infant, he thinks, "These words are a shadow of his idea that if faith is true, then nothing that is true is in conflict with faith" (246). Scott describes this faith: "The Christian imagination does not shrink, in other words, from the tangibility, from the gross concreteness, of our life in time, and it is not afraid to face the limited, conditioned nature of human existence" (110). Eccles admonishes the deluded Rabbit, "Christianity isn't looking for a rainbow. If it were what you think it is we'd pass out opium at services. We're here to *serve* God, not *be* God" (125). In Updike's fiction, faith is neither fixed nor detached from the everyday world. Distancing oneself from reality erodes faith, for the transcendent reveals itself through the mundane. When Rabbit despairs over his daughter's death, Eccles counsels, "Be a good husband. A good father. [. . .] We must work for forgiveness; we must *earn* the right to see that thing behind everything" (259).

Hunt's description of the humorist who "retreats to the shared laughter and acknowledged foibles of common humanity rather than confront the highly individual demands that faith requires" (75) fits Eccles. Chagrined, the minister seeks relief for his pain in society, significantly, at "the drugstore in the center of town": "He feels at home; Eccles feels most at home in public places. He [. . .] drinks two Coca-Cola glasses of miraculous clear water" (160). After enduring humiliation, this humorist locates the "miraculous" within the two (expressing his double vision) glasses of humble water. Moreover, the clergyman's association with a pharmacy reinforces his identification with the Caldwell-like pharmakos figure. Eccles' surname is doubly significant: etymologically, it means "assembly of citizens, church," reflecting this activist minister's commitment to the ethical sphere that requires participation in society; it also is the name of the street that Leopold Bloom lives on in *Ulysses*, thereby associating the clergyman with Joyce's own bumbling scapegoat and comic hero.

Like Caldwell, Eccles never attains the religious sphere (he reappears only in the revised *Rabbit Redux* of *Rabbit Angstrom: A Tetralogy*, no longer a minister but a fundraiser), but at this point he serves as a model for someone like Rabbit, confined to the aesthetic sphere. Despite his doubts, Eccles through his social ministry displays his faith. When the task of informing Rabbit of the death of his child falls to Eccles, the minister reflects: "One of the uses society seems to have for him is to break tragic news and the cave of his mouth goes dry as he braces for the familiar duty. *No man, having put his hand to the plough*" (247). The passage from Luke (9.62), which concludes, "and looking back, is fit for the kingdom of God," illustrates that though faith is subject to doubt, a Christian perseveres nonetheless.

Aptly, the image of plowing locates faith in the quotidian. Likewise, it is fitting that Eccles describes his function in terms of "uses society seems to have for him "and "duty" because they indicate his acceptance of his role in society no matter how distasteful. Eccles' pronoun indicates his empathy: "Harry. A terrible thing has happened to us"(248). Discussing hell, Eccles informs Rabbit, "'What we live in you might call'—he looks at Harry and laughs—'inner darkness'" (120). Eccles' ability to laugh despite his keen awareness of the human plight proclaims his faith. At novel's end, Rabbit associates Eccles with laughter—"He imagines her telling Eccles about how he slapped her fanny and thinks he hears Eccles laughing and himself smiles. He'll remember Eccles as laughing" (276)—a defining image for the Kierkegaardian humorist.

Eccles begins Rabbit's regeneration by directing him toward the reinvigorating green world. Symbolically, the green world is associated with the minister: his "olive Buick" (97), the "green" of the rectory lawn, Lucy's "green eyes" (110), the living room's "heavy green" furniture (117), and "the green alleys" of the golf course (123). Moreover, Eccles finds Rabbit the gardening job with Mrs. Smith where the flowers "seemed to belong to a different climate, to a different land" (128). Working outdoors with his hands and, without realizing it, revitalizing the lonely Mrs. Smith, Rabbit renews himself by his involvement with the natural process of birth, growth, and death: "Sun and moon, sun and moon, time goes" (127). This experience awakens in him a sense of how life should be lived.

Discussing the importance of such pastoral interludes within novels primarily set in urban locales, Leo Marx concludes: "the hero explores the possibility of a simpler, more harmonious way of life. At some point, invariably, there is an idyllic interlude when the beauty of the visible world inspires him with a sense of relatedness to the invisible order of the universe" (253). In comic terms, Rabbit begins to discern the congruity beneath the surface chaos. Caring for Mrs. Smith's prize rhododendrons ("dozens of great rectangular clumps like loaves of porous green bread") and her "evergreen" bushes (128), Rabbit perceives the presence of the divine in nature: "He loves folding the hoed ridges of crumbs over the seeds. Sealed, they cease to be his. The simplicity. Getting rid of something by giving it to itself. God Himself folded into the tiny adamant structure. Self-destined to a succession of explosions, the great slow gathering out of water and air and silicon: this is felt without words in the turn of the round hoe-handle in his palms" (127–28). In this humble work, after at first complaining about the "poor" pay, he discovers the peace and harmony he had imagined finding in his romantic dreams of Florida. The reference to the "seeds" that are buried to be resurrected recalls the seeds in *The Centaur* that symbolized the hope of rebirth. This "is felt without words," that is, in a very profound sense.

Rabbit's faith, however, is severely tested by the accidental drowning of his daughter. When the Angstroms, with the family intact, seem to have surmounted their problems, disaster strikes. The description of the drowning dramatizes its suddenness and the fumbling frustration of the mother as the infant slips out of her soapy hands. One moment baby Rebecca is perfectly healthy and the next, lifeless. Rabbit must rebuild his faith from the trials and tribulations of everyday life. Early on, he recognizes, "There is this quality, in things, of the right way seeming wrong at first. To test our faith" (37). At one point, Tothero declares, "Right and wrong aren't dropped from the sky. We. We make them" (257). The immature Rabbit has difficulty accepting this counsel: "Tothero's revelation chilled him. He wants to believe in the sky as the source of all things" (258). The passage describing Janice's recognition that her frantic prayers for her child's life will go unanswered echoes others in the novel as well as elsewhere in Updike's fiction: "Though her wild heart bathes the universe in red, no spark kindles in the space between her arms; for all of her pouring prayers she doesn't feel the faintest tremor of an answer in the darkness against her" (243–44).

Rabbit also despairs. Returning to the apartment, he stares at the water remaining in the bathtub and effortlessly reaches down to pull the plug: "He thinks how easy it was, yet in all his strength God did nothing. Just that little rubber stopper to lift" (255). His frustration recalls Peter Caldwell's when "a tiny gap" defeats his attempts to attach tire chains during a blizzard. These three passages also echo Ruth Leonard's self-pity when Rabbit abruptly leaves their bed: "It's like when she was fourteen and the whole world trees sun and stars would have swung into place if she could lose twenty pounds what difference would it make to God Who guided every flower in the fields into shape?"

(179). The lack of divine intervention undermines faith, but it is essential for maturity that human beings accept that there is no traditionally concerned God to intercede in their behalf.

Rabbit finds no solace in establishment religion: on Palm Sunday, "Out on the street people leave church carrying wands of green absent-mindedly at their side" (90). As in *The Centaur*, orthodoxy is undermined in other ways as well, including the minister Eccles' doubts, Kruppenbach's lack of charity, the missing Dalai Lama, and the darkened church at the end of the novel. Lacking faith in a traditionally concerned God, Rabbit struggles to comprehend the paradoxical and unfathomable events of life, such as when Tothero, earlier the victim of life-threatening strokes, attends Rebecca's wake: "Tothero, leaning on a cane and his face half-paralyzed; but talking, walking, alive. And the baby dead" (257). Schiff notes, "Updike's God is dualistic and paradoxical" ("Updike's Domestic God" [51]). As the numb Angstrom family paces the local streets, during the mourning period for the infant, Rabbit ponders his existence:

> The houses, many of them no longer lived in by the people whose faces he all knew, are like the houses in a town you see from the train, their brick faces blank in posing the riddle, Why does anyone live here, why is this town, a dull suburb of a third-rate city, for him the center and index of a universe that contains immense prairies, mountains, deserts, forests, cities, seas? This childish mystery— the mystery of "any place," prelude to the ultimate, "Why am I me?"—ignites panic in his heart. (260–61)

As with Caldwell, Rabbit's pain leads him to question his fate. The terms "riddle" and "mystery" fit, for comedy presents life as perplexing; moreover, it is appropriate that a familiar, everyday and ordinary scene of neighborhood houses inspires Rabbit's inquiries. In contrast, Rabbit had earlier arrogantly insisted that "it," the meaning of life, transcended an ugly housing development that he and Eccles pass. Now, Rabbit's musings suggest a heightening of consciousness, for comedy celebrates open minds and ridicules closed ones.

After the drowning, Rabbit reflects upon why he stayed away from his home on the day of the accident: "What held him back all day was the feeling that somewhere there was something better for him than listening to babies cry and cheating people in a used-car lot and it's this feeling he tries to kill" (250). The reference to killing is appropriate, for the immature Rabbit must die for him to mature. Gradually, Rabbit comes to recognize the primacy of parenthood: "Or maybe just being a father makes everyone forgive you, because after all it's the only sure thing we're here for" (187); Janice too "seems to accept herself with casual gratitude as a machine, a white pliant machine for fucking, hatching, feeding" (216).

Later, when Rabbit takes Nelson to a playground, the familiar sounds and smells of childhood activities produce not nostalgia this time but a revelation: "He feels the truth: the only thing that has left his life has left irrevocably; no search would recover it. No flight would reach it. It was here, beneath the town, in these smells and these voices, forever behind him. The fullness ends when we give Nature her ransom, when we make children for her. Then she is through with us, and we become, first inside, and then outside, junk. Flower stalks"(208). Rabbit's youth is gone and no flight, whether to Florida or to a nostalgic paradise lost, can recapture it. The final image directly connects this insight to the repeated images of decaying flower stalks, especially his experience in Mrs. Smith's garden, where, as part of his duties, he cut and burned the "crumbled stalks."

Rabbit, too, belongs to the natural process of life. At one point Rabbit alludes to a local event called "Fosnacht Day." The origin and specific details of this holiday are vague in his mind for it is a vestige of an earlier time, a folk custom, and dying out. Rabbit does, however, remember that when he was a child his grandfather would purposely delay coming downstairs in order that his grandson would not be the Fosnacht:

> "What was the penalty for being a Fosnacht?"
> "I forget. It was just something you didn't want to be. Wait. I remember, one year, I was the last downstairs and my parents or somebody teased me and I didn't like it and I guess I cried, I don't know. Anyway that's why the old man stayed up." (118–19)

The term "Fosnacht" is never defined in the novel, but its scapegoat connotations are suggested by the translation of two German words: *Fastnacht*, meaning "Shrove Tuesday," and *Fasernackt*, meaning "stark naked." As the Hamiltons point out, the golf match with Eccles where Rabbit suffers the humiliation of his embarrassing play and the minister's sarcasm occurs on Shrove Tuesday (147). Edith Kern alludes to the "German *Fastnachtspiele* that combines scapegoat rites with celebrations of nature's changing seasons in such a way that the fool as a central figure is frequently killed and later resurrected" (11). Linking the European Middle Ages with modern America, the preservation of this ritual reflects the comic notion that the essential concerns of humanity do not change. Like the pharmakos associations with Caldwell and Eccles, the grandfather's behavior represents the older generation's self-sacrifice on behalf of the younger. On the golf course, the chastened Rabbit looks to the sky as he had when as a child he would look upstairs for his grandfather's protection; now, however, his grandfather is dead and it is Rabbit's turn to assume the adult's protective role.

An episode occurs that shows Rabbit momentarily accepting this role. Fittingly, the event is both minor and farcical. After reconciling with Janice, he has accepted his father-in-law's offer to work in his used car lot and thus must quit the gardening job with Mrs. Smith. By doing so, he sacrifices his own happiness for the obligation to support his family. On Rabbit's farewell visit with Mrs. Smith, Nelson, who has accompanied his father, bites into a piece of chocolate candy that she has offered him. The taste, however, is too rich for him and Rabbit allows the boy to spit out the "bits of chocolate shell and stringy warm syrup and the broken cherry" into his hand (207). Significantly, Rabbit accepts "this mess" of his son's in contrast to his earlier fleeing the muddle of his home life. As a result, he is left with a hand "full of melting mashed candy" as Mrs. Smith, unaware of this occurrence, embraces him. The intent is not to undercut the real emotion in the scene but to indicate Rabbit's willingness, at least in a small way, to sacrifice himself for his son.

Yet Rabbit remains far from ready for the demands of the ethical sphere. Near the end of the novel, the confused Rabbit, once again on the run, allays his guilt: "Two thoughts comfort him, let a little light through the dense pack of impossible alternatives. Ruth has parents, and she will let his baby live; two thoughts that are perhaps the same thought, the vertical order of parenthood, a kind of thin tube upright in time in which our solitude is somewhat diluted" (282). Rabbit's "two thoughts," which provide some consolation, indicate his inchoate double vision. Through acceptance of their duties in society, especially parenthood, human beings create order within the surrounding chaos and in a sense transcend the limitations of the finite. Yet, maturing remains an ongoing challenge. At the cemetery when his daughter's tiny casket is lowered into the ground, he panics and flees again. Understandably, he has difficulty accepting the infant's death and his responsibility for it. The novel's epigraph is Pascal's *Pensee* 507: "The motions of grace, the hardness of the heart; external circumstances." In "Ungreat Lives," a review of Andre Dubus' *Voices From The Moon*, Updike describes "our homely, awkward movements of familial adjustment and forgiveness as being natural extensions of what Pascal called 'the motions of grace'" (652). Rabbit recognizes that his desertion of Nelson "is a hardness he must carry with him" (282–83). Unable to cope with his circumstances, he hardens his heart, rejecting the motions of grace.

The tension in Rabbit between his sense of responsibility and his selfishness reflects the human condition. In "One Big Interview," Updike asserts, "I feel that to be a person is to be in a situation of tension, is to be in a dialectical situation" (501). At the end of the book, Rabbit tries to determine his course: "On this small fulcrum he tries to balance the rest, weighing opposites against each other: Janice and Ruth, Eccles and his mother, the right way and the good way, the way to the delicatessen—gaudy with stacked fruit lit by a naked bulb—and the other way, down Summer Street to where the city ends." When he looks toward the church, its window is dark: "There is light, though, in the street-lights" (283). For the comic hero, understanding his role in life will come from everyday experience, not supernatural revelation. In the words of the Stevens poem, "Let the rabbit run." Galligan, citing as an example the ending of *Huckleberry Finn* with Huck fleeing civilization, notes that "comedies end in a symbolic gesture rather than a summary assertion" (X). The novel concludes as it began, with Rabbit, intimidated by reality, attempting to escape from it. This immature Rabbit still has a long way to run.

· 3 ·

THE COMIC HERO'S RENEWAL
IN *RABBIT REDUX*

"Being crazy's what keeps us alive."

*"Because I love my country and can't stand to have
it knocked."
"'If you loved it you'd want it better,' Jill says."
"'If it was better I'd have to be better,' he says
seriously, and they all laugh, he last."*

*R*abbit Redux resumes the story of Harry Rabbit Angstrom in 1969, ten years after *Rabbit, Run*. During the interim Rabbit has returned home to his wife Janice and their son, Nelson, now thirteen years old; after the death of the infant Rebecca, the Angstroms have not had any other children. They live in the same vicinity but now own a house in a new development not unlike the one Rabbit had scorned in the earlier novel. Rabbit toils as a printer at the plant in Brewer where his father works. At 36, Rabbit is in a rut, with a stale marriage and a dead-end job; moreover, he feels increasingly alienated by the social and political turmoil of the 1960's. The first novel introduced a confused young man attempting to escape his responsibilities by pursuing romantic illusions; the opening of *Redux* presents a deadened figure who has submerged his individuality and retreated into conformity and drudgery. The death of his daughter has left Rabbit devoid of hope and faith. No longer on the run, he now hides in obscurity. This time Janice leaves Rabbit for an affair with the car salesman Charlie Stavros. At loose ends, the demoralized Rabbit visits a black bar on the other side of town, where he encounters Jill, a runaway 18-year-old from an affluent background. Although wary initially, he soon welcomes Jill into his house and bed.

During her stay, Jill functions both as a wife and as a daughter for Rabbit as well as a sister and as a lover for Nelson. Next, a black revolutionary, drug dealer, and fugitive called Skeeter also moves in. In effect, the 1960's come home to Rabbit: the counter culture, political and social radicalism, the sexual revolution, illicit drugs, and especially black militancy. Through lectures and communal readings, Skeeter educates Rabbit about American racism and imperialism; meanwhile, he supplies Jill with heroin. Although at times the household forms a community, eventually, with Jill's despair and increasing drug use and Skeeter's messianic delusions, the situation deteriorates.

Nevertheless, despite the tension in the household and threats from bigoted neighbors, Rabbit tolerates the presence of his visitors. One night, however, while Rabbit and Nelson are away, the house is firebombed. Although Skeeter escapes, Jill dies in the fire. Homeless, Rabbit returns with Nelson to his parents' house. Shortly afterwards, Rabbit suffers another blow when he loses his job. Meanwhile, the arrival of Rabbit's worldly sister, Mim, from Las Vegas enlivens the depressed household. During her visit, Mim counsels Rabbit and also helps end Janice's affair with Stavros. At the conclusion of the novel, Janice and Rabbit begin a reconciliation by spending an afternoon at a motel. The book ends with a hopeful if uncertain peace between them: "He. She. Sleeps. O.K?" (407).

The comic nature of life is much more conspicuous in *Redux* than in *Run*. The first novel in the series provides only glimpses of subtle cracks in society's infrastructure; in contrast, *Redux* abundantly foregrounds the social and political upheavals of the 1960's. While *Run* focuses its attention on the narrow context of Rabbit's home town, the sequel broadens its canvas to include the diverse and problematic worlds of black America, the counter culture, the elderly, a developing suburbia, the desert playland Las Vegas, and even outer space. Moreover, the power of the McLuhanesque media, obtrusive and ubiquitous, overwhelms the average person like Rabbit, exacerbating his confusion and despair. *Run*, set in the insular 1950's, centers on the individual within the nuclear family, but the sequel focuses on the individual's place within the extended family, the community, the nation, the world, and even, given the moon expedition, the universe.

As husband, father, and citizen, Rabbit will gradually begin to understand his place and his family's in a fluid society where private and public domains overlap. The continual domestic realignments—Janice's moving-in with Charlie Stavros, the arrival of Jill and Skeeter, Rabbit's eventual return to his parents' home, Mim's visit from Las Vegas, and Rabbit and Janice's reconciliation—illustrate the interconnectedness and mobility within society that cut across class, racial, ethnic, ideological, social and generational divisions. Exposure to the bohemian Jill, the black community, the revolutionary Skeeter, the worldly-wise Stavros, the sophisticated Mim, and his aging parents broadens Rabbit's perspective and contributes to his renewal. This inclusiveness is appropriate since the central comic theme is the integration of the individual into society. Moreover, the doubleness associated with comedy is evident in the novel's focus on both female and male heroes. Janice, no less than her husband, seeks to find her way in a rapidly changing world.

Within *Redux*, the humor that reflects the comic nature of life is also far more prominent than in *Run*. When Rabbit's father exults, "Uncle Sam is on the moon!" his wife shrugs, "That's just. The place for him" (93). This wry indictment of the government for slighting its earthly affairs in favor of euphoric space exploration underscores the comic notion that mankind's "place" is here on earth: that Uncle Sam is more at home on the moon points up the dire state of society. Overall, farce predominates. In this teeming novel, anything goes, from Jill's shocking the neighbors by casually sunbathing topless to Rabbit's clumsy lovemaking with the "wall-eyed" Peggy Fosnacht to Skeeter's revisionist history: "The Southern assholes got together with the Northern assholes and said, Let's us do a deal. What's all this about democracy, let's have here a dollar-cracy" (232). When Jill joins Rabbit's household, he imagines a tabloid headline: "CLINIC FOR RUNAWAYS OPENED. *Fathers Do Duty On Nights Off*" (144). With its zaniness, *Redux* is closer in spirit to *The Centaur* than to *Run*. Here, changes in society turn the larger world inside out; Janice's departure and the arrival of Jill, Skeeter, and Mim turn Rabbit's private world upside down. Now he experiences fully the topsy-turvy nature of life merely adumbrated in *Run*. By upsetting the normal state of affairs, farce bares mankind's essential condition. Kern quotes Bakhtin: "The influence of the carnival spirit was irresistible: it made a man renounce his official state as monk, cleric, scholar, and perceive the world in its laughing aspect" (9). By renouncing, in one way or another, their "official state," Janice and Rabbit arrive at a better understanding of the world's "laughing aspect" and their place within it.

Present in *Redux* are trickster figures who instigate carnivalesque activities, "whether Lords of Misrule, jesters, clowns, devils, or saintly prophets" (Kern 117). Tricksters have a dark side, but their mischief ultimately is redemptive. For Janice, her lover and mentor, Charlie Stavros, plays this role; for Rabbit, these figures include Jill, Skeeter, and Mim. In the judgment of Rabbit's father, Stavros is a shady character ("This son of a bitch looks slick" [177]), but in Janice's estimation he "is remaking her from the bottom up," and "the whole base of her feels made new, mud made radiant" (382). The word "radiant" is associated with the heavens, while Stavros' surname suggests the Greek word for cross (*stauros*), thus connoting Christ's redemption. When Janice fears that her affair with him has destroyed her world, Stavros coolly reassures her, "You can get it back" (383). Similarly, Rabbit at times brands Jill a whore, drug abuser, and spoiled "bitch," but her mysticism intrigues him and "Her cooking has renewed his taste for life" (171).

Skeeter's identification with the carnivalesque is explicit: *Slavery*, one of his assigned readings, "seems a small carnival under Skeeter's slim hand" (242). He is portrayed as a devil ("So he is evil" [208]), but also as a streetwise prophet ("'By many false prophets,' Skeeter tells him, 'you shall know my coming, right?'" [224]), clown ("He entertained us" [327]), and Lord of Misrule (after the fire, the destroyed house appears to Rabbit "a hellish fun house" [329]). For Skeeter, in effect expressing the dichotomy between the comic hero and the meticulous man, "Chaos is God's body. Order is the Devil's chains" (275). The novel clearly identifies Mim as well with the carnivalesque: the references to her "clownish" clothing (352) and "clown costume" (358); her name, which suggests mime; her dazzling mannerisms, which make even smoking a cigarette a performance ("Pop is enchanted by the routine, struck dumb" [353]); the comic "act" in which she impersonates a Disneyland Abraham Lincoln and a mechanical guide conducting a tour of George Washington's house; her dubious career in Las Vegas ("only I take on the audience one at a time" [360]); her flamboyant life style ("I used to be a den mother for a pack of Hell's Angels" [363]); and, most of all, her revitalizing the household by overturning it. By challenging conventionality, these tricksters serve to remind Rabbit and Janice of their existence *sub specie aeternitatis.*

In the world of carnival, speech and gesture are coarse and candid (Kern 9). The language of *Redux*, mingling topical references, ribaldry, street lingo, technical jargon, and the inflated argot of the media, celebrates vitality, variety, and democracy as well as zaniness. Bakhtin, citing Rabelais, observes that farce often makes vulgar reference to sexuality, but that these allusions are "not obscene" but "positive" because they celebrate life (qtd. in Kern 18). With a vulgarity that nonetheless conveys his appreciation of women's vitality and resiliency, Rabbit expresses how Janice's discontent reflects the frustrating biological disparities between men and women: "Women, fire in their crotch, won't burn out, begin by fighting off pricks, end by going wild hunting for one that still works" (104). When *Redux* begins, Rabbit is psychologically comatose. For Bakhtin, farce is "hostile to all that was [. . .] completed" and "laughed at rigidity" (qtd. in Kern 11). Rabbit's renewal begins when he opens himself to new experiences that, though painful, prove liberating. According to Bakhtin, "Carnival laughter is the laughter of all the people" (qtd. in Kern 8). Rabbit's interactions with the likes of Skeeter and Jill—like Caldwell's with the drunk and hobo—serve to reconnect him to "the people."

Over the last ten years, Rabbit has distanced himself from God as well: "No belief in an afterlife, no hope for it, too much more of the same thing" (104). Unlike *Run*, here clergymen, churchgoing, and theological discussions are absent. Yet, as the novel unfolds, there are indications of God's subtle presence within the quotidian. Skeeter muses upon Vietnam, "It is where God is pushing through" (261). At Jimbo's Friendly Lounge, the pianist Babe hymns, "in a voice that is no woman's voice at all and no man's, is merely human, the words of Ecclesiastes. A time to be born, a time to die. A time to gather up stones, a time to cast stones away. Yes. The Lord's last word. There is no other word, not really." Significantly, the last word locates the transcendent within everyday reality: the Lord's word sung in a bar. Babe's powerful rendition "frightens Rabbit with its enormous black maw of truth yet makes him overjoyed that he is here" (125). Her voice transcends all categories, even gender, and expresses the fundamental truth that human beings must accept their place in time. This scene recalls the pivotal passage in *The Centaur*, also set in a bar, when Caldwell's clergyman father, with the language evoking the 100th Psalm, affirms that the raucous laughter reveals that "All joy belongs to the Lord" (220). In both scenes God emerges from within the sordid and even menacing commonplace. Later, Jill, whom Rabbit meets at Jimbo's, instructs him, in Blakean terms, that "God is in the tiger as well as the lamb" (162).

Elsewhere, Rabbit's mother, the person who understands him best, inquires whether he prays, and his reply, "Mostly on buses" (197), denotes God's place within everyday life. Rabbit's response is not flippant; he does indeed pray on buses, the prosaic setting where black teenagers and "fat Dutch housewives" confront one another. Like Reverend Eccles in *Run*, whose piety is more evident when driving his car than preaching, Rabbit here finds buses more conducive than church for prayer. (In the 1995 edition of *Redux*, Rabbit encounters the former minister Eccles while waiting for a bus and they ride for a few stops together.) Furthermore, the discrediting of the increasingly egomaniacal Skeeter indicates that finally God is found within ordinary reality rather than the surreal. Rabbit recognizes Skeeter as a prophet, but finally rejects him as a savior: "'I shall return,' Skeeter promises, 'only in glory.'" Reflecting comedy's ultimate predilection for normalcy, Rabbit pleads, "When you do, leave me out of it" (336). From his carnivalesque exposure to Jill and Skeeter, Rabbit absorbs the message of Christianity (emphasized by Updike's italics): *"We must be nice to her, we must be nice to the poor, the weak, the black. Love is here to stay"* (153). Bakhtin quotes a 1444 letter from the Paris School of Theology: "This is why we permit folly on certain days so that we may later return with greater zeal to the service of God" (qtd. in Kern 14). Rabbit's tolerance of his visitors, despite their unconventional, even criminal behavior, stems from his gradual perception of the common humanity he shares with them. Increasingly, he recognizes that in order to transcend his own life of quiet desperation, he must learn to love others.

Through his unsettling experiences, Rabbit rediscovers a sense of his place within humanity. Earlier, he had noted the lack of any sense of community in his suburb: "Their neighbors in Penn Villas are strangers, transients—accountants, salesmen, supervisors, adjusters—people whose lives to them are passing cars and the shouts of unseen children" (61). The inhabitants "do not connect" (76). This environment is as cold and soulless as the moon. The arrival of Jill and Skeeter brings tension, violence, madness, and even death, but also vitality, truth, freedom, and joy. A community evolves, a new family to replace Rabbit's splintered one: "Their laughter makes a second wave to reassure him they are not laughing at him, they are laughing in relief at the gift of truth, they are rejoicing in brotherhood, at having shared this moment, giggling and cackling; the house is an egg cracking because they are all hatching together" (213).

Just as an egg cracks in order to produce life, this rebirth will not be without friction. In this scene Rabbit, uneasy about Skeeter's intrusion, has come to blows with him. The arrival of Nelson with his pal Billy Fosnacht, however, interrupts the scuffle. Skeeter seizes the opportunity to defuse the ugly mood by mocking the teenage Billy, with his acne and orthodontia, as "grotesque." This gibe breaks the tension and results in laughter, joy, and a sense of brotherhood. The scene illustrates Frye's insight that the prevailing emotions of comedy are sympathy and ridicule (*Anatomy* 43). Together these two attitudes convey the double vision of comedy. Billy's last name, "Fosnacht," is the name of the scapegoat ritual, "Fosnacht Day," that Rabbit obliquely alludes to in *Run*. Now forgotten, the ritual subtly reappears with Billy assuming, momentarily, the role of the pharmakos. Eventually, however, in this novel it is Jill, with her drug use and death in the firebombing of Rabbit's house, who is identified with the pharmakos figure. Comedy does not fix blame; rather, it suggests that all human beings are like the pharmakos, both guilty as well as innocent.

Eventually, Rabbit accepts his own complicity in Jill's death. Reconciling with Janice at novel's end, Rabbit resignedly acknowledges the blame he and his wife share: "Her trip drowns babies; his burns girls. They were made for each other" (395). Rabbit's frankness in admitting his flawed human nature contrasts with the stance of Jill's haughty mother when she finally descends from her Connecticut suburb to claim her dead daughter's possessions. With her single vision, she resembles the self-important "gods" who torment Caldwell. Although Mrs. Aldridge must bear at least some of the responsibility for her disaffected child's fate, she instead blames Rabbit. Rabbit, wiser from his experiences, recognizes this meticulous figure's wish to distance herself from the quotidian: "She wanted to stay out of harm's way. She wanted to have some fun and not be blamed. At the end she wanted not to have any apologizing to do to any heavenly committee. Right now she wanted to tame the ravenous miracle of her daughter being cast out and destroyed" (347). The use of religious imagery—"heavenly," "miracle," and "cast out and destroyed"—connects this world and the next. Christianity recognizes humanity's inherently flawed nature, what comedy terms foolishness, as the result of original sin. The comic hero stumbles repeatedly but accepts his shortcomings as an integral part of his humanity; the worst sin is despair, which, as a form of pride, denies forgiveness and renewal. In comedy, characters do not wear their faith on their sleeves; they live it. Rabbit justifies exposing Nelson to the antics of Jill and Skeeter: "And life is life, God invented it, not him" (231). In such a fashion, Updike seamlessly weaves God and faith into the quotidian.

In the aftermath of the fire, Rabbit tries to articulate the human condition: "But it is all life, sex, fire, breathing, all combination with oxygen, we shimmer at all moments on the verge of conflagration, as the madhouse windows tell us" (346). Now, however, it is not only the madhouse windows that reveal the instability of society; the media accomplishes this merely by reporting the news of the day: "These things happen all the time in the papers" (18). In the 1950's *Run*, news of the larger world is in the background—just brief bulletins interrupting the music on Rabbit's car radio during his drive south—while the focus is on the turmoil in Rabbit's private life. By contrast, in *Redux* reports of war, riots, demonstrations, scandals, crime, space explorations, and changing mores and life styles overflow in the print and electronic media. Indeed, the power of the media threatens to overwhelm reality. When moviemakers choose Brewer as a location for a film about "MIDDLE AMERICA," Rabbit comes upon the scene and feels "dim, dim and guilty, to see how the spotlights carve from the sunlight a yet brighter day, a lurid pastel island of heightened reality around which the rest of us—technicians, policemen, the straggling lake of spectators including himself—are penumbral ghosts, suppliants ignored" (184).

Moreover, the speed and sensationalism with which the media report the news serve to accelerate the pace of events and to emphasize the helplessness of the individual in the face of such flux. Watching the space launch on television in a bar, Rabbit and the other patrons are made aware of their obsolescence: "They have not been lifted, they are left here" (7). The inhuman jargon transmitted from space reinforces these feelings of alienation:

"Nine zero four thirty-four forty-seven."

"Roger, copy, Tranquility. That gravity align looked good. We see you recycling."

"Well, no. I was trying to get time sixteen sixty-five out and somehow it proceeded on the six-twenty-two before I could do a BRP thirty-two enter. I want to log a time here and then I'd like to know whether you want me to proceed on torquing angles or to go back and re-enter again before torquing. Over." (96)

Unlike the philosophical and literary epigraphs included in *The Centaur* and the other *Rabbit* novels, each of the four sections of *Redux* begins with an epigraph quoting dialogue of transmissions from either American or Soviet missions in space. Throughout the novel, television, radio, and newspapers—Rabbit works as a linotyper and sees reports transposed into type before his eyes—blare the news. Characters discuss, argue, and analyze current events. Mostly, Rabbit finds this news dismaying and alienating. The media's comparison of the moon expedition with Columbus' discovery of America baffles him: "They keep mentioning Columbus but as far as Rabbit can see it's the exact opposite: Columbus flew blind and hit something, these guys see exactly where they're aiming at and it's a big fat nothing" (29).

In the 1960's no one escapes the turmoil: "Next day, Friday, the papers and television are full of the colored riots in York, snipers wounding innocent firemen, simple men on the street, what is the world coming to?" (57). As one of those "simple men on the street," Rabbit defends the Vietnam War and a beleaguered America against liberals like Charlie Stavros and radicals like Skeeter; later in the novel, Rabbit confronts the racial bigotry of his Penn Park neighbors. Unrest in the black community is evident not only in the type he sets for newspaper articles about black power but in the "pushy" youths he encounters on buses. Eventually, technological advances make his printing job obsolete. Even the sports world, once Rabbit's refuge, has changed. Attending a baseball game, Rabbit finds, "something has gone wrong. The ball game is boring." The ballplayers "seem specialists like any other, not men playing a game because all men are boys time is trying to outsmart" (83–84). Worse, blacks now dominate basketball, "his sport," with their flashy style, and, on the TV screen, the few remaining white players appear out of place.

The blurring of the private and public sectors is evident in Updike's use of the *Ulysses*-like technique, in which Rabbit imagines his life as bizarre headlines: "LINOTYPER'S WIFE LAYS LOCAL SALESMAN. *Greek takes Strong Anti-Viet Stand*" (74). Gradually, images from the media invade Rabbit's thoughts. After Janice's departure, Rabbit expresses his loneliness by comparing his home to a spacecraft: "But the spacecraft is empty: a long empty box in the blackness of Penn Villas, slowly spinning in the void, its border beds half-weeded" (99). Elsewhere, Rabbit refers to Janice's affair with Stavros as a "fucking coalition government" (181). Social and political unrest exacerbates Rabbit's confusion: "Things go bad. Food goes bad, people go bad, maybe a whole country goes bad. The blacks now have more than ever, but it feels like less, maybe. We were all brought up to want things and maybe the world isn't big enough to take all that wanting. I don't know. I don't know anything" (80). Even progress is undercut. At this point in his life, Rabbit views scientific advances reductively, "but then being smart hasn't amounted to so much, the atom bomb and the one-piece aluminum beer can" (13).

Moreover, the revisionism of Stavros and Skeeter subverts Rabbit's political naiveté, exposing him to the darker side of American history and current realpolitik. Appropriately, this demythologizing, along with Rabbit's memories of childhood ("And Rabbit remembers, it's a myth they never fought" [367]), exemplifies the comic truism that in both the public and private spheres the past resembles the problematic present. Even nostalgia provides no haven. At one point Rabbit watches a TV skit about the Lone Ranger that at first evokes warm memories of his childhood: "those generous summer days, just enough dark to fit sleep into, a war being fought across oceans just so he could spin out his days in such happiness, in such quiet growing. Eating Wheaties" (22). Rabbit's memory glosses over the horrors of World War II, but the comedy sketch, at first "pretty funny," returns him to reality. In this campy version of the heroic western, the foolish Lone Ranger's disgruntled wife, behind her husband's back, carries on an affair with his sidekick, Tonto. Rabbit "laughs, but underneath the laugh this final gag falls flat, maybe because everybody still thinks of Tonto as incorruptible, as above it all, like Jesus and Armstrong" (24). Aside from the skit's uncomfortable parallel with the Angstroms' own domestic problems, Rabbit finds himself questioning what he had once taken for granted: America's moral preeminence: "Where has 'the side of right' gone?" (24). When Stavros condemns America for the imperialism that began with the usurpation of the Indians, Rabbit explodes self-righteously: "'What were we supposed to do, let 'em have the whole continent for a campfire site?' Sorry, Tonto" (49). The unspoken apology at the end of his outburst reveals Rabbit's ambivalence, an attitude, according to Frye, characteristic of comedy (*Anatomy* 181). With his private and public worlds askew, Rabbit finds it difficult to relinquish his traditional beliefs; yet he recognizes the unfairness of his jingoism. Just as *Run* undercuts Rabbit's religious orthodoxy, the sequel causes him to reexamine his unquestioning patriotism.

Rabbit, an average American ("He's a normal product" [47]), is ripe for change in his life. With his basketball glory long forgotten, Rabbit is a ghost of his former self. When Jill asks him, "You don't think much of yourself, do you?" Rabbit admits, "Once the basketball stopped, I suppose not" (200). The lingering sadness of the baby's death, his stale marriage, the drudgery of his job, and the characterless development Rabbit lives in have sapped his spirit. Only a vestige of his charisma remains:

> The small nose and slightly lifted upper lip that once made the nickname Rabbit fit now seem, along with the thick waist and cautious stoop bred into him by a decade of the linotyper's trade, clues to weakness, a weakness verging on ano-

nymity. Though his height, his bulk, and a remnant alertness in the way he moves his head continue to distinguish him on the street, years have passed since anyone has called him Rabbit. (4)

His vitality has faded along with his nickname. Unlike in *Run*, Rabbit feels almost comfortable in his trap. When the self-pitying Rabbit whines that he has sacrificed his life by working "day after day for ten years," his blunt sister is unsympathetic: "Mim tosses this off. 'You felt like it. It was the easiest thing to do'" (370). In effect, Rabbit has used his occupation as a means of numbing himself emotionally.

All of the *Rabbit* novels, as well as *The Centaur*, focus on work, but none more so than *Redux*. Each of the four chapters begins either with Rabbit at work or leaving work. All four epigraphs quote men at work in space. The novel continually depicts aspects of work: the intricacy of Rabbit's typesetting; the camaraderie of the workers at the print shop; the details of Mim's life as a call girl in Las Vegas; the neighbor Peggy Fosnacht's difficulty as an older woman in finding employment; the baseball players who approach their game as a job; the fatigue of mission control during the long hours of the space launch; the horror of slavery as depicted in *The Life and Times of Frederick Douglass*; the routine of housework; the role of unions; the exploitation of workers like Rabbit's father; the nature of capitalism as explained by Skeeter; and the workplace as a setting for socialization (Janice's affair with Stavros begins upon her return to work at her father's lot; a co-worker invites Rabbit to join him at Jimbo's).

Work, however, can be misused. Retreating to the cocoon of work, Rabbit has distanced himself from human contact. After the death of Becky, Rabbit has neglected his wife: "You've taken Janice for granted ever since—the time" (6). Like the inhabitants of *The Waste Land*, Janice and Rabbit "had become locked rooms to each other" (54). The once lusty Rabbit is now, as both Janice and Mim note, priggish. His squeamishness, discernable in *Run*, has become pronounced: Rabbit "lifts his head fastidiously" when his father swears (7); elsewhere, Janice reflects that her husband is "too fastidious, hates sex, really" (57). The references to "fastidious" identify him as an anti-comic meticulous man. Now, it is Janice's sexual appetite that intimidates Rabbit: "he had fled her cunt as a tiger's mouth" (27). His preference for technology over human contact is apparent when, as he absentmindedly touches Janice in bed, "He thinks of feathering the linotype keys, of work tomorrow, and is already there" (27).

Illustrating the cyclic nature of life, Janice becomes adventurous while Rabbit withdraws into himself. Dismayed by her "provincial" (39) and "clinging" (34) husband, she reenacts his flight in *Run*. The "dumb mutt" of the earlier novel renews herself: "One of the nice things about having a lover, it makes you think about everything anew. The rest of your life becomes a kind of movie, flat and even rather funny"(53). With vulgar reductiveness, Janice acknowledges her averageness: "I'm just a cunt, Harry. There are billions of us now"(33). She expresses this observation not resignedly, but objectively; the significance lies in her new boldness. Struck by the change in Janice, Mim describes her evolvement in comic terms: "Janice can be quite funny about herself, which is a new thing" (375).

As Janice matures, she learns to love life. When Rabbit drives erratically, Janice warns him, "If you want to kill yourself, go ahead, but don't kill me; I'm just getting to like being alive" (400). By the end of the novel, Janice sheds her identification with death and becomes life-giving. During their final tryst, Janice "must make a miracle" in order to save Charlie's life when he suffers a heart attack. By saving Charlie, she also exorcises the stigma that has haunted her since the drowning of her infant daughter: "The mark upon her as a giver of death has been erased" (387). This emergency parallels the description of the drowning infant in *Run*, except that this time Janice's efforts are successful. The scene depicts the trial-and-error experience of the average person rising to the occasion. Foolishly, Janice at first blunders and brings the choking Stavros cold pills instead of his heart medicine. For a moment she panics and the description evokes the soapy infant slipping from her wet grasp: she "very stupidly lets the faucet water run to get cold, wetting her palm in turning it off, so the pills there blur and soften and stain the creased skin they are cupped in" (386). Undeterred, Janice persists in her efforts and ultimately saves Charlie through force of will.

In *Self-Consciousness*, Updike observes that the crucial difference between tragedy and comedy is that comedy offers second chances (241). Ten years after the drowning of Rebecca, Janice makes the most of a second opportunity. Charlie's nickname for her, "Tiger," along with Rabbit's association of her sexuality with a tiger, links Janice to Jill's insight that God exists in the tiger as well as the lamb. In Blakean terms, the tiger alludes to experience that, while often harsh and painful, is also enlightening. Janice's bitter experiences in *Run* have toughened her. Her boldness in defying conventionality in the sequel has provided her with the chance to save another's life and thereby redeem her own. After rescuing Charlie, Janice recognizes that their affair has run its course. Prudently, comedy does not push its luck: "Next time she might not be able to keep him up. Miracles are granted but we must not lean on them. This love that has blown through her has been a miracle, the one thing worthy of it remaining is to leave" (388).

The reference to "miracles" reflects Janice's comic faith that discerns the transcendent within the quotidian. Strong enough now to end the affair with Stavros, Janice next initiates the reconciliation with Rabbit. For everything there is a time. Earlier, in Molly Bloom-like stream of consciousness, Janice had reflected upon her life, the average woman's eight Shakespearian stages of birth, infancy, adolescence, marriage, motherhood, prime, old age, and death:

> How silly. How silly it all is. We're born and they try to feed us and we get breasts and menstruate and go boy-crazy and finally one or two come forward to touch us and we can't wait to get married and have some babies and then stop having them and go man-crazy this time without even knowing it until you're in too deep the flesh grows more serious as we age and then eventually that phase must be over and we ride around in cars in flowered hats for a while to Tucson or seeing the leaves turn in New Hampshire and visit our grandchildren and then get into bed like poor Mrs. Angstrom [. . .] and then we die and it wouldn't have mattered if we hadn't bothered to be born at all. (55)

Eventually, however, her experiences foster in her an appreciation of "silly" ordinary life. Yet even here, Janice perceives that larger events are mostly peripheral in the individual's life: "And all the time there are wars and riots and history happening but it's not as important as the newspapers say unless you get caught in it" (55). Comedy pays attention to public events only insofar as ordinary people "get caught" in them. The verb "caught" is telling. Not only does its use recall Rabbit's ensnarement in *Run*, but also its voice signifies the traditional passivity of the comic hero.

Passivity, however, ought not to be confused with lifelessness. For much of *Redux*, Rabbit has resigned himself to failure and a circumscribed existence. Only his characteristic expressiveness belies his despair: "Thirty-six years old and he knows less than when he started. With the difference that now he knows how little he'll always know. He'll never know how to talk Chinese or how screwing an African princess feels" (22). Rabbit has closed his eyes to life's possibilities. Unlike Janice, his experiences have made him timid: "I once took that inner light trip and all I did was bruise my surroundings. Revolution, or whatever, is just a way of saying a mess is fun" (172). When his mother implores him to "Pray for your own rebirth" and once more "Run" (197–98), Rabbit associates these imperatives with death: "He feels she is asking him to kill Janice, to kill Nelson. Freedom means murder. Rebirth means death" (198). Rabbit's fears are valid, for rebirths are accomplished only with pain and loss. True to comedy's penchant for the prosaic, Rabbit recognizes this fact while eating a casserole of chicken pieces: "No avoiding it: life does want death. To be alive is to kill" (311). Nevertheless, turbulent change is preferable to stagnation. Acutely, Janice notes Rabbit's deterioration: "You were a beautiful brainless guy and I've had to watch that guy die day by day" (74). To become healthy, Rabbit must once again "run," that is, venture new experiences.

Three comic discussions depict Rabbit's evolvement. The first occurs when Rabbit grudgingly accompanies Janice and Nelson to a Greek restaurant in an unfamiliar part of Brewer. Rabbit has begun to suspect his wife of having an affair with Charlie Stavros and his suspicions mount when the salesman enters the same downtown restaurant where the Angstrom family is dining. Significantly, the restaurant is Greek, outside Rabbit's usual boundaries; in contrast, Stavros, of Greek descent, feels at home. When Rabbit, guessing randomly, orders "the *paidakia*," Charlie snaps authoritatively, "I don't think so. It's marinated lamb, you need to order it the day before, for at least six" (42). For Rabbit, this ethnic restaurant with its incomprehensible menu, strange cuisine, and immigrant customers illustrates the threatening changes overwhelming his romanticized America. When a large Greek family enters ("They cackle their language, they giggle, they coo, they swell with joy of arrival"), Rabbit "feels naked in his own threadbare little family" (40).

The families here represent larger social entities: Rabbit's family is the traditional white Protestant majority that now feels threatened by such newcomers. During a debate over politics, Rabbit takes the role of the foolish alazon with the cagey Charlie as the realistic eiron. Although Rabbit had done his best to avoid the Korean War and was relieved to serve his Army duty in Texas, here he embodies one of the stock alazon figures, the swaggering soldier, as he defends American military intervention around the globe: "Bully for you. You're what made America great. A real gunslinger" (47). Stavros' use of the term "bully" is apt, for alazons are bullies forcing their point of view in the face of reason. By ignoring reality, Rabbit's arguments defend the indefensible just as his family outing barely hides the marital rift between him and Janice and her affair with Stavros. Uncomfortably, Rabbit cannot help noticing how close his wife and Stavros sit together.

In comedy, where change is natural and cyclic, any outlook that denies change is certain to prove shortsighted. Neatly, Charlie turns the tables on his adversary when Rabbit, "a defiant bastion," defends 19th century manifest destiny: "'Fair enough,' Stavros says. 'Now you're in their way'" (50). Repeatedly, Rabbit betrays his ignorance: labeling the American-born Stavros a foreigner, airing his racial and ethnic prejudices, and displaying his simplistic notions of history and current events ("If we don't send somebody in the other side sure as hell will, the Greeks can't seem to manage the show by themselves" [44]). His tirade proclaims his foolishness: "That's one of my Goddam precious American rights, not to think about politics" (44). Comedy exposes foolishness rather than evil. Yet Rabbit's behavior, given his background, is understandable: "His tongue is reckless; but he is defending something infinitely tender, the star lit with his birth" (47). His blustering, however, cannot prevent the truth from inevitably emerging. After the heated discussion, both sides attempt to smooth things over with Rabbit apologizing and Charlie paying the bill, "everyone now anxious to please" (51). Then, abruptly, Charlie destroys Rabbit's "keen family happiness" by unwittingly exposing Janice in an incriminating lie that reveals their intimacy. Despite all attempts at a cover-up, the discussion ends with the affair between Janice and Stavros out in the open. Comedy's allegiance is to the truth. Stavros has displaced Rabbit and the latter, in topsy-turvy fashion, is now the cuckold and outsider.

Another comic discussion finds Jill and Rabbit arguing foreign policy. After Rabbit, cynically, advocates fear as the most powerful motivation, Jill counters, "Let's try love for a change" (170). Rabbit, squeezing her slender wrist tightly, again personifies the bullying alazon: "Then you better find yourself another universe. The moon is cold, baby. Cold and ugly. If you don't want it, the Commies do. They're not so fucking proud" (170). When the distraught Nelson asks his father why he is so contentious, Rabbit's answer is self-incriminating:

> "Because I love my country and can't stand to have it knocked."
> "If you loved it you'd want it better," Jill says.
> "If it was better *I'd* have to be better," he says seriously, and they all laugh, he last. (171)

The joke is on Rabbit, but finally he too joins in the mirth. His laughing at himself exemplifies Galligan's notion that the comic vision requires human beings to acknowledge their own foolishness (XII): "Thus, through lame laughter—she still rubs her wrists, the hand he hit her with begins to hurt—they seek to reconstitute their family" (171).

Later, a third comic discussion suggests a change in Rabbit. During this scene two neighbors, Showalter and Brumbach, attempt to intimidate Rabbit into removing Skeeter from his home. There is a ludicrous quality to this confrontation: "Showalter has a way of bending, as if dance music is playing far away and he wants to cut in between Rabbit and Eddie" (286). These two characters, comic and menacing simultaneously, recall the murderers in Hemingway's "The Killers." Brumbach's handshake chills Rabbit: "*I twist bodies to my will. I am life. I am death*" (287–88). As the conversation proceeds, "Rabbit sees the structure: one man is the negotiations, the other is the muscle." This division of responsibilities reflects each man's incompleteness: "An age of specialization and collusion" (289). Showalter, the spokesman, is "in the hardware end" of computers; Brumbach, "the muscle," is a scarred Vietnam veteran who personifies the swaggering soldier: "He stands the way guys in the Army used to, all buttoned in, shoulders tucked back, an itch for a fight between their shoulder blades" (286).

Nevertheless, Rabbit cannot help liking the man, in part because he respects Brumbach's war service, "where he himself should have been fighting had he not been too old, too old and fat and cowardly" (290), but also because his own broadened experience has increased his tolerance for divergent points of view. As a result, Rabbit attempts, jokingly, to reach a compromise: "I'll keep my kid from looking in your windows, and you keep yours from looking in mine." His visitors, however, reject this offer, warning Rabbit to "fucking barricade the whole place" (289). At the end of the confrontation, Brumbach at last shows his ruined face: "The cocky little man keeps his arms stiff at his sides. Instead he turns his head, so the ruined jaw shows. The scar is not just a red L, Rabbit sees, it is an ampersand, complicated by white lines, where skin was sown and overlapped to repair a hole that would always be, that would always repel eyes" (290–91).

Brumbach too has suffered. The human comedy includes him and Showalter as well. Although misguided, they are not depicted without sympathy. Brumbach has the final word, and he speaks movingly: "I earned this face," he says. "I got it over there so I could have a decent life here. I'm not asking for sympathy, a lot of my buddies made out worse. I'm just letting you know, after what I seen and done, no wiseass is crowding me in my own neighborhood" (291). For most of this episode the two visitors, with their bullying and closed minds, embody blustering alazons while Rabbit, as he parries their threats, assumes the role of the reasonable eiron. Moreover, Brumbach's fear of being crowded reveals his anti-comic attempt to thwart change.

Comedy, however, resists neat categorizing. Although the neighbors' behavior is reprehensible, their fears have validity: Skeeter, after all, is a heroin dealer and felon. Brumbach's heartfelt expression of his sentiments makes it apparent that Rabbit has taken his visitors' concerns too lightly. At the same time, the episode shows Rabbit that his barren development does constitute a community. Rabbit recognizes this fact when, in the midst of the negotiations, out of the corner of his eye he is surprised to observe a mail truck appear "Out of nowhere" and a postman collect "a torrent, hundreds it seems, of letters" (290) from the mailbox that Rabbit is leaning against. Earlier, Rabbit had reflected that, unlike his old neighborhood of Mount Judge, where "people were always mailing Valentines" (289), in this development the mailbox seems unused. The humble quotidian, represented by ordinary mail, presents the underlying congruity beneath the incongruity that the best comedies reveal. Countering the neighbors' anti-comic divisiveness, the presence of community reassures Rabbit.

In the paperback edition, Updike provides a dictionary definition of *redux* that gives its primary meaning as a return to health. Rabbit's recuperation begins when he accepts his black coworker Buchanan's invitation to meet him for a drink. Desperation prompts him: "Something in what Buchanan said. He was lying down to die, had been lying down for years"(103). Grudgingly, he respects Janice's decision to leave: "At least she had the drive to get out" (104). For Rabbit, crossing the bridge to the downtown area is venturing into terra incognita: "Beyond the lake of light, unfriendly darkness" (113). Like Peter Caldwell, the spiritually dying Rabbit will make a metaphorical descent to the underworld in order to be renewed. In this unlikely locale, a black bar, Rabbit will start to better comprehend the comic nature of life. He will begin to transcend the provincialism that is stifling him ("I don't think this fella's ever gotten above Twelfth Street, have you Harry?" [127]). Rabbit starts to view blacks as people. Before entering the bar, *black* was a "political word"; here Rabbit meets individuals who also yearn for a better life. Buchanan points out their common humanity: "What I am is a man trying to get from Point A to Point B, from the cradle to the grave hurting the fewest people I can. Just like Harry here" (131).

Paradoxically, this ghetto locale provides a pastoral interlude. As the apprehensive Rabbit enters the murky maze-like bar, he is at first unnerved by the presence of so many blacks. His anxiety is eased, however, when he notices "the idyllic green felt" of a pool table. Play, an essential element of comedy, "reassures Rabbit. Where any game is being played a hedge exists against fury" (115). Soon, another form of play occurs when the pianist Babe performs:

What does Babe play? All the good old ones. All show tunes. "Up a Lazy River," "You're the Top," "Thou Swell," "Summertime." [. . .] "My Funny Valentine," "Smoke Gets in Your Eyes," "I Can't Get Started," starting to hum along with herself now, lyrics born in some distant smoke, decades when Americans moved within the American dream, laughing at it, starving on it, but living it, humming it, the national anthem everywhere. Wise guys and hicks, straw boaters and bib overalls, fast bucks, broken hearts, penthouses in the sky, shacks by the railroad tracks, ups and downs, rich and poor, trolley cars, and the latest news by radio. Rabbit had come in on the end of it, as the world shrank like an apple going bad and America was no longer the wisest hick town within a boat ride of Europe and Broadway forgot the tune, but here it all still was, in the music Babe played, the little stairways she climbed and came tap-dancing down, twinkling in black, and there is no other music, not really. [. . .] As Babe plays she takes on swaying and leaning backwards; at her arms' ends the standards go root back into rag-time. Rabbit sees circus tents and fireworks and farmers' wagons and an empty sandy river running so slow the sole motion is catfish sleeping beneath the golden skin. (123–24)

Just before crossing the bridge to this side of town, Rabbit, with time on his hands, wanders the downtown streets of Brewer. The mood is lethargic: "fat men in undershirts loiter, old ladies move between patches of gossip with the rural waddle of egg-gatherers, dogs sleep curled beside the cooling curb, and children with hockey sticks and tape-handled bats diffidently chip at whiffle balls and wads of leather" (113). This passage recalls Mark Twain's description in *Life on the Mississippi* of the sleepy riverside town before the arrival of the steamboat; in contrast, Babe's music evokes the animated mood of Twain's town when it awakens. The images of "circus tents and fireworks and farmers' wagons and an empty sandy river" suggest the excitement and vitality produced by an event like the appearance of a glamorous steamboat. What Rabbit remembers from baseball games of his youth ("There was a beauty [. . .] a game whose very taste, of spit and dust and grass and sweat and leather and sun, was America" [83]) is present in the music. Babe's songs locate something Rabbit and America have lost: the jaunty comic spirit of accepting life as it comes, rolling with the punches, and yet hoping and striving for something better. The assessment, "there is no other music, not really," associates the comic spirit expressed in these popular songs with the words from Ecclesiastes that Babe sings afterwards: "The Lord's last word. There is no other word, not really" (125). The concluding "really" links faith with reality.

Somewhere, the "American dream" has been misplaced, just as Rabbit's hopes have faded. Musing about blacks earlier, Rabbit had conceded, "at least they remember how to laugh" (12). Here the pool table and the evocativeness of Babe's music furnish Rabbit with a glimpse of the idyllic green world. Slyly, Updike reinforces this incongruous linking by later matter of factly listing in a police report the pianist Babe's last name as Greene. The distance Rabbit and America have traveled in the ten years since *Run* is illustrated in the contrasting settings of the green world: the first Rabbit novel located it in Mrs. Smith's garden; now, it exists in the inner city among blacks invisible in *Run*. Seeds, the symbol of rebirth in *The Centaur* and *Run*, are repeatedly associated with blacks: Skeeter declares, "We black men [. . .] are the future's organic seeds" (275).

In Jimbo's, the mood created by the music and the camaraderie, along with the drinks and marijuana, engulfs Rabbit in happiness: "he brims with joy, to be here with these black others, he wants to shout love" (125). Abruptly, however, this euphoria evaporates. After Babe ends her mesmerizing performance, Skeeter pimps her to Rabbit. Comedy visits the green world, but its home remains the problematic present. Rabbit's experience in the bar is not entirely upbeat; he must endure the insults of Skeeter and the jibes of Buchanan. Nor will his new life be blissful: to be reborn is painful as well as exhilarating. The American dream evoked in Babe's songs took the bad with the good, recognizing that life inevitably is filled with ups and downs and that people cannot insulate themselves from reality. Rabbit is impressed by Buchanan's comic live-and-let-live philosophy: "Funny man, Buchanan. No plan, exactly, just feeling his way [. . .] maybe that's the way to live" (146). When Rabbit and Jill leave together, Babe plays "There's a Small Hotel," the title adumbrating the motel that will be the site of Rabbit's reconciliation with Janice. The final line, *"With a wishing well"* (135), plaintively underscores the need for hope.

From Jill, Rabbit learns about a world as foreign to him as the black community: the counter culture with its mysticism, anti-materialism, casual drug use, free sex, vegetarianism, and pacifism. The epigraph to the second section of the novel, entitled "Jill," quoting Neil Armstrong's awed feelings after reaching the moon, presages the ambivalent effect this young woman shall have on Rabbit: *"It's different but it's very pretty out here."* A free spirit, Jill teaches the "cynical" Rabbit that "our egos make us deaf. Our egos make us blind" (159). Jill helps Rabbit understand the class system and his place within it. She explains Janice's behavior to the confused Rabbit: "She wants to be alive while she is alive" (273). Also, her presence enflames the oedipal rivalry between Rabbit and his son. At first Jill functions as Rabbit's wife and as Nelson's missing sister, but before long she and the boy are lovers. Observing their closeness, Rabbit begins to feel "Jealousy, perhaps" (153). When Jill perishes in the fire, the grief-stricken Nelson berates his father: "You fucking asshole, you've let her die. I'll kill you. I'll kill *you*" (320). Just as the infant Rebecca's drowning drives Rabbit and Janice apart, Jill's death prompts the long cold war between father and son.

Rabbit's education intensifies when Skeeter moves in. The black agitator's sense of urgency reflects comedy's emphasis on the present: "You just don't know, Chuck. You don't even know that now is all the time there is" (263). Skeeter fills Rabbit's empty book shelves with paperbacks: *The Selected Writings of W.E.B. Du Bois, The Wretched of the Earth, Soul on Ice, The Life and Times of Frederick Douglass,* others, history, Marx, economics, stuff that makes Rabbit feel sick, as when he thinks about what surgeons do, or all the plumbing and gas lines there are under the street" (226). As a symptom of his fastidiousness, Rabbit prefers to remain removed from reality: "He is immature" (246). From a revisionist point of view, Skeeter analyzes Western history, slavery, racism, Vietnam, capitalism, socialism, black power, and Christianity. During his rambling lectures, Skeeter cajoles Rabbit and Nelson into reading from his texts and playacting the part of blacks.

In comedy, play is instructive. Reading the account in Douglass' autobiography of the author's humiliating experience as a slave moves Rabbit. He cannot but compare Douglass' plight and rebirth to his own life: "'*A man without force,*' Rabbit intently reads, '*is without the essential dignity of humanity. Human nature is so constituted, that it cannot honor a helpless man, though it can pity him, and even this it cannot do long if signs of power do not arise*'" (282). The comic hero is passive, not supine. Douglass renews himself by standing up to the cruel and dehumanizing overseer: "*It was a resurrection from the dark and pestiferous tomb of slavery, to the heaven of comparative freedom. I was no longer a servile coward, trembling under the frown of a brother worm of the dust, but my long-cowed spirit was roused to an attitude of independence*" (282–83). By empathizing with "a brother worm of the dust," Rabbit draws strength for his own resurrection.

Finally, however, Rabbit can learn only so much from his visitors. By challenging the status quo, the carnivalesque liberates human beings from stagnation and complacency. Since meeting Skeeter and Jill, Rabbit has broadened his perspective and deepened his understanding of life. Although they have not radicalized him, he has tempered his conservatism and increased his tolerance for divergent points of view: "Pop, all they're saying is they want the killing to stop" (349). For everything there is a time: now, it is time for stability. Comedy's place is the middle ground of compromise, not the extremes of either the right or the left; ultimately, it functions on a human level that transcends ideology.

From a comic perspective, there is not that much difference between Ho Chi Minh and Everett Dirksen lying in state: "Dignitaries look alike" (236); and President Nixon, "He's just a typical flatfooted Chamber of Commerce type who lucked his way into the hot seat and is so dumb he thinks it's good luck" (225). The references to "typical" and "type" suggest Nixon's ordinariness despite his high office. Eventually, Rabbit recognizes that it is now time for the restoration of normalcy. When the frightened Nelson, during one of Skeeter's outbursts, points at his father and screams, "'I want to grow up like *him*'—his father, Harry, the room's big man—'average and ordinary'" (262), it is a plea for domestic law and order. After the firebombing of the house, the police remove Nelson to his grandparents' home, where he "seems relieved to be at last in the arms of order, of laws and limits" (326).

Recalling Rabbit's reaction to his daughter's drowning, this fresh disaster reminds him of his guilt: "So again in his life the net of law has slipped from him. He knows he is a criminal, yet is never caught" (329). Paradoxically, however, the purging fire also is liberating: "His house slips from him. He is free" (332). A kindly old watchman, another wise, ordinary person, informs Rabbit that the mortgage insurance will pay for most of the damage. More encouragingly, the "geezer," by twice addressing him as "young fella," reminds Rabbit that he remains youthful enough for a fresh start. Later, as he "hallucinates," Rabbit locates his position in time: "The freshening sky above Mt. Judge is Becky, the child that died, and the sullen sky to the west, the color of a storm sky but flawed by stars, is Nelson, the child that lives. And he, he is the man in the middle" (330). Now Rabbit recognizes that he belongs in the middle, the comic present between the past of Becky and the future of Nelson. Human beings learn from the past and plan for the future but live in the present. When he enters the wreckage of the house to salvage something, he rejects the "resaleable" television set in favor of a "dumb bench" that Janice "always loved" (332). The epithet "dumb," identifying the bench with his "dumb mutt" wife, suggests his unconscious intention of reuniting with Janice.

The novel's final chapter dramatizes the sunset of one stage in Rabbit's life and the dawn of another. Rabbit has lost his wife, house, the surrogate daughter/lover Jill, and any closeness with his son. In response, he buries himself in the routine of his job: "Rabbit is at his machine. His fingers feather, the matrices rattle on high, the molten lead comfortably steams at his side" (339). The consolation that this familiar work affords him is apparent not only in the language and imagery, but also because he is matter-of-factly engaged in typesetting the news story reporting his home's firebombing and Jill's death. The antiseptic tone of the report, reminiscent of the obituary for Caldwell, mirrors Rabbit's detachment. He still clings to his machine as a means of insulating himself from reality. When the supervisor Pajasek interrupts his work to inform Rabbit that he is fired, the reason underscores life's uncertainty: "You learned the skill and now the bottom's dropping out" (340–41).

Even the selection of the survivors appears capricious. Just as the elderly Tothero outlives the infant Rebecca and Rabbit's bedridden mother revives while the teenage Jill dies, Rabbit, not his retirement-age father, loses his job. This news appears the final nail in his coffin: "Die I guess would be the convenient thing" (342). The pragmatic supervisor dismisses such talk and, like the watchman, attempts to bolster Rabbit by emphasizing his youth ("young buck") and urging him to make a fresh start. Callously, Pajasek advises: "Leave the mess behind you. Forget that slob you married. [. . .] Kid, schmid. You can't live your life that way. You got to reason outwards from Number One. To you, you're Number One, not the kid" (342).

Unlike the conclusion of *Run*, however, now Rabbit owns up to his responsibilities. Minimizing Janice's blame for the "mess" and admitting his own, he acknowledges: "I can't go anywhere, I got this kid" (342). Jill's death has made Rabbit more aware of his parental responsibilities. Meeting with Jill's mother at the local police station, Rabbit recognizes the woman's culpability for Jill's demise. The police chief seconds Rabbit's verdict: "Rich bitch, if she'd given the girl half a reason to stay home she'd be alive today." With "A coach's paternal punch on the arm ," the chief cautions, "Keep your nose clean, Angstrom, and take care of your own" (348). The veteran police chief, whose own sense of duty is evident in his voluntarily responding to a fire out of his district " on behalf of my esteemed colleague the sheriff of Furnace Township who rolled over and went back to sleep" (328), appears a more reliable counselor than the single-vision Pajasek. Nevertheless, the supervisor's image of the firing as a "sacrifice" (348) is accurate, for Rabbit's new life will arise only from the embers of the old.

True to the cyclic nature of comedy, he returns to his childhood home. The familiar setting replenishes him: "It has been his salvation, to be home again" (349–50). Here, Rabbit enjoys a second adolescence: "An appetite for boyish foods has returned" (350) and he finds himself "faithfully masturbating" (377). Now he is mature enough to find his father's predictable rants, examples of comic uncremental repetition, amusing. In return, Rabbit's presence brightens his parents' lives as well. Reductively, his ailing mother allows: "Harry's being home, she claims, is worth a hundred doses of L-dopa" (350). Rabbit's boyhood family becomes complete when his sister, Mim, arrives from Las Vegas for a visit. The homely tableau that Rabbit in *Run* felt excluded from is now intact. Once Mim, a female Charlie Stavros, breezes into town in a flashy "borrowed" Toronado, Rabbit's education accelerates. Taking charge, Mim pulls them out of the gloomy house to dinner and a film: "Though Mom's head waggles and she has some trouble cutting the crust of her apple pie, she manages pretty well and looks happy: how come he and Pop never thought of getting her out of the house?" (369).

Ultimately, however, Mim focuses her attention on her floundering brother: "To help her help *you*. How can I help *her*, I'm no doctor" (368). She paves the way for the Angstroms' reconciliation by diverting Stavros' attention to herself as well as by initiating negotiations with Janice. Reflecting the cyclic nature of comedy, the elder sibling, once the star of the family, now learns from the younger sister who earlier had lived in his shadow. She is "Miss Fix-It" to his "Mister Muddle"(369). While Rabbit has played it safe, Mim has taken risks and crossed boundaries: "Mim knows things, Rabbit realizes proudly. Wherever you go in some directions, Mim has been there" (356).

In her earthiness, openness to experience, resiliency, and playfulness, Mim personifies the comic hero: "Be crazy to keep free" (358). Rabbit's mother also helps him rebound with a comic proverb: "Inch by inch. [. . .] Life is a cinch. Yard by yard, life is hard." When Rabbit wonders where he "went wrong," his mother explains succinctly, "You're. Growing up" (373). Gazing out his mother's bedroom window at the familiar street, Rabbit has a revelation: "Time is our element, not a mistaken invader. How stupid, it has taken him thirty-six years to begin to believe that" (373–74). This passage parallels the scene in *Run* when Rabbit views his familiar neighborhood anew after the death of his daughter. That locale, awing Rabbit with its "mystery," inspires questions about life; here, he finds answers. Human beings exist in time: any attempt to evade this reality is futile.

At the end of the novel, as Rabbit gingerly reconciles with Janice, he explains that he is "too rational" to believe in Skeeter's apocalyptic viewpoint; instead, he offers, "Confusion is just a local view of things working out in general" (405). Overall, their diverse experiences, undergone separately (they never meet in the middle two chapters), have given them a greater appreciation of life. Fittingly, since comedies traditionally conclude with a marriage, the end of *Redux* finds Rabbit and Janice reconciling. Symbolizing their rebirth, the Angstroms in effect reenact their high school courtship. Arranging to meet, ostensibly to discuss their divorce, they appear nervous teenagers. Significantly, both now live with their parents. For the occasion, Rabbit chooses to wear his old athletic jacket with the Mount Judge High School colors and lettering discovered in his parents' attic. The burning of his adult clothing in the fire represents the old Rabbit's death, and the resurrection of this jacket, the symbol of his greatest glory, his rebirth. At the same time, Janice's appearance also signals her renewal: "Yet she too is wearing something too young for her, with a hairdo reverting to adolescence, parted way over like those South American flames of the forties. Chachacha" (393). The allusions to "South American flames" and "Chachacha" suggest Janice's new Mim-like boldness and sensuality, born out of her adventurousness. For both Rabbit and Janice, this playacting indicates hopefulness, resiliency, and an awareness of the cyclic nature of life. It also puts the past into perspective: wearing his athletic jacket, Rabbit recognizes that "it was an ice-cream world that he made his mark in" (393). The resolute Janice, once disdained by Rabbit as inept, organizes their rapprochement. By presenting him with the keys to the family car that she had taken with her when moving in with Stavros, she symbolically restores her husband to his former position as head of the family. Now, however, power will be shared: while Rabbit drives, Janice navigates. Their meandering progress through Brewer recalls their original courtship, when the teenage couple searched for trysting places. Although the nervous Rabbit is ready to flee at any moment, Janice's new-found strength sustains them.

In flashes, Rabbit recognizes that his old ways are dead, no longer viable. Cruising, they pass Summer Street, the direction of Rabbit's flight in *Run:* "At the end of Summer Street he thinks there will be a brook, and then a dirt road and open pastures; but instead the city street broadens into a highway lined with hamburger diners, and drive-in sub shops, and a miniature golf course. [. . .] He has been here before" (398). Unlike Huck Finn or even his younger self, the older Rabbit finds no open territory for escape in middle-aged America. With his flight blocked, Janice instead steers her timid husband to the aptly named "Safe Haven Motel." Comedy promotes accommodation and compromise. At the motel, Janice's judgment is vindicated when the couple, to Rabbit's surprise, have no difficulty, despite a lack of luggage, registering for a room. The desk clerk, a friendly codger like his counterpart in *The Centaur,* notes Rabbit's youth and remonstrates with him for thinking that he will never visit distant places like Santa Fe: "Don't say that, young buck like you" (402). The old man's use of the term "young buck" (echoing Pajasek and the watch-man) and his description of the couple as resembling "haah school" students on a "honeymoon" encourage the possibility of a fresh start.

Registering, Rabbit "must lie" in listing as his address his burnt-out house. Doing so reveals his burgeoning faith in the quotidian because in Updike's fic-tion "lies" are necessary to make the leap of faith between hope and reality. In this instance, despite the fact that the house no longer exists, "The junk mail and bills have been getting to him from that address." Impressed, Rabbit re-flects that the postal service is "wonderful" and "Supernatural, that it works" (400). Just as the mail pick-up during the confrontation with his neighbors had revealed the community existing within the seemingly soulless development, here the unexpected arrival of bills and junk mail, an example of the quintes-sentially mundane, illustrates the comic faith that miracles occur within the context of ordinary life. These thoughts confirm Rabbit's skepticism about the limitations of radicalism: "Young punk revolutionaries, let them try to get the mail through, through rain and sleet and dark of night" (400–01). Subcon-sciously, Rabbit's awe over the wonderment of ordinary life encourages him to pursue reconciliation with Janice, despite their problems, rather than to flee to some fantasy.

Inside the motel room, when Rabbit acknowledges his guilt, Janice cautions him not to overreact: "Relax. Not everything is your fault" (406). Gradually, Rabbit "feels them drift along sideways deeper into being married" (405). The novel ends with them curled up together asleep. However tentatively, they have reconciled: for the first time since their breakup, husband and wife are together. The final sentence of the novel's epigraph, the transmission of the cosmonaut Colonel Shatalov as he prepares to dock his spacecraft, expresses the Angstroms' experience: "It took me quite a while to find you, but now I've got you." Rabbit falls asleep against her stomach, "his babies from her belly" (407), suggesting that the strongest link between them is their shared parent-hood. The punctuation of "He. She. Sleeps" symbolizes the gap that lingers between them, one that will take time to bridge. The final utterance "O.K.?"—its colloquialism reflecting the fondness of both this novel and com-edy in general for the vernacular—conveys measured optimism as well as, with its question mark, a hard-earned respect for life's uncertainty. For now, at least, Rabbit and Janice have returned to health.

· 4 ·

THE ROLE OF COMEDY
IN DISPELLING ILLUSION
IN *RABBIT IS RICH*

"Whatever Reality Is, It's Not That."
— FRYE, *The Anatomy of Criticism*

"Life is sweet. That's what they say."

In *Rabbit Is Rich*, set in the 1979 America of oil shortages and hostages, the 46-year-old Rabbit has become prosperous. Now a co-owner with his wife, Janice, and her mother, Bessie, of Springer Motors, his late father-in-law's Toyota dealership, he makes a comfortable living; moreover, he enjoys his status as "the star and spearpoint of all these two dozen employees and hundred thousand square feet of working space" (4). As a measure of his success, Rabbit belongs to the Flying Eagle, a *nouveau riche* country club. Here the Angstroms socialize primarily with the Murketts, the successful contractor Webb and his much younger wife, Cindy, and the Harrisons, Rabbit's long-time adversary, Ronnie, and his wife, Thelma. Although Rabbit loathes Ronnie and finds Thelma unappealing, he tolerates their company because of his regard for Webb and his lust for Cindy. Despite fears of aging and worries about holding on to his money, Rabbit avers, "Still, life is sweet" (6). When he reads the obituaries and thinks about how the dead "were multiplying," including his parents and his old coach, Tothero, during the interim since *Rabbit Redux*, "For the first time since childhood, Rabbit is happy, simply, to be alive" (10). Toward the deceased like Fred Springer, Rabbit feels grateful: "The great thing about the dead: they make space" (5).

Two unsettling occurrences, however, disturb Rabbit's serenity. First, he suspects that a young woman shopping for a car at his lot is his grown daughter, the baby born out of his affair with Ruth in *Run*. Hopeful that he has a daughter after all, Rabbit sets about to learn whether this teenager is his child. His sleuthing leads to the discovery of the location of the widowed Ruth's farm, but Rabbit lacks the courage to confront Ruth. Next, and more ominously, his son, Nelson, returns home, announcing his plans to quit college and work in the family business. His son's behavior puzzles Rabbit until the arrival of Nelson's pregnant girlfriend, Pru.

Despite Rabbit's reservations about the union between Nelson and Pru, eventually they marry with Rabbit paying for the wedding. Now the Angstroms, senior and junior, live with Janice's mother in her crowded house. Although Rabbit resists employing his son at Springer Motors, Janice and Ma Springer overrule him, and Nelson replaces Charlie Stavros at the lot. The tension between father and son increases when Nelson, on his own initiative, invests the firm's money in exotic stock such as convertibles, sports cars, and even a snowmobile. Meanwhile, Rabbit grows richer by investing first in gold and then silver. Even more thrilling, the country club set plans a vacation in the Caribbean, where Rabbit feels certain that he will at last bed Cindy. Before leaving, however, Rabbit and Janice, using the profits from their investments in precious metals, purchase their own home.

In the Caribbean, the couples, exulting in the freedom from routine, agree to swap mates for the last two nights of their stay. Rabbit, however, is disappointed when he ends up with the plain Thelma instead of the lustrous Cindy. Nevertheless, the night proves a revelation, for Thelma and Rabbit achieve intimacy. The next morning, Janice greets Rabbit with the dismaying news that, because Nelson is missing, they must return to Brewer immediately. There will be no night of ecstasy after all. At the airport, Ma Springer relates glad tidings: Pru has given birth to a daughter. Once home, Rabbit pays a last visit to Ruth's farm, where he finally questions Ruth about the identity of her daughter's father. Although the resentful Ruth steadfastly maintains that the girl is not his, he remains unconvinced. Later, Nelson returns to Kent State while Pru and the baby remain at Ma Springer's. At the novel's conclusion, Rabbit and Janice move into their new house. *Rabbit Is Rich* ends with Rabbit holding his granddaughter: "Fortune's hostage, heart's desire, a granddaughter. His. Another nail in his coffin. His" (467).

Like the first two novels in the series, *Rabbit Is Rich* begins with Rabbit again attempting to evade his responsibilities. This time, however, it is success not failure that prompts him. His reluctance to accept his place in time and society is evident in the novel's three main plot lines: his yearning to have a daughter;

his infatuation with the much younger Cindy; and, most of all, his rivalry with Nelson. For the first time since his high school basketball stardom, Rabbit has achieved a modicum of success, and, after so much failure, he fears any changes that threaten his position. The greatest menace to Rabbit's happiness is his grown son, Nelson, who represents the oncoming young generation: "Because Nelson has swallowed up the boy that was and substituted one more pushy man in the world, hairy wrists, big prick. Not enough room in the world" (226). The comic world, however, is dynamic, not static. Over the course of the novel, circumstances will impel Rabbit to give up his delusions and accept reality. At the same time, however, Rabbit will obtain a better sense of the possibilities available within his own life. Wisely, Stavros advises, "You got freedom you don't even use" (272).

Eventually, Rabbit convinces Janice that they should leave her mother's and buy their own home; afterwards, the daring Caribbean adventure proves enlightening. Near the novel's conclusion, a wiser Rabbit reveals his faith when he counsels his mother-in-law: "Let go; the Lord knows best" (385). As he ages, Rabbit's sense of humor becomes more acute. His running joke about the Rotarians as just kids "dressed up in fat and baldness and money like a cardboard tuxedo in a play for high-school assembly" (275) achieves the status of anecdotal permanence. Increasingly, he perceives life as play. At Nelson's wedding reception, "He sounds to himself, saying this, like an impersonator; life, just as we thought, is playing grownup" (250). Rabbit even has some fun at the expense of his creator: "'D'you ever get the feeling everything these days is sequels?' He asks in turn. 'Like people are running out of ideas'" (403). Nevertheless, the joke is on Rabbit when he forgets that he too is part of the human comedy. Rabbit imagines bliss with the dreamy Cindy as "his certain destination" (393), but comedy punctures illusions. When the Caribbean vacationers disembark from the airplane, Rabbit's first encounter with the aromatic tropical air transfixes him, "but Ronnie Harrison ruins the moment by exclaiming distinctly, behind his ear, 'Oh boy. That's better than a blow job'" (394). Worse, all the women, even his idealized Cindy, laugh.

Rabbit Is Rich presents a world beset by fear, uncertainty, and frustration. America in 1979 is a helpless giant, held hostage economically by its dependence on foreign oil and politically by the seizure of its embassy in Tehran. Nelson sums up the nation's ineptitude: "We can't do *any*thing anymore" (378). The opening of the novel, with Rabbit and his associate Charlie Stavros trading anecdotes about people's frantic behavior in the throes of the energy crisis, immediately conveys the hysteria of the times. The frustration is evident as motorists, vying for the limited supplies of gas, run amok. Despite his own prosperity, Rabbit cannot ignore society's disintegration: "On the news there is rioting in Levittown over gasoline, people are throwing beer bottles full of gasoline; they explode, they look like old films of Vietnam or Budapest but it is Levittown right down the road, north of Philadelphia" (49).

Even the Pope comes under fire. John Paul II's doctrinaire stand on birth control during his visit to the United States ignites heated discussion among Rabbit's set: "'He's running scared,' Rabbit offers. 'Like everybody else'" (293). Just as the exile of the Dalai Lama reflects Rabbit's own flight in *Run*, here the Pope's defense of tradition in the face of social change parallels Rabbit's attempt to maintain his position against Nelson's encroachment. More than ever, life appears inexplicable. The Dalai Lama's fate suggests this: "Not only is the Pope coming but the Dalai Lama they bounced out of Tibet twenty years ago is going around the U.S.A. talking to divinity schools and appearing on TV talk shows" (231). The resilient Dalai Lama, after fleeing Southeast Asia for his life, years later emerges on the American lecture circuit and television. His resurfacing emphasizes the similarity between Rabbit's fate and his own. In *Run*, Rabbit listens to radio news of reports of the Dalai Lama's exile and even, in his hubris, compares himself to the religious leader. Now, after twenty years of ups and downs, the international figure and the average person are both survivors who, for the moment at least, have landed on their feet.

Rabbit Is Rich, as its title suggests, focuses on the economic aspect of life. With affluence, however, comes insecurity: both Rabbit and America fear the loss of their accumulated wealth. The volatility of money contributes to the sense that life is capricious. The appreciation of Rabbit's investments in precious metals mocks how his father had once slaved for a pittance: "Poor Pop, he didn't live to see money get unreal" (402). For Rabbit now, money symbolizes the mystery of life: "He loves money, though he doesn't understand how it flows to him, or how it oozes away" (139). Eventually, the relationship between wealth and poverty expresses life's paradoxical nature: "And through the murk he glimpses the truth that to be rich is to be robbed, to be rich is to be poor" (375). The predominance of money undermines institutions such as higher education and the professions. According to Nelson, "College is a rip-off, the professors are teaching you stuff because they're getting paid to do it, not because it does you any good" (208); Rabbit thinks dentistry is a "Hellish way to make a living. Maybe there's no entirely good way" (203).

Throughout, the middle-aged Rabbit voices his confusion and frustration: "In middle age you are carrying the world in a sense and yet it seems more out of control than ever" (189). Reflecting the generational conflict at the novel's heart, Rabbit blames the current turmoil on his son's emerging generation: "Khomeini and Carter both trapped by a pack of kids who need a shave and don't know shit, they talk about old men sending young men off to war, if you could get the idiotic kids out of the world it might settle down to being a sensible place" (354–55). These sentiments project Rabbit's own uneasiness with Nelson. Increasingly, Rabbit's tone echoes that of the weary George Caldwell. At 46, Rabbit complains, "if a meaning of life was to show up you'd think it would have by now" (231). He finds existence increasingly problematic: "Life. Too much of it, and not enough. The fear that it will end some day, and the fear that tomorrow will be the same as yesterday" (354). Yet, as elsewhere in the series, a reflex pessimism is no more adequate than optimism in predicting the future. After the initial panic, the energy crisis abates.

Rabbit's attempt to retell a joke to his friends epitomizes the frustrating and uncertain nature of the world. Sure that his circle will enjoy the pun "A mercy killing, or murder most foul" heard in a radio account about a golfer's killing of a goose, Rabbit eagerly retells it. Instead, the joke falls flat because his friends either do not listen, or interrupt, or miss the point. Nevertheless, the joke gains anecdotal permanence with allusions to it recurring. Months later, the Harrisons triumphantly produce a newspaper clipping detailing the incident that is the basis of the anecdote. This item, however, is a factual account minus the pun and when Rabbit protests that he had been making a joke, the Harrisons, pedantically, focus on the discrepancies between the two versions: " 'The point is, Harry,' Thelma says, 'it's so *different.* You said he was from Baltimore and this says he was from Washington. You said the ball hit the goose accidentally and the doctor put him out of his misery' " (291–92). Later, after returning from the Caribbean, the Angstroms receive in an envelope without a return address another clipping, this one from a golf magazine, describing how a doctor had been fined for killing a goose on a golf course. This version concludes ironically that the doctor had "cooked his own goose" (454).

For Janice, however, this clipping has disturbing implications: She recognizes that it is Thelma who has sent it. Rabbit's little joke has evolved into a reminder of Thelma's affection for him, which could threaten the Angstroms' marriage: "Janice was vehement. 'I'm *furious* with her, doing such a flirtatious thing, so soon after' " (455). Overall, the different versions of the incident, from the radio gag to the earnest account in an advice column to the arch report in the golf magazine, reflect the vagaries of existence. Galligan notes that "the effect of most jokes is to affirm apparently irrational orders" (11). Near the end of the novel, Rabbit concludes one of his catalogues of the dead, which includes his parents, daughter, Jill and Skeeter from *Redux*, various celebrities like Mamie Eisenhower and John Wayne, and Skylab, with "the goose" (462).

Despite his affluence, Rabbit remains the comic hero: bumbling, as, for example, in his capsizing of the sailboat in the Caribbean; attractive, as indicated by Thelma's unrequited affection for him ("I adore you. *Adore* you" [216]); vital ("You're so glad to be alive" [418]); and a survivor: ("Now the dead are so many he feels for the living around him the camaraderie of survivors" [139]). Furthermore, Rabbit's middle age positions him between youth and old age and reflects comedy's predisposition for the midpoint between extremes. Like Dante, as well as George Caldwell, this comic hero finds himself midway through life's journey. With his new-found prosperity, however, Rabbit has become "smug and satisfied" (317). A parody of Robert Browning's "God's in his heaven—/ All's right with the world!" (1.222–23) indicates Rabbit's complacency: "He is in his bed, his molars are in their crowns" (86).

At the same time, his wealth makes him uneasy: "I pretty much like what I have. The trouble with that is, then you get afraid somebody will take it from you" (72). This lethal combination conspires to make him fearful of change. In particular, the passage of time threatens Rabbit for it reminds him of his own mortality. Regressing from *Redux*, he again views time as an enemy rather than as his element. Even the change of the seasons, which once had reinvigorated Rabbit, ultimately depresses him, "but then again reminding him he's suffered another promotion, taken another step up the stairs that has darkness at the head" (171). Above all else, Nelson's emergence as a young adult represents the ravenous nature of time. For much of this novel, Rabbit resists Janice's sound advice: "Nelson's not your enemy. He's your boy and needs you" (125).

The novel's two epigraphs convey Rabbit's smugness and uneasiness. The first connects Rabbit to Sinclair Lewis' George Babbitt, another businessman and member of the bourgeoisie: "At night he lights up a good cigar, and climbs into the little old 'bus, and maybe cusses the carburetor, and shoots out home. He mows the lawn, or sneaks in some practice putting, and then he's ready for dinner." Over the years, Rabbit, as Ruth observes, has become one of the fat cats he once disdained, "A regular Brewer sharpie. A dealer. The kind of person you used to hate. Remember?" (443). When he thinks of his parents' economic struggles during his childhood, "Rabbit basks above that old remembered world, rich, at rest" (69). Learning of Skeeter's death, Rabbit feels relieved that this agitator can no longer threaten society. Nelson accuses his father, "All you think about is money and things" (119).

Befitting the cyclic nature of comedy, Rabbit has regained his status as a big fish in a small pond. The relationship between the sports glory of his teenage years and his current self-satisfaction is underscored by the newspaper clippings and pictures celebrating his high school basketball exploits that adorn his office walls. The nightmarish headlines in *Redux* blaring his misfortunes and humiliations have been replaced by actual ones saluting past heroics: "Angstrom hits for 42. *'Rabbit' Leads Mt. Judge Into Semi-Finals.*" These memorabilia, "Resurrected from his dead parents' attic [. . .] had been Fred Springer's idea, along with that phrase about an agency's reputation being the shadow of the man up front" (4). Now once again Rabbit is "the man up front." He relishes his comeback: "He likes being part of all that; he likes the nod he gets from the community that had overlooked him like dirt since high school" (6).

Nevertheless, a disconcerting hint of temporality is present: "Even under glass, the clippings keep yellowing" (4). The other epigraph, from Wallace Stevens' "A Rabbit as King of the Ghosts," hints at Rabbit's insecurity: "The difficulty to think at the end of the day/ When the shapeless shadow covers the sun/ And nothing is left except light on your fur—" (1–3). This shadow is as ominous as the omen of the eagle is for Chiron in *The Centaur*. The phrases "end of the day" and "nothing left" convey Rabbit's sense of time running out. At the beginning of the novel ("king of the lot" [5]) and at the end ("Harry was king of the castle" [456]), images depict Rabbit as a monarch. For most of the novel, however, it is an uneasy head that wears the crown. Fearful of relinquishing his place in the sun, Rabbit desperately wishes to maintain the status quo: "Take over, young America. Eat me up. But one thing at a time, Jesus. There's tons of time" (122). Like Peter Caldwell, Rabbit wishes to stop time. Ultimately, however, Rabbit learns that not only is this impossible, but that, paradoxically, freedom is achieved by accepting one's place in time. Together, the epigraphs reflect Frye's two comic emotions: ridicule and sympathy. On one hand, Rabbit's Babbitt-like complacency is foolish; on the other, his concern for his own finitude is natural and understandable.

The opening of the novel reveals Rabbit's hopes of staying outside the hurly-burly of the quotidian:

> Running out of gas, Rabbit Angstrom thinks as he stands behind the summer-dusty windows of the Springer Motors display room watching the traffic go by on Route 111, traffic somehow thin and scared compared to what it used to be. The fucking world is running out of gas. But they won't catch him, not yet, because there isn't a piece of junk on the road gets better mileage than his Toyotas, with lower service costs. (3)

America is suffering the frustrations and fears of the energy crisis, but Rabbit, significantly separated from the street scene by a window, feels insulated by his lucrative association with the foreign-made energy-efficient Toyotas. As in *Redux*, Rabbit hopes to use his work—as Peter Caldwell tries with his art—to distance himself from the demands of life. Rabbit's gazing through a window here recalls a similar passage in *Run* when, as a young father, he peered enviously through his parents' kitchen window at the homely tableau of his mother, father, sister, and son eating dinner. Then, Rabbit, feeling incapable of providing in his own home the romanticized familial bliss he imagines before him, fled in despair; now, the scene before him is one of confusion and panic, and he is glad to remain removed from it. Eventually, Rabbit will discover that his affluence will not protect him from life's vicissitudes. Already, the qualification "not yet" indicates a dim suspicion that he cannot indefinitely remain detached from the encroaching world.

His longing for a daughter reflects the newly affluent Rabbit's Gatsby-like desire to recreate the past. In part, he vaguely hopes to replace his two dead daughters, the drowned baby Rebecca and the burnt surrogate daughter Jill. Moreover, he hopes to assuage his guilt for abandoning Ruth by funding the girl's education: "It's not for you, it would be for her. I can't give a lot. I mean, I'm not that rich" (447). Rabbit's obsession with the girl also reflects nostalgia for his youthful love affair with Ruth: "He does not know if he loved her or not, but with her he had known love, had experienced that cloudy inflation of self which makes us infants again and tips each moment with a plain excited purpose" (112). When Annabelle enters his showroom, she reminds the blunt Rabbit of Ruth: "A little touch of the hooker about her" (14). Finally, Rabbit's desire for a daughter reflects his rivalry with Nelson. When Ruth asks Rabbit why he has no interest in claiming either of her two sons as his child, he snaps: "'I have one boy. He's enough'—the phrase just comes—'bad news'" (444). His refusal to confront Ruth confirms that his desire for a daughter amounts to wishful thinking: "It's true, he could have looked her up, he even knew she lived around Galilee. But he hadn't. He hadn't wanted to face her, the complicated and accusing reality of her" (112). Galligan distinguishes between wishfulness and wishful thinking: "Comedy is the mode for realistic, wishing but not wishful, imaginations" (34). Early on, Janice exposes her husband's fantasizing: "You *always* want what you don't have instead of what you *do*. Getting all cute and smiley in the face thinking about this *girl* that doesn't exist while your *real* son, that you had with your *wife*, is waiting at home right now and you saying you wished he'd stay in Colorado" (72).

Rabbit's crush on Cindy Murkett also amounts to wishful thinking. For Rabbit, fantasizing about younger women is a way of escaping his role in time. Ogling the comely Cindy, Rabbit focuses on her youthfulness (Babbitt also had an ideal "fairy girl"). Although she is almost thirty, Rabbit views her as a teenager, "still smelling of high school" (57). He envies Webb Murkett, old enough to be Cindy's father. Despite his sexual attraction to Cindy, Rabbit cannot ignore entirely the age gap between them. On the plane to the Caribbean, "Cindy seems, in this confusion, amiable but remote, a younger sister" (393). At the wedding of Nelson and Pru, meeting the bride's mother reminds Rabbit that he belongs with women of his own generation: "Rabbit realizes with a shock that she is his proper date: old as she seems this woman is about his age and instead of naked in dreamland with stacked chicks like Cindy Murkett and Grace Stuhl's grandson's girlfriend he should be in mental bed with the likes of Mrs. Lubell" (250).

The references to "dreamland" and "mental bed" suggest an awareness of the fanciful nature of his desires. Significantly, this recognition occurs at Nelson's marriage, a ceremony Rabbit had opposed because it signifies his son's coming of age. Before the wedding, both young women Nelson brings home, his classmate Melanie and his fiancée, Pru, pique Rabbit's interest. Melanie, who returns with Nelson from Kent State to watch over him for her friend Pru, keeps Rabbit at a distance; nevertheless, he envies the middle-aged Stavros' intimacy with her. Although Stavros sensibly recognizes that his affair with Melanie will be short-lived, his audacity in vacationing with a young woman thirty years his junior, as well as the account of Melanie's father dropping out of a successful law career to live "out there on the West Coast fucking Indian maidens" (272), impresses Rabbit. When he recognizes that Pru is pregnant, Rabbit "is touched by her, turned on: *he* wants to be giving her this baby" (184). This reaction combines the three elements of Rabbit's wishful thinking: his attraction to younger women, his desire for another child, and his rivalry with Nelson.

Ultimately, the shallowness of Rabbit's infatuation with Cindy becomes apparent. For all his lustiness, Rabbit remains essentially prudish; echoing Janice's characterization of her husband in *Redux*, Thelma remarks, "You're such a sweet prude, Harry" (412). When Rabbit discovers hidden photos of the Murketts having sex, the pornographic images of Cindy shock as well as excite him: "who would have thought sweet Cindy could be so dirty? It takes some doing to realize that other boys are like you are, that dirty, and then to realize that girls can go right along with it takes more than one lifetime to assimilate" (308). Except for fantasizing about Cindy, Rabbit's interest in sex has dwindled. Early in the novel, a farcical scene occurs when an inebriated Janice, intent on sex, interrupts Rabbit as he avidly reads *Consumer Reports* in bed: "Naked, she lurches onto the bed where he is trying to read the July issue of *Consumer Reports* and thrusts her tongue into his mouth. He tastes Gallo, baloney, and toothpaste while his mind is still trying to sort out the virtues and failings of the great range of can openers put to the test over five close pages of print" (50). In her lustiness, Janice embodies the earthy comic figure antithetical to the fastidious Rabbit.

Now it is money that titillates him. After purchasing thirty Krugerrands, Rabbit becomes excited during foreplay with Janice amid the coins: "She is still examining the coin, stroking its subtle relief, when he wants her attention to turn to him. He hasn't had a hard-on just blossom in his pants since he can't remember when" (217). Rabbit estimates even the idealized Cindy in terms of monetary value. When the idea of swapping spouses is broached to Webb, "The old fox knows he has the treasure to barter" (407). For Rabbit, Cindy's youth and beauty are her currency, and, just as the value of gold and silver fluctuates with time, so will she. The day after his night with Thelma, Rabbit reevaluates Cindy in her bathing suit, "She is getting fatter, day by day. Better hurry, he tells himself" (423). On the flight home, Janice confides to her husband, "Webb says she's not that wonderful" (427).

Finally, the chief manifestation of Rabbit's wishful thinking is his refusal to accept Nelson as an adult. Early on, Rabbit recalls that his uneasiness with his son began when Nelson reached puberty: "From about that time on he began to feel crowded, living with the kid" (212). He admires Webb for distancing himself from his own grown children; his two young children with Cindy never disturb the Murketts' parties or even appear in the novel. For Rabbit, "Two glimpses mark the limits of his comfort in this matter of men descending from men." He remembers at age thirteen seeing his father dressing and being dismayed by the sight of "the mute and helpless flesh"; in contrast, as a father himself, he recalls accidentally surprising the fourteen-year-old Nelson as the boy emerged from a shower: "he had pubic hair and, though his body was still slim and pint-sized, a man-sized prick, heavy and oval, unlike Rabbit's circumcised and perhaps because of this looking brutal, and big. Big" (212).

Unlike the paragon George Caldwell, who sacrifices himself for his son, Rabbit views Nelson as an adversary: "It's great to have an enemy. Sharpens your senses" (125). Despite the wise counsel of Stavros ("Don't give up on the kid. He's all you got" [27]) and Janice, Rabbit girds himself for Nelson's challenge. He begins jogging in preparation for "The big bout" (142), with the adjective underscoring the life and death nature of this struggle in Rabbit's mind:

> "It's now or never," he tells her, the blood of fantasy rushing through his brain.
> "There's people out to get me. I can lie down now. Or fight."
> "Who's out to get you?"
> "You should know. You hatched him." (142)

With "the blood of fantasy rushing through his brain," Rabbit dehumanizes his son. Rabbit's overreaction is evident in his vow "To press against. Your own limitations" (142). This bravado is closer to tragedy than comedy. As Scott notes, tragic figures like Oedipus and Lear "soon exhaust themselves in the effort to gain release from the restrictions that are a consequence of their finitude" (90). In contrast, the down-to-earth Janice has no difficulty accepting Nelson's maturing: "Typical of the way things have gone, that the kid's growing up should seem a threat and tragedy to him and to her an excuse to steal a T-shirt" (138).

In Rabbit's overheated imagination, the son's ascension signals his own immediate demise. Ironically, Nelson's desertion of his own family dashes Rabbit's last opportunity for bliss with Cindy. On the plane ride home a gloomy Rabbit senses that he has reached his apex and from now on can only fall: "He has risen as far as he can, the possibility of such women is falling from him, falling with so many other possibilities as he descends" (428). Martin Grotjahn elaborates on the nature of the oedipal syndrome in comedy:

> The psychodynamics of the comedy can be understood as a kind of reversed Oedipal situation in which the son does not rebel against the father but the son's typical attitudes of childhood longing are projected upon the father. The son plays the role of victorious father with sexual freedom and achievement, while the father is cast in the role of the frustrated onlooker. The reversed Oedipus situation is repeated in every man's life when the younger generation grows up and slowly infiltrates and replaces the older generation in work and life. The clown is the comic figure representing the impotent and ridiculed father. (273)

Nelson enjoys sexual relations with both Melanie and Pru in the house where, since Fred Springer's death, Rabbit has ruled; now Rabbit, attracted to both young women and desirous of impregnating Pru, becomes the frustrated on-looker. Significantly, at Nelson's wedding, the father feels the urge "to play the disruptive clown" (244). Moreover, unlike Rabbit, who never had the oppor-tunity to attend college or travel, Nelson goes away to school at Kent State University and hang-glides in Colorado. In contrast to the provincial father, the son, who thinks nothing of hitchhiking across the United States, majors in geography. Worst of all, Rabbit must now accept Nelson's entry into the fam-ily business. Just as Fred Springer had prepared the way for his son-in-law, who, as Ma Springer points out, was at that time no more promising than Nel-son is here, it is time that Rabbit "make room" for his son.

Rabbit's sense that everything is running out—energy, time, money—stems from his narcissistic fear of his own mortality. Spitefully, Rabbit welcomes the world's end: "It gives him pleasure, makes Rabbit feel rich, to contemplate the world's wasting, to know that the earth is mortal too" (12). Comedy, however, undercuts such selfishness; instead, it celebrates a generous live-and-let-live attitude. Rabbit himself admits, "The world keeps ending but new people too dumb to know it keep showing up as if the fun's just starting" (88). Over the course of the novel, Rabbit will gradually learn that there is enough energy, time, and space for both his generation and the next, for him and Nelson. Once again Mim, fittingly at Nelson's wedding, enlightens her brother: "You must let go, Harry. The boy's life is his, you live your own" (241). Nelson's marriage symbolizes his coming of age: "I feel like I'm becoming a man" (208). Frye observes, "The appearance of the new society is frequently symbolized by some kind of party or festive ritual" (*Anatomy* 163). The wedding proves a joy-ous event, and despite the expense, even Rabbit becomes philosophical amid the gathering of family and friends: "What the hell, we're all going down the chute together"(249). Pru's pregnant condition emphasizes the marriage's celebration of life: "The secret knowledge shared by all that she is pregnant enriches her beauty" (242–43). According to Langer, comedy celebrates Comus, a fertility god who is "a symbol of perpetual rebirth, eternal life" (124).

In comic fashion, Rabbit's acceptance of Nelson's individuality helps lead to his own liberation. At the crowded reception in Ma Springer's gloomy Victorian home, it occurs to him: "He'd like a house some day with lots of light, splashing in across smart square surfaces. Why bury yourself alive?" (253). Stavros prods him, "How come you and Jan keep living in that shabby old barn with her mother?" (272). In order to enrich their lives, human beings must take chances and cross boundaries. Elsewhere, Stavros succinctly articulates the comic creed: "Being crazy's what keeps us alive" (90). In *Rich*, "crazy" becomes an honorific term. Nelson reminds his father how, in order to sell used cars in "the good old days," Charlie and "old man Springer used to do all these crazy things, they'd give away stuffed animals and crates of oranges" (165) When Nelson purchases large American cars and a British Triumph for resale, Rabbit denigrates these vehicles as "crazy cars"; eventually, however, Nelson's business instincts prove correct and the cars sell at a profit.

During the quarrel between father and son over this investment, after Nelson, in a fit of pique that expresses his hostility, crashes these cars "comically fast," Rabbit charges that this behavior "borders on crazy" (172). Springer Motors symbolizes Rabbit's power, and continually throughout the novel Nelson attacks his father by wrecking cars from the dealership. Unexpectedly, however, Rabbit's reaction to his son's destructiveness reveals his subconscious sympathy with Nelson's rebellion. Rather than outraging Rabbit, Nelson's attack brings forth "These strange awkward blobs of joy bobbing in Harry's chest." This incident too achieves anecdotal permanence: "Within a week, at the club, it has become a story he tells on himself" (170). Rabbit's joking, like Caldwell's, indicates his growing sense of the comic nature of life. Vaguely, Rabbit recognizes that his intransigence is as inhibiting for himself as for his son. Later, after evading Ruth's collie while spying on her farm, Rabbit reflects, "He hasn't felt so close to breaking out of his rut since Nelson smashed those convertibles" (282). When Rabbit at last approaches Ruth's door, he momentarily panics ("This is crazy. Run!" [437]), before overcoming his fears.

Crowded in Ma Springer's house, Rabbit finally recognizes that, as the realistic Pru urges, "it's natural [. . .] to want your own space" (358). Granting his son space, Rabbit creates more room for himself. This greater independence is mental as well as physical: "He thinks in this room he might begin to read books, instead of just magazines and newspapers, and begin to learn about history, say" (453). His new home "hints to him of many reforms and consolidations now possible in his life, like new shoots on a tree cropped back" (453). The simile is apt for in the two preceding novels in the series, plant stalks had been used as symbols of rebirth. Symbolically, Rabbit and Janice choose New Year's Day as the date to tell her mother about their new house and new life. Even the elderly Ma Springer, distraught by Rabbit and Janice's desertion, rebounds from despair. On their return from the Caribbean, the Angstroms find "her at the terminus of the last great effort of her life. Henceforth, she is in their hands" (429). This verdict, however, turns out to be premature. On the next page, the old woman, in order to replace the vanished Nelson, "wasn't so totally thrown by events that she didn't have the wit to call up Charlie Stavros and have him come back to the lot" (430).

Rabbit's rebirth entails more than a new house. Here, as in the other novels, God is an elusive presence. Early in the book, Rabbit fleetingly muses, "Rain, the last proof left to him that God exists" (125). The successful Rabbit thinks about God as little as possible. Doing so makes him uncomfortable because he associates God with death: "He doesn't want to think about the invisible anyway, every time in his life he's made a move toward it somebody has gotten killed" (162). At the same time, God's remoteness is unsettling. Discussing their concern over Nelson, Janice assures Rabbit that as parents they have done their best. She concludes by noting, "We're not God." In reply, Rabbit concurs, "'Nobody is' [. . .] scaring himself" (312). Joyce Carol Oates warns, "When the comic vision is weak in Updike's writing, a terrible nihilism beckons" (67). For much of the novel, Rabbit and God are estranged: "Sometimes he prays a few words at night but a stony truce seems to prevail between himself and God" (140). Rabbit's inability to pray is linked with his diminishing sexual powers. In bed at night, he finds it difficult either to pray or maintain an erection. For Rabbit, both God and sexuality are discomforting reminders of mortality. During the arrangement of a church wedding for Nelson and Pru, Rabbit envies the homosexual minister, Archie Campbell: "He walks on water; the mud of women, of making babies, never dirties his shoes. You got to take off your hat to him: nothing touches him. That's real religion" (202).

Rabbit's wishful thinking extends to religion as well. He longs for a faith that will insulate him from life, where he can walk on water and never soil his shoes. Earlier in this scene, upset by Nelson's atheism, Rabbit at first responds portentously, "Hell, what I think about religion is—" before concluding, with everyone's eyes on him, weakly "—is without a little of it, you'll sink" (198). As the meticulous figure, Rabbit hopes to compartmentalize God. In the fearful Rabbit's view, a "little" of religion is necessary to safeguard human beings from harm, from "sinking" into unpleasant reality. In contrast, Reverend Campbell instructs Nelson and Pru: "Marriage is not merely a rite; it is a sacrament, an invitation from God to participate in the divine. And the invitation is not for one moment only. Every day you share is meant to be sacramental" (201).

These words define the role of the divine within the quotidian; fittingly for the unpredictable nature of comedy, they come from, in Rabbit's judgment, an unlikely source. Rabbit disdains the clergyman as "prissy" and, likening him to *Mad* magazine's Alfred E. Newman, foolish. Yet, it is this "fag" who articulates God's involvement in everyday life, including procreation: " 'I was born in January,' Archie Campbell says, rising. He grins to show his seedy teeth. 'In my case, after much prayer. My parents were *an*cient. It's a wonder I'm here at all' " (202). The reference to his "seedy" teeth, repeated during the wedding scene, connects Campbell with the image of seeds that in Updike's fiction represents vitality and rebirth.

As in the previous novels in the series, Rabbit renews himself when he dares to cross boundaries. En route to his Caribbean holiday, Rabbit describes the Brewer airport in carnivalesque terms:

> Ever since the airport he has been amazed by other people: the carpeted corridors seem thronged with freaks, people in crazy sizes and clothes, girls with dead-white complexions and giant eyeglasses and hair frizzed out to fill a bushel basket, black men swaggering along in long fur coats and hip-hugging velvet suits, a tall pale boy in a turban and a down vest, a dwarf in a tam-o'-shanter, a woman so obese she couldn't sit in the molded plastic chairs of the waiting areas and had to stand propping herself on a three-legged aluminum cane. Life outside Brewer was gaudy, wild. Everyone was a clown in costume. Rabbit and his five companions were in costume too. (389–90)

Unlike *Redux*, where, amid the euphoria of the expedition to the moon Rabbit was one of those "left behind" in earth-bound deadening routine, here he embarks on an exhilarating visit to another world. Significantly, Ollie and Peggy Fosnacht, their last name the name of the pariah figure in *Run*, though present at Webb's party when this vacation is planned, are excluded. Away from his routine, Rabbit gives himself to the moment and plunges into a new lifestyle: playing, partying, spending freely, gambling recklessly, and even sailing. Although Webb shoots the best golf, Rabbit loses $300 at the casino, and the sailboat overturns, Rabbit is reinvigorated. Crossing boundaries is risky and fraught with danger—Rabbit "feels shaky and humiliated" (398) after losing at blackjack and the sailing "episode is inglorious" (405)—but there is no gain without pain. Like George Caldwell, Rabbit learns anew that humiliation and embarrassment are part of the human condition. Moreover, venturing outside his safe niche allows Rabbit to discern the difference between fantasy and possibility. All of these new experiences are prologue to his overriding goal:

sleeping with Cindy. True to the spirit of comedy, the outcome shall be quite different from the anticipation (Rabbit observes in another context, "As with many joys it does not come exactly as envisioned" [213]). Instead, life provides him with a far more valuable experience

In the airplane to the Caribbean, "Joy makes his heart pound. God, having shrunk in Harry's middle years to the size of a raisin lost under the car seat, is suddenly great again, everywhere like a radiant wind" (390). On the island, Rabbit and his friends cross another kind of boundary when they arrange to swap spouses for the evening. Fittingly, this episode begins with the band serenading the newly aligned couples with the strains of "Where Are the Clowns?" (409). In a scene that parallels George Caldwell's religious experience outside a rough New Jersey saloon and Rabbit's own within the black bar in *Redux*, intimacy with Thelma provides Rabbit with a revelation:

> That void, inside her. He can't take his mind from what he's discovered, that nothingness seen by his single eye. In the shadows, while humid blue moonlight and the rustle of palms seep through the louvers by the bed, he trusts himself to her as if speaking in prayer, talks to her about himself as he has talked to none other: about Nelson and the grudge he bears the kid and the grudge the boy bears him, and about his daughter, he thinks he has, grown and ignorant of him. He dares confide to Thelma, because she has let him fuck her up the ass in proof of love, his sense of miracle at being himself, himself instead of someone else, and his old inkling, now fading in the energy crunch, that there was something that wanted him to find it, that he was here on earth on a kind of assignment. (419)

Only comedy would have the audacity to portray its hero rediscovering his faith through anal sex. Although God is not explicitly mentioned, the wording "speaking in prayer," "sense of miracle," and "confide," a cognate of faith, reveal the spiritual nature of this experience; moreover, the expression "here on earth on a kind of assignment" suggests that earthly life is temporary and ancillary to a transcendent existence. Finally, Thelma's comment after the above passage, " 'It makes you'—the word is hard for her to find—'radiant'" (419), employs the same adjective that Rabbit used on the airplane to describe God's reappearance as "a radiant wind" (390). The importance of this word, with its connotations of the heavens, is emphasized by Thelma's deliberate search for the precise term.

Rabbit's sex with Thelma reaffirms his faith: "Since fucking Thelma up the ass he's felt freer, more in love with the world again" (430). Although this experience itself is hardly Caldwellesque, it does result in a greater appreciation of everyday life. Earlier in the novel, in a moment of despair, Rabbit had thought, "From a certain angle the most terrifying thing in the world is your own life, the fact that it's yours and no one else's" (182). At the same time he had complained, "The problem is, even if there is a Heaven how can there be one we can stand forever?" (181). This question, framed in the comic vernacular, echoes the stately lines from Stevens' poem "Sunday Morning": "Is there no change of death in paradise?/ Does ripe fruit never fall? Or do the boughs/ Hang always heavy in that perfect sky,/ Unchanging" (76–79). This poem explores the religious yearnings that exist even within a nonbeliever and hedonist. Rabbit, while lacking the sophistication of the persona in "Sunday Morning," resembles her in his estrangement from God and his position within the self-centered confines of Kierkegaard's aesthetic sphere. The frustrated Rabbit feels trapped within his routine but receives no comfort in contemplating a sterile afterlife.

In "Sunday Morning," without death and change, all sensuous experience cloys. Until this point in the novel, Rabbit fears death. Girding himself for unappetizing sex with Thelma, he imagines his own death—"as he will be before the undertakers undress him for the last time" (413). When Rabbit first penetrates Thelma's anus, he finds "there is no sensation: a void, a pure black box, a casket of perfect nothingness" (417). Rather than horrifying Rabbit, these images impress upon him that death and change are integral to life. The sex with Thelma renews him, not primarily because of its sensuality (which is downplayed), but because it reconnects Rabbit to reality. In contrast to his earlier adolescent fantasies, Thelma represents mature love, reminding him that he should be interested in women his own age ("You should want to fuck *me*, I'm your generation, Harry. I can *see* you. To those girls you're just an empty heap of years and money" [420]); moreover, Thelma, who has lupus, accepts death as a part of life ("I'm dying, you know that, don't you?" [415]). When Thelma and Rabbit finally fall asleep, it is "as if not a few stolen hours but an entire married life of sanctioned intimacy stretches unto death before them" (422). In the ten years between this novel and the next novel of the series, Thelma becomes Rabbit's mistress; in *Rest*, her identification with death is reinforced when she dies and Rabbit attends her funeral, the only funeral, aside from the infant Rebecca's in *Run*, depicted in the series.

The telling phrase, however, is "sanctioned intimacy," suggesting the sacramental nature of their relationship, which harkens back to the minister Campbell's description of marriage. The intimacy that Rabbit and Thelma experience during their evening together is in effect marriage-like. Reflecting the doubleness of comedy, Thelma functions as a second wife for him in this novel as Ruth did in *Run* and Jill did in *Redux*. Rabbit's sense that the middle-aged Thelma better suits him than does his dream girl, Cindy, represents an acknowledgment of his place in time. This evening replenishes Rabbit spiritually. Later, the memory of this experience empowers Rabbit to approach Ruth's farmhouse and confront her about his "daughter": "he takes that step, drawing heart from that loving void Thelma had confided to him" (437). When Ruth denies that he is the father, Rabbit takes her word at face value: "Let go. God has never wanted him to have a daughter" (450). Afterwards, he offers, "Maybe God is in the universe the way salt is in the ocean, giving it a taste" (462). This remark reflects God's subtle but ubiquitous presence within everyday life. Earlier in the novel, Rabbit recalls his feelings as a basketball player "when you're down ten points and less than five minutes left on the clock and you've just taken one too many elbows in the ribs, and all the muscles go loose suddenly and something begins lifting you and you know nothing is impossible, with faith" (165). In *Rich*, until this episode with Thelma, Rabbit had lost this faith.

Significantly, both spiritual experiences, on the basketball court and on holiday, take place within the framework of play (Thelma is "playful" making love [415]). Aptly, Thelma during the evening, characterizes herself: "I'm crazy, Harry. I got to get you out of my system" (416). Like Stavros, Thelma wisely recognizes that unconventional behavior keeps human beings vital. In her combination of innocence and experience (symbolized by the demure schoolteacher exterior that masks her passionate nature and sexual expertise), her Job-like fate as a sufferer of a debilitating disease, and especially her willingness to sacrifice herself ("The one thing I'm absolutely not supposed to do is go out in the sun. I was crazy to come down here, Ronnie tried to talk me out of it" [415–16]), Thelma represents the pharmakos. Describing her unrequited love for Rabbit, she refers to him as "My little hairshirt" (421).

Again, Updike reinforces the identification of a character with this figure by subtly alluding to the word's root meaning. In the Harrisons' bathroom Rabbit discovers a wealth of pharmaceuticals: "Plain as she is, Thelma carries a hefty medicine kit, and beauty aids, plus a sun block called Eclipse, and Solarcaine. Vaseline, too, for some reason. Tampax, in a bigger box than Janice ever buys. And a lot of painkiller, aspirin in several shapes and Darvon and more pills in little prescription bottles than he would have expected" (412). Before long, Rabbit learns why Thelma carries Vaseline with her. Discussing the pharmakos, Frye declares, "But the element of *play* is the barrier that separates art from savagery, and playing at human sacrifice seems to be an important theme of ironic comedy" (*Anatomy* 46). By jeopardizing her health through exposure to the sun, Thelma on this holiday is "playing at human sacrifice." Through sexual play with Thelma, as he had achieved by playing basketball, Rabbit gains a greater respect for the sacredness of life.

As in the other novels, Rabbit's renewal will not be accomplished without a visit to the revivifying green world. Teasingly, Updike locates it in a number of settings. These include Ma Springer's Poconos cottage, where Rabbit, refreshed by nature, "feels love for each phenomenon and not for the first time in his life seeks to bring himself into harmony with the intertwining simplicities that uphold him" (138); the Flying Eagle Tee and Racquet Club, with "its fairways and terraced tennis courts" (61) and chlorinated pool, where the staff wear green uniforms and Rabbit in his green bathing trunks enjoys his privileged status; and Ruth's farm with the repeated references to the house's "green door" (157). Yet, finally, none of these green worlds sustains Rabbit. Nelson intrudes upon his father's cozy domestic arrangement; not only do circumstances thwart Rabbit's pursuit of Cindy, but eventually he has misgivings about the country club clique; and as indicated by the various descriptions of Ruth's farmhouse green door as needing "its green paint refreshed" (112), "scabby" (157), and its "paint a poisonous green" (438), Rabbit has no future there either. After at last confronting Ruth, he departs knowing that he will never return: "Both know, what people should never know, that they will not meet again" (450).

Ultimately, the pregnant Pru represents the green world. Repeatedly, Pru is associated with the color green: Rabbit notices her "eyes, a flourishing green" and their "uncanny green clarity" (183); she regularly drinks crème de menthe ("a little bright green gleam of it appears by Pru's elbow at surprising times" [192]); in Nelson's jaundiced view, she wears "horrible green platform shoes" (336); and her crotch is "like the center of a flagrant green flower" (338). With child, Prudence represents fertility and vitality. Frye notes, "In the rituals and myths the earth that produces the rebirth is generally a female figure"(*Anatomy* 183). On his initial meeting with Pru, Rabbit quickly senses that she is pregnant. This recognition changes his world. The walls of the Springer house "change meaning, containing this seed between them"; even the old room's furnishings revive: "all these souvenirs of the dead bristle with new point, with fresh mission, if as Harry imagines this intruder's secret is a child to come" (184). "This seed," the image recurrent in Updike's fiction, promises rebirth for Rabbit as well. Rabbit finally gains a female descendant: "Fortune's hostage, heart's desire, a granddaughter. His. Another nail in his coffin. His" (467). The wording conveys Rabbit's range of emotions: a sense of the continuity between generations, his awareness that all along he had desired a female descendant, and an acceptance of his own mortality.

Rabbit Is Rich ends with Rabbit renewed. Expressing a deeper faith grounded in reality, he reaffirms: "Life is sweet. That's what they say" (463). With Nelson back at Kent State, "The kid was no threat to him for now. Harry was king of the castle" (456). Accepting his role has resulted in an enlarged kingdom, his own home and a granddaughter, as well as a richer appreciation of life. Now Rabbit understands the comic wisdom of living in the present: "No point in keeping secrets, we'll all be dead soon enough, already we're survivors, the kids are everywhere, making the music, giving the news"

(462). This novel's depiction of the gradual succession of the generations reflects Frye's description of the fundamental dynamic of comedy:

> Thus the movement from pistis to gnosis, from a society controlled by habit, ritual bondage, arbitrary law and the older characters to a society controlled by youth and pragmatic freedom is fundamentally, as the Greek words suggest, a movement from illusion to reality. Illusion is whatever s fixed and definable, and reality is best understood as its negative: whatever reality is, it's not *that*. (*Anatomy* 169–70)

Rabbit's experiences have exposed his wishful thinking: "whatever reality is, it's not *that*." Just as Rabbit felt trapped in a "net" in *Run*, in this novel the aptly named Webb Murkett (web, murky), with his glamorous wife, showy house, and authoritative manner, had for a time captivated the impressionable Rabbit. According to Kerry Ahearn, Webb is a "devilish character" who "embodies self-containment and unquestioned power in marriage and family" (77). Now, however, Rabbit sees through the smug, univocal Webb: "Harry suddenly hates people who seem to *know;* they would keep us blind to the fact that there is nothing to know" (425).

As Rabbit watches the Super Bowl, the halftime performers, "born, can you believe it, around 1960 at the earliest," sing "Energy is people" and "People are en-er-gy" (465). According to Lynch, comedy sings "the song of the indestructibility of the people" (107). Galligan elaborates: "Perhaps the plainest illustration of his concept of the generative finite is the aging process. The best way to understand, or at least to dissipate the confusion of one age, is to proceed into the ages that follow" (26). No longer threatened by the younger generation, Rabbit acknowledges his place in time. He recognizes the necessity of preserving his history, the fading clippings of his high school basketball exploits, as well as his health: "At his age you wear a hat" (434). At the same time, he is more keenly aware of the possibilities contained within the quotidian: "Nelson having stolen his Corona, Harry has allocated to himself a grape-blue Celica Supra, the ultimate Toyota" (434). The cars' names are telling. If Nelson has reached for his father's crown, Rabbit in turn has achieved transcendence: "This blue buzzard has charisma" (434). At the conclusion, Rabbit, holding his granddaughter, understands that he is indeed rich. Rabbit's love of life finally proves his greatest asset in *Rabbit Is Rich*. In comedy, appreciating the value of everyday life amounts to true wealth.

· 5 ·

THE COMIC HERO ACCEPTS HIS MORTALITY IN *RABBIT AT REST*

"There Comes a Time."

"what to make of a diminished thing." — FROST, "THE OVEN BIRD"

Rabbit at Rest begins just before New Year's 1989 with the semiretired Rabbit and Janice residing half the year in their Florida condominium while Nelson manages Springer Motors in Brewer. By now, Rabbit has become acutely conscious of death, with news of disasters like the Lockerbie bombing exacerbating his sense of foreboding. Strained relations between father and son add to Rabbit's uneasiness. During a post-Christmas visit, Nelson behaves erratically, becoming easily irritable and disappearing for hours. Adding to the mystery, Rabbit is perplexed that the recent used-car sales figures from the dealership are much lower than normal. Although Rabbit is kept in the dark, Pru confides to Janice that Nelson is using cocaine. Meanwhile, the dutiful grandfather takes eight- year-old Judy and four-year-old Roy on day trips. On one such excursion, Rabbit and Judy go sailing. Far from shore the boat capsizes and Rabbit, in his efforts to rescue his granddaughter, suffers a heart attack. Afterwards, as Rabbit convalesces from a coronary bypass, his doctor outlines a strict diet and exercise program for him.

The second chapter returns to Pennsylvania. On his farewell visit to the dying Thelma Harrison, his long-time mistress, Rabbit learns about his son's drug addiction. Late one night Pru frantically rouses Rabbit and Janice from bed because Nelson, in his frenzy for cocaine, has assaulted her. Next, Rabbit discovers that his son, to pay for his habit and medicine for his AIDS-stricken friend and coworker Lyle, has been stealing from the Toyota agency.

Confronted, Nelson reluctantly agrees to enter rehabilitation. During the same period, Rabbit undergoes an angioplasty in the Brewer Hospital, where, coincidentally, he encounters a young woman working as a nurse whom he suspects is his daughter. On his release from the hospital, Rabbit returns to his son's home. That evening, after the children are asleep, Rabbit finds himself alone in the house with the distraught Pru. When she visits his bedside to talk over her problems, solace becomes intimacy: they make love.

In the last chapter, with Nelson undergoing rehabilitation, Rabbit resumes managing Springer Motors. Soon, however, a series of events changes his life forever. Suddenly, Thelma dies; next, despite Rabbit's efforts to revive the family business, an executive from Toyota arrives to announce his company's decision to disenfranchise Springer Motors; finally, Rabbit learns that Pru has revealed their liaison to an outraged Janice and Nelson. Rather than confronting his resentful family, Rabbit, once more, flees south. Alone in Florida, he explores Deleon neighborhoods off the beaten track. On one of these forays, he challenges a teenager to a strenuous one-on-one basketball game. On the final play, as Rabbit launches the winning shot, he collapses with a violent heart attack. When Janice and Nelson reach Rabbit's bedside, they find him dying. The novel ends with a one word sentence: "Enough" (512).

The comic hero's life-long journey to maturity culminates in *Rabbit at Rest*. As the average person confronting illness and aging, Rabbit gradually recognizes that he too is mortal: now it is his turn to "make room" for the next generation. A number of occurrences diminish Rabbit's appetite for life, but the determining factor in his acceptance of death is his concern for the welfare of his son's family. Now, Rabbit intuits that his presence inhibits Nelson's maturation. Despite being a parent himself, Nelson remains feckless: he still blames his father for his problems and neglects his responsibilities. By sacrificing his own life for his family, Rabbit, late in the game, approaches Caldwell-like maturity. In comic fashion, his life has played out in a very different way from what he earlier had imagined. Instead of finding freedom through self-indulgence, Rabbit ultimately liberates himself through self-sacrifice. Moreover, through the prism of his experiences, Rabbit glimpses the congruity that exists beneath the surface chaos. Before dying, Rabbit subtly affirms his faith: the transcendent manifests itself in the quotidian.

In *Rest*, the comic world rolls on, unrelentingly frustrating, absurd, confusing, and, more than ever, uncertain. Events in both his private life and in the world at large exasperate Rabbit. After becoming separated from the rest of the family at the airport, Rabbit and his granddaughter have difficulty locating their car in the vast airport parking lot. When Judy sobs in panic, Rabbit empathizes, "He too wouldn't mind having a cry" (23). The ominous image depicting the scene that confronts Rabbit, "a brutal river" of cars (20), presages the subsequent ordeal in the "dark water" when the sailboat overturns. In both instances, the presence of others, either entering and exiting the lot or sailing and water-skiing near the capsized sailboat oblivious to Rabbit's plight, heightens his frustration.

At home, life is unsettling as well. Rabbit's grown son "frightens him" (24). His relationships with women remain problematic. Rabbit laments that he and his wife live "in a world of mostly mixed signals" (90) and he resents Janice's returning from her women's group with fresh accusations of male chauvinism. After their tryst, Pru also sends him mixed signals: "Women, no telling which side they want to dance on" (445). At times even his beloved grandchildren show Rabbit scant respect: little Roy exclaims, "Grampa looks ridiculous" (53). Nor does a comfortable retirement insulate Rabbit from life's frustrations: "Some people have it made; not for them a condo where they steal your view of the Gulf from the balcony. No matter how hard you climb, there are always the rich above you, who got there without effort. Lucky stiffs, holding you down, making you discontent so you buy more of the crap advertised on television" (484–85).

As a way of dealing with his irritations, Rabbit consoles himself with food. Eating—especially overeating—becomes a recurring motif. Immediately, the novel condemns the sedentary Rabbit's rich diet: one of its epigraphs warns, "Food to the indolent is poison, not sustenance." Exemplifying this quotation (from *The Life and Times of Frederick Douglass*), which first appeared in *Redux*, Rabbit avoids exercise while continually binging on lethal junk food. Despite the edicts of his doctors ("Ma'am, teach this stubborn bastard to *eat*" [172]) and the good example of his nutrition-conscious daughter-in-law as well as the irony of Charlie Stavros ("It's your funeral" [242]), Rabbit continually violates the diet his doctors have prescribed. Now, food is more alluring than sex. He rhapsodizes about macadamia nuts: "his tongue feels the texture of the fissure, miraculously smooth, like a young woman's body" (240–41). Nevertheless, no matter how much he eats, his appetite remains unsated. Adding to his frustration is the paradox that worrying about his health makes him hungry: "Harry finds that every time he thinks of his death it makes him want to eat—that's why he hasn't lost more weight" (218). His inability to give up junk food underscores the paradoxical nature of existence: "If God didn't want us to eat salt and fat, why did He make them taste so good?" (177).

The state of society is as unsound as Rabbit's diet: "Everything falling apart, airplanes, bridges, eight years under Reagan of nobody minding the store, making money out of nothing, running up debt" (9). The rebellious Rabbit of the earlier novels flouted society's mores; now, "He resents the fact that the world is so full of debt and nobody has to *pay*—not Mexico or Brazil, not the sleazy S and L banks, not Nelson. Rabbit never had much use for old-fashioned ethics but their dissolution eats at his bones" (400). These sentences—linking international, national, and familial instances of fiscal irresponsibility—combine Rabbit's public and personal frustrations. By the 1980's the extent of society's disintegration is evident in the irony that by now Rabbit feels morally superior to the larger community. Retirement only exacerbates his dissatisfaction. Reflecting on the aimlessness of modern existence, Rabbit muses, "Most of American life is spent driving somewhere and then driving back wondering why the hell you went" (29). The Florida landscape contributes to Rabbit's feelings of anomie: "Between these paths there's somehow nothing, a lot of identical palm trees and cactus and thirsty lawn and empty sunshine, hotels you're not staying at and beaches you're not admitted to and inland areas where there's never any reason to go" (88). Man's attempts to dominate nature seem futile: "The skin men have imposed on bleak nature is so thin it develops holes" (85).

Ironically, he finds the headline of a newspaper article, "Circus *Redux*," puzzling: "He hates that word, you see it everywhere, and he doesn't know how to pronounce it. Like *arbitrageur* and *perestroika*" (50). Rabbit's difficulty in keeping pace with the modern world indicates a growing fear of being left behind: "He is still trying to keep up with America, as it changes styles and costumes and vocabulary as it dances ahead ever young, ever younger" (280). The older Rabbit gets, the more the world awes him. Florida's dazzling natural marvels reinforce this sense of wonder. As Rabbit and Janice take the grandchildren on a tour of the Thomas Alva Edison Winter Home, Rabbit reflects upon the guide's rhapsodic description of the exotic trees on the grounds: "*Why did God bother,* Harry wonders, *to do all these tricks, off by Himself in the Amazon jungle?*" Whereupon the tour guide's practiced spiel supplies the answer: "They are chocolate brown on one side and white on the other and because of their unusual shapes and lasting qualities are in great demand for dried floral arrangements. You can purchase these leaves in our gift shop" (94). Afterwards, at Jungle Gardens, the colorful flamingos remind Rabbit of the diversity in life that makes relationships among individuals problematic:

Flocks of flamingos, colored that unreal orange-pink color, sleep while standing up, like big feathery lollipops, each body a ball, the idle leg and the neck and head somehow knitted in, balanced on one pencil-thin leg and wide leathern foot. Others, almost as marvelous, are awake and stirring, tenderly treading. "Look how they drink," Harry tells his grandchildren, lowering his voice as if in the presence of something sacred. "Upside down. Their bills are scoops that work upside down." And they stand marveling, the four human beings, as if the space between farflung planets had been abolished, so different do these living things loom from themselves. The earth is many planets, that intersect only at moments. Even among themselves, slices of difference interpose, speaking the same language though they do, and lacking feathers, and all drinking right side up. (103)

Rabbit, more than ever, is acutely conscious of the precariousness of life. Sailboats capsize; planes crash; Hurricane Hugo threatens Florida; Nelson's accountant, Lyle, dies of AIDS; the energetic baseball commissioner and former president of Yale University, Bartlett Giamatti, "*Only fifty-one*" (447), after lunch in his summer home, suffers a fatal heart attack; on the drive south, Rabbit reflects upon road-kill: "Just think, he lay down for lunch and that was it" (449). Unthinkably, "Now Springer Motors is *kaput, finito*. Down the tubes just like Kroll's. Nothing is sacred" (464). Images of "sinking" recur: the boat, Nelson's house, Springer Motors (Rabbit imagines a *Redux*-like newspaper headline, *Joint Scam Sinks Family Concern*" [258]), and Rabbit himself. Even within the confines of his snug Pennsylvania residence, Rabbit feels vulnerable. When drug dealers telephone his home seeking payment for Nelson's debts, the menacing voices undermine any sense of security: "But the caller has hung up, leaving Harry with the sensation that the walls of his solid little limestone house are as thin as diet crackers, that the wall-to-wall carpet under his feet is soaked with water, that a pipe has burst and there is no plumber to call" (230). By now, Rabbit perceives the flimsiness of man's institutions. Near the end of the novel he ponders:

> He knows when the bottom fell out. When they closed down Kroll's, Kroll's that had stood in the center of Brewer all these years, bigger than a church, older than the courthouse, right at the head of Weiser Square there, with every Christmas those otherworldly displays of circling trains and nodding dolls and twinkling stars in the corner windows as if God Himself put them there to light up this darkest time of the year. [. . .] When he worked there back in Shipping you saw the turnover, the hiring and firing, the discontinued lines, the abrupt changes of fashion, the panicky gambling of all this merchandising, but still he believed in the place as a whole, its power, its good faith. So when the system just upped one summer and decided to close Kroll's down, just because shoppers had stopped coming in because the downtown had become frightening to white people, Rabbit realized the world was not solid and benign, it was a shabby set of temporary arrangements rigged up for the time being, all for the sake of money. You just passed through, and they milked you for what you were worth, mostly when you were young and gullible. If Kroll's could go, the courthouse could go, the banks could go. When the money stopped, they could close down God Himself. (461)

Rabbit's history with Kroll's reflects his evolvement: in his childish imagination, the store with its magical Christmas displays represented the harmonious workings of God and man ("As a little kid he couldn't tell what God did from what people did; it all came from above somehow" [461]) that created a stable meaningful universe; as a young man employed there, he recognized the store as a human enterprise subject to economic forces, but nevertheless he retained an overall trust "in the place as a whole, its power, its good faith"; ultimately, as a mature adult, when "the system" abruptly closes Kroll's, he perceives the essential instability and uncertainty of human institutions. Nothing is sacred: "When the money stopped, they could close down God Himself" (461). Rabbit now knows better than to place his "faith" in the permanence of man's creations. With time, the old order changes: Soviet communism collapses and the defeated Japan outstrips the victorious U.S.A. Helpfully, the Toyota executive who announces his company's decision to disassociate itself from Springer Motors, confides to Rabbit: "'Things change,' says Mr. Shimada. 'Is world's sad secret'" (393). Though Rabbit pleads, "with a tired joke, 'I'm too old for flux'" (398), he has little choice but to keep rolling with the punches.

Death dominates Rabbit's thoughts. In particular, the specter of sudden, violent death, like the horror of the Lockerbie bombing, haunts him:

> Imagine sitting there in your seat being lulled by the hum of the big Rolls-Royce engines and the stewardesses bringing the clinking drinks caddy and the feeling of having caught the plane nothing to do now but relax and then with a roar and giant ripping noise and scattered screams this whole cozy world dropping away and nothing under you but black space and your chest squeezed by the terrible unbreathable cold. (8)

The vividness of his stream of consciousness reveals Rabbit's identification with the Lockerbie victims. The comfortable images of the "Rolls-Royce engines" and "the clinking drinks caddy" reflect Rabbit's own affluence and leisure financed by Springer Motors. Yet, given the paradoxical nature of the world, one is most vulnerable to life's vicissitudes when there is "nothing to do now but relax." His fears prove prophetic. The fatal heart attack occurs when Rabbit experiences once more his basketball glory during a moment of triumphant play. The rendering of this horror recalls his description of the Lockerbie disaster: "Up he goes, way up toward the torn clouds. His torso is ripped by a terrific pain, elbow to elbow. He bursts from within" (506). Rabbit too will plummet abruptly and helplessly to his death.

A comic discussion reveals Rabbit's reluctance to confront his own mortality. During a lull at work, Rabbit chats with Benny Leone, one of his salespeople. Here, Rabbit personifies the bullying alazon figure as he insists on turning the conversation to sports even though he knows Benny has no interest in the topic: "Maybe he enjoys bullying him with it, boring him" (351). Rabbit's imposing title of Chief Sales Representative associates him with what Cornford calls the "professional types" (122), who hold a superior position in society over their listeners. Rabbit begins by lavishly praising Mike Schmidt, the veteran Philadelphia Phillies baseball star, for abruptly electing to retire in midseason despite forfeiting a large portion of his salary: "He knew what he had to do and couldn't do it, and he faced the fact and you got to give him credit. In this day and age, he put honor over money" (351). Before Benny can respond, the other salesperson interrupts: "'An error each in the last two games against the Giants,' Elvira inexorably recites. 'And hitting .203, just two hits his last forty-one at bats'" (352). This dry recounting of indisputably damning statistics neatly undercuts Rabbit's romanticized version of Schmidt's retirement. Meeker notes, "The comic point of view is that man's high moral ideals and glorified heroic poses are themselves largely based upon fantasy" (26). By downplaying the reality of the athlete's diminishing skills, Rabbit assigns Schmidt too much credit, but Elvira, representing the pragmatic eiron, matter of factly sets the record straight: "They would have cut him by August, the way he was going. He spared himself the humiliation" (352).

Rabbit too feels the pressure of time on his own diminished powers. Earlier, in the hospital after his first heart attack, he had struck a heroic pose: "determined to be debonair—Bogey at the airport in Casablanca, Flynn at Little Big Horn, George Sanders in the collapsing temple to Dagon, Victor Mature having pushed apart the pillars" (172). Rabbit's self-aggrandizement is clear in his selection of glamorous movie stars in romantic roles as the models of his own heroism. At the same time, his identifying with images of actors playing parts and with the ballplayer Schmidt fits comedy's sense of life as play. Galligan, citing the importance of play as a means of understanding life, explains: "An acceptance of limitations with a concomitant rejection of 'magical' solutions and 'angelic' powers point towards a delight in games (with all their arbitrary rules about fair and foul balls) and in unabashed pretense" (37). Now, Rabbit too must come to terms with the limitations of existence. Unlike another famous aging ballplayer, Pete Rose, Mike Schmidt at least knows when to quit. Ultimately, Rabbit salutes his decisiveness: "Schmidt did what Rose is too dumb to: quit, when you've had it. Take your medicine, don't prolong the agony with all these lawyers" (356).

By now Rabbit ruefully acknowledges that he can no longer count on an older generation to shield him from life's slings and arrows: "When he was a kid and had growing pains he would be worried and the grownups around him laughed them off on his behalf; now he is unmistakably a grownup and must do his own laughing off" (7). The wording indicates the individual's changing role over time. The phrase "growing pains" refers to his gradual maturing, a process that inevitably entails suffering; the image "laughing off" aptly describes the comic perspective that accepts these "pains." "Grownups," having reached maturity, bear their responsibilities "on behalf of" the younger generation. As he ages, Rabbit more and more resembles George Caldwell. Expressing their bewilderment, they sound alike: in *The Centaur*, Caldwell complains, "if I knew what the hell the point of it all was. I ask and nobody'll tell me" (102); Rabbit confesses, "Well I don't know what the hell's going on" (83). Just as Caldwell's antics in the classroom are celebrated, Rabbit's blunder in mistakenly eating bird food on a family outing becomes legendary: "they begin the long day that for years to come will be known in fond family legend as The Day Grandpa Ate the Parrot Food, though it wasn't exactly for parrots, and he didn't eat much of it" (92). This "natural" mistake reflects humanity's intrinsic foolishness.

Another parallel occurs when Rabbit dresses up as Uncle Sam for a Fourth of July parade, "though he has become more corpulent than our national hero should be" (362). In *The Centaur*, Peter has a disconcerting dream in which the local town fails to remember his father although "he was Uncle Sam and led the parade" (136). Both Rabbit's impersonation and Peter's nightmare reflect the comic hero's position in the generations. As Rabbit marches, he notices that there has been "a bubbling up of generation on generation since the town brought him forth" (369); nevertheless, "They remember him," and cheer him, calling "his old nickname" affectionately. Rabbit has consented to participate in the parade "for Judy's sake"; he experiences "an exalted sacrificial feeling" although, en route, "He feels giddy, ridiculous, enormous." Here too he achieves mythic status: "He is a legend, a walking cloud" (370). The reference to sacrifice is telling. Though weary and fearful of having cancer, Caldwell continues working in order to sustain his family; after his heart attack, Rabbit musters the strength to replace his son at Springer Motors. Like Caldwell, Rabbit humbly recognizes man's inherent limitations: "Nobody's perfect. We're only human. Look at Jim Bakker. Look at Bart Giamatti" (454). Coupling such diverse figures (recalling Caldwell's linking of Bing Crosby with St. Paul), the convicted television evangelist and the scholar, reflects the inclusiveness of comedy: "We're all just human, bodies with brains at one end and the rest just plumbing" (410).

In Florida, Rabbit interacts with Jews for the first time and their equanimity intrigues him: "*Tell me how you've got on top of sex and death so they don't bother you*" (71). As in *Redux*, where Rabbit learns from the black experience, here, by negotiating the boundary between Jews and gentiles, he deepens his own understanding of life: "He is still getting used to the Jews down here, learning from them, trying to assimilate the philosophy that gives them such a grip on the world" (6). Bernie Drechsel, after "making money and children," accepts retirement as just another stage of life: "and now he's at the other end of life's rainbow, and this is what you do: Bernie endures retirement fun in the way he's endured his entire life, sucking that same acrid wet-cigar taste out of it" (66). These Jews live in the comic present: "Rabbit is impressed by this ability Jews seem to have, to sing and to dance, to give themselves to the moment" (61). With their long history, Jews understand the human condition: "He in turn treasures their perspective; it seems more manly than his, sadder and wiser and less shaky" (57). Their comic perspective has helped them survive. Near the end, the isolated Rabbit briefly entertains the notion of a flirtation with Mrs. Zbritski, a widow in her 60's and a survivor of the holocaust: "Didn't he read somewhere that even in the Nazi death camps there were romances?" (488). Like the blacks in *Redux*, Jews have not forgotten how to laugh. Listening to Rabbit's uneasiness about Nelson's behavior, Joe Gold says: "Here's a Jewish joke for you. Abe meets Izzy after a long time no see. He asks, 'How many children do you have?' Izzy says, 'None.' Abe says, 'None! So what do you do for aggravation?'" (72–73).

Rabbit's willingness to cross boundaries is most apparent in the shocking episode of his lovemaking with his daughter-in-law. His defense of his actions ("It was just a crazy moment that didn't hurt anybody" [433]) employs the same epithet "crazy" that recurs in *Rich* as an honorific term for bizarre but ultimately justifiable behavior. Rabbit and Pru are "weary and half crazy with their fates" (361). On this night of passion, the demoralized Pru feels abandoned by her crack-addicted husband ("I love coke, Mom. And it loves me" [154]) and Rabbit feels similarly deserted by his ambitious spouse. Noting that "Eros" dominates comedy, Frye includes both "Oedipus and incest themes" (*Anatomy* 181). This scene merges both the oedipal and, in a sense, the incestuous, but suggests that human needs override society's taboos.

The storm raging outside during the scene serves as an objective correlative for the powerful and spontaneous passion that overwhelms them: "As if in overflow of the natural heedlessness" (346). Rabbit insists, at the time "it seemed sort of natural" (342). There is an Edenic quality to this episode: "a piece of paradise blundered on, incredible" (342). The verb "blundered" connects this scene with Rabbit's "historic blunder" in eating the parrot food: his behavior here too is natural and unpremeditated, if also foolish. Associating the lovers with childhood—"His gesture has the presexual quality of one child sharing with another an interesting discovery" (345)—suggests innocence. Moreover, Updike atypically refrains from detailing the sexual act; the chapter closes with Pru and Rabbit ready to make love. Finally, there is Rabbit's version afterwards: "She was hard-up and I was at death's door. It was her way of playing nurse" (434). This reductiveness conveys the flavor of this episode far more accurately than does Janice's rigid moralizing and Nelson's self-pity.

According to Frye, self-righteousness is antithetical to comedy (*Anatomy* 167); Potts observes that comedy is not moralistic: "But for the moralist to condemn any comedy because of its subject matter is an error in judgment. Its business is to satisfy a healthy human desire: the desire to understand the behavior of men and women toward one another in social life, and to judge them according to their own pretensions and standards" (207). As with the night of intimacy with Thelma in *Rich*, this daring sexual experience proves salutary. The disclosure of this experience leads directly to Rabbit's "revelation" of what course he should follow. Pru also ultimately benefits. The revitalization of her marriage is signaled by the news that she and Nelson will try to have a third child; moreover, Pru establishes some distance from her manipulative mother-in-law with her scheme of uniting all three generations under the same roof.

Pru is not misnamed. The word "prudence" implies the capacity for judging in advance the possible results of one's actions. At times, circumstances warrant radical measures. Entering Rabbit's room with a condom in her bathrobe, Pru initiates events: "It was her show" (354). Pru, a survivor in her own right, knows what she's doing. With her world crumbling, she cannot afford to play it safe. Driven by her "slum hunger," she succeeds in saving her marriage. The depiction of Pru, along with that of Mim, Thelma, Ruth, the mature Janice, and, later, Annabelle Beyer, reveals that Updike does portray strong and sympathetic female characters in his fiction.

At the beginning of *Run*, when Rabbit, on his flight south, asks for directions, an old farmer gives him enigmatic advice. In the final section of *Rest*, when Rabbit flees to Florida once more, he unsuccessfully attempts to revisit the site where he encountered the rustic sage three decades ago: "Rabbit wants to see once more in Morgantown, a hardware store with two pumps outside, where a thickset farmer in two shirts and hairy nostrils had advised him to know where he was going before he went there. Well, now, he did. He had learned the road and figured out the destination" (438). The duality associated with this speaker (the "two pumps," "two shirts," and "nostrils") identifies him as a comic authority possessing double vision. Now, the seasoned Rabbit appreciates this counsel. Through a lifetime of trial and error, the comic hero gradually finds his way. His dual nature, balancing passivity with venturesomeness, allows him both to absorb the lessons of life and, when the situation calls for it, to act boldly. When an indignant Janice confronts her husband about his sleeping with Pru, Rabbit acts. Rejecting Janice's summons to present himself for a "family therapy session," Rabbit departs for Florida instead. Like Caldwell at the conclusion of *The Centaur*, now Rabbit's course is clear.

External circumstances motivate Rabbit. First, Janice develops a new life for herself that increasingly excludes her husband: "He is alone" (6). When Bessie Springer dies, her daughter inherits everything. Now "Janice is rich"

(5). Nelson's accountant thwarts Rabbit's attempts to investigate the firm's books because he knows, as Janice boasts, "I'm the only one who counts" (225). Similarly, Nelson refuses to deal with his cocaine addiction until Janice threatens to take legal action against him. Although she feels remorse for her firmness with her wayward son, "This numbness she feels must be the *power* her woman's group in Florida talks about, the power men have always had"(315). When disaster threatens, Janice exhibits her comic faith: "You *are* taking it hard. Don't. Daddy used to say, 'For every up there's a down, and for every down there's an up'" (395). Her emergence stems from finally escaping the shadow of her parents: "but of course if they were alive she wouldn't be doing this, she wouldn't have the mental space. They were wonderful parents but had never trusted her to manage by herself" (312). After learning of Rabbit's sleeping with Pru, her voice on the telephone "sounded comically like her mother" (435).

With her independence, Janice begins adapting to a life alone even before Rabbit is gone. While he convalesces in Brewer Hospital, she relishes her freedom: "Maybe being a widow won't be so very bad is the thought she keeps trying not to think"(309). Also, she notices that in talking about her husband, "There is this subtle past tense that keeps creeping into her remarks about him" (363). Expressing its comic focus on today, the *Rabbit* series employs the present tense throughout; now Janice consigns its hero to the past. Philosophically, she allows, "Well, sometimes in life you have to give up things that you love" (396). No longer does she rely on Rabbit for information about the world: "He hears in the things she says, more and more, other voices, opinions, and a wisdom gathered away from him" (395). He feels that these new influences in her life "seem an invasion as devious as that televised catheter nudging forward into his shadowy webbed heart" (336). As he had feared all along, Rabbit's most formidable rival turns out to be his son. Janice's bond with Nelson excludes Rabbit: "Their complicity is complete now" (153). Her willingness to sell Rabbit's beloved Penn Park house to bail out Nelson illustrates that her ultimate loyalty is to her son. When she hears of Rabbit's second heart attack, at first she reflexively starts to pray for his recovery, but, on second thought, "With him gone, she can sell the Penn Park house. '*Dear God, dear God,*' she prays, '*Do what You think best*'" (510).

Others close to Rabbit also fade from his life. On Rabbit's return to Florida, he visits Thelma, his mistress of ten years during the interval between *Rich* and this novel: "She didn't sound happy to hear from him, but not distressed either: resigned, merely" (192). The scene has a morbid air. The dark, "motionless stuffed" living room depresses Rabbit: "This room is so finished, he feels in it he should be dead. It smells of all the insurance policies Ron sold to buy its furnishings" (196). Even Thelma's refreshments seem anti-life. Coffee and tea are "no-nos" so Rabbit settles for a soft drink, but the Diet Coke is "tasteless": "First they take the cocaine out, then the caffeine, and now the sugar" (197). The quintessential American drink is now as diminished as Rabbit. In discussing their illnesses, Thelma reveals that her health is rapidly deteriorating: "I'm losing it, Harry." Her sexual recklessness now frightens Rabbit, "because it suggests a willing slide into death." She senses his reluctance to make love: "On her own she sees he isn't up to it" (203). When he, clinging, embraces her, "Thelma goes dead, somehow, in his arms" (207). As he leaves, Thelma announces that their affair is over. When Rabbit protests, "Without you, I don't have a life," she is adamant: "Maybe Nature is trying to tell us something. We're too old to keep being foolish" (207).

In light of Stavros' credo "Being crazy's what keeps us alive," Thelma's remark implies a death wish. This scene parallels Rabbit's final encounter with Ruth in the previous novel, when the two former lovers recognize that they would never again meet. Subtly, Updike provides a link between these two episodes by means of the image of "yellow school buses" outside Thelma's house. (Ruth's yard also contains parked yellow school buses once driven by her husband.) The buses on Thelma's street with their cargos of "shrilly yelling children" symbolize the succession of generations: as the aging lovers' lives draw to a close, a new generation emerges as the children "release" from the school buses.

Rabbit's flamboyant sister, Mim, appears only briefly here in a phone conversation with her brother. Although only fifty, the flippant Mim dismays Rabbit with her own sense of aging: "That's cow pasture. That's hang-it-up time, if you're a woman. You don't get the stares anymore, it's like you've gone invisible" (287). When Rabbit, seeking the reassurance of nostalgia, whimsically inquires about the lyrics of a childhood song ("What's the line that comes after 'Makes your eyes light up, your tummy say "howdy"'?"), Mim abruptly cuts him short: "I have no fucking idea" (289). At Thelma's funeral, Rabbit meets Cindy Murkett, his "dream girl" in *Rich*. Observing her now, with her beauty faded, Rabbit muses, "He had wanted Cindy and wound up with Thelma. Now both are beyond desiring" (375). While in Brewer Hospital, Rabbit learns that his nurse is Annabelle Byers, Ruth's daughter, whom he suspects is his as well. From Annabelle, Rabbit learns that Ruth is rejuvenated, living and working in Brewer and has "lost a lot of weight and dresses real snappy." Nevertheless, he resists Annabelle's invitation to meet her: "He is suddenly tired, too tired for Ruth. Even if the girl is his daughter, it's an old story going on and on like a radio nobody's listening to" (278).

On his return to Brewer, Rabbit, needing advice, seeks out Charlie Stavros, now retired from Springer Motors. Rabbit feels, however, that "It's not quite like the old days, when they had all day to kill, over in the showroom" (240).

Inevitably, Pru as well distances herself from Rabbit. After their night together, Rabbit and Pru "are severely polite with each other" and "It was now as if it had never been" (361). During Rabbit's last conversation with his family, Nelson reveals that he and Pru have decided to have a third child: "Not only for Judy and Roy, but for our*selves*. We love each other, Dad" (482). This news produces mixed feelings in Rabbit, but the overriding emotion is "relief." Pru belongs with Nelson. By the novel's conclusion, Rabbit feels totally estranged from family and friends. When Pru inquires his whereabouts, Rabbit answers evasively, "Far away, where everybody wants me" (444).

Additionally, Rabbit is left without an occupation to sustain him. The elderly but still vital Dr. Morris informs Rabbit: "A man needs an occupation. He needs something to do. The best thing for a body is a healthy interest in life" (476). On his drive south alone, Rabbit, mulling over his life, recognizes that most of all it is work that has fulfilled him:

> What he enjoyed most, it turns out in retrospect, and he didn't know it at the time, was standing around in the showroom, behind the dusty big window with the banners, bouncing on the balls of his feet to keep up his leg muscles, waiting for a customer, shooting the bull with Charlie or whoever, earning his paycheck, filling his slot in the big picture, doing his bit, getting a little recognition. That's all we want from each other, recognition. Your assigned place in the rat race. (451)

True to comedy, Rabbit locates happiness within the quotidian, "filling his slot in the big picture." The canny Florida Jews understand the relationship between happiness and the quotidian. Bernie Drechsel notes: "'There are two routes to happiness,' he continues, back at the wheel of the cart. 'Work for it, day after day, like you and I did, or take a chemical shortcut'" (58). When Rabbit asks where is the happiness "after you've gone the distance," the answer is "Behind you" (58). Now, Rabbit's happiness is behind him. The workplace dramatizes the succession of the generations. Nelson condemns his father as an anachronism: "That was *then*, Dad, this is *now*. You were still in the industrial era" (39). Finally, there is no role for Rabbit in Nelson's business schemes. When Rabbit ridicules his son's decision to sell aqua motorcycles called Waverunners at the lot, Nelson counters with a pointed, "People can adjust, if you're under a certain age" (416).

Rabbit's obsolescence is made clear in the scene depicting the visit of the Toyota executive, Mr. Shimada, to announce his company's decision to sever its ties with Springer Motors. The passage emphasizes the contrast between the "impeccable" Shimada, his only imperfection his English, and Rabbit. Just before Shimada's arrival, Rabbit decides to clean up the litter in the lot. When the limousine pulls in, Rabbit, "Puffing, his heart thudding," his suit "pulling at the buttons," rushes to greet his visitor and shakes hands "with a hand unwashed of street grit, dried sugar, and still-sticky pizza topping" (385). With the Caldwell-like Rabbit personifying the down-to-earth comic hero, Shimada represents the meticulous anti-comic figure. Touring the facility, Rabbit refrains from introducing the visitor to the assistant parts manager "for fear of besmirching Mr. Shimada with a touch of grease" (387). From "a single sheet of stiff creamy paper, sparsely decorated with typed figures" (390), Shimada announces Springer Motors' death sentence. His data sheet—"single" suggesting his univocal vision and "stiff" indicating his inflexibility—serves as an objective correlative for Shimada's humorless perspective. Exiting, Shimada callously makes "a little Japanese joke," advising Rabbit to purchase a luxury "Rexus at dealer price" while still eligible for the discount. In return, Rabbit "gives the manicured hand a gritty squeeze" and makes an ironic rejoinder of his own: "Don't think I can afford even a Corolla now" (394). Nevertheless, this comic discussion, as usual, ends by revealing the true state of affairs. Soon, "all joking falls away and he abruptly feels fragile and ill with loss" (394). The younger employees find other positions, but for Rabbit this day ends his working life. Later, at home talking on the phone to Nelson at the lot, Rabbit rues his retirement: "Hanging up, Harry pictures the showroom, the late-afternoon light on the display windows, tall to the sky now with all the banners down, and the fun going on, amazingly, without him" (419).

Finally, the retired Rabbit's failing health diminishes his zest for life. Even before the heart attacks, Rabbit connects his weakening eyesight with his ennui: "And the lenses are always dusty and the things he looks at all seem tired; he's seen them too many times before" (56). Aptly, given the state of Rabbit's health, the novel opens in Florida with its "sunstruck clinics—dental, chiropractic, arthritic, cardiac, legal, legal-medical—that line the boulevards of this state dedicated to the old" (4). After his heart attack, Rabbit's life must change drastically: a strict diet, regular exercise, medicine, and, inevitably, more surgery. For Rabbit, once an athlete, the diminishing of his physical powers is especially dispiriting. Since the first operation, Rabbit has not been the same: "Ever since they invaded his arteries with dyes and balloons, he has aches and pains in remote and random joints, as if his blood is no longer purely his own. Once you break the cap on a ginger-ale bottle, there is never again as much fizz" (289–90).

Watching his operation on a monitor, Rabbit feels that the doctors are invading a place where "God or whoever never meant human hands to touch" (269). Rabbit rejects his doctor's suggestion of more surgery: "In fact when you think about it, his whole life from here on in is apt to be insulting. Pacemakers, crutches, wheelchairs. Impotence" (475). Rabbit cannot hide his distaste for the infirmities of aging: "He does hope he never reaches the point where he has to think at the time about shitting. Ma Springer, toward the end, got to talking about her bowel movements like they were family heirlooms, each one precious" (489). During the climactic basketball game in Florida, the panting Rabbit refuses his opponent's gracious offer to stop play. Scornfully, he berates himself: "No big deal you're too out of shape for this. No big deal you aren't good even for a little one-on-one" (505).

As his present and future dim, Rabbit retreats into the past. In a poetic passage, he recalls playing as a child: "Then as now, waking from twilight dreams, he discovered himself nearer a shining presence than he thought, near enough for it to cast a golden shadow ahead of his steps across the yard; then it was his future, now it is his past" (191). As Rabbit reminisces, his maturation is evident. When he thinks of that long-ago feud between "that long dead Methodist neighbor of theirs on Jackson Road" and his mother, "he smiles" (183). Now he possesses the double vision to put this overblown incident in perspective. The aging Rabbit identifies with the past: "things he remembers personally, VE day or the Sunday Truman declared war on North Korea, are history now, which most of the people in the world know only about from books" (183). When Rabbit plays basketball with the youths in Florida, one of them prophetically "taunts him, 'you're history'" (491); before the final game, when his opponent, Tiger, deduces that Rabbit "played once," Rabbit dates himself, "Long time ago" (503).

His interest in sports, as either participant or spectator, wanes. He gives up his beloved golf: "The kids out there at the Flying Eagle don't want an old man in the foursome" (396). As for spectator sports, "You can't live through these athletes, they don't know you exist" (233). For the comic hero, a diminished playfulness is an ominous sign. Increasingly, the past overwhelms the fragile present: "he feels a stifling uselessness in things, a kind of atomic decay whereby the precious glowing present turns, with each tick of the clock, into the leaden slag of history" (420). Later, hearing of problems at work, he feels relieved, "Thank God, Harry no longer has to care" (499); more and more, everyday events are "Not his problem. Fewer and fewer things are" (340). Working in his garden, he feels himself drawn to the earth: "In his mood of isolation and lassitude he is drawing closer and closer to the earth, the familiar mother with his infancy still in her skirts, in the shadows beneath the bushes" (395). In *Run*, his gardening for Mrs. Smith had acquainted him with the cyclic natural process that includes all life; now, older and weary, he himself is ready to mix with the dirt.

Foremost, it is the plight of his grandchildren that motivates Rabbit. In the sailboat episode, he risks his life to ensure Judy's safety. Unlike the drowning of baby Rebecca, Rabbit, although in great pain from a heart attack, succeeds in saving Judy: "Joy that Judy lives crowds his heart" (133). (Whether Judy was actually in danger is doubtful, but Rabbit assumed she was.) Early on, however, he notices Judy's unhappiness: "*At her age, this girl should be happier than she is,* Harry thinks" (49). In Pennsylvania, when summoned by Pru in the middle of the night because of Nelson's abusive behavior, Rabbit reflects, "Nobody has brought this child a present for some time. Her childhood is wearing out before she is done with it" (263). Afterwards, Janice, enlisting her husband's support for Nelson's rehabilitation, nudges Rabbit, "Weren't those children dear? Harry, you don't want them to live in one of those sad one-parent households" (269). Upon Nelson's return from the clinic, Rabbit remains dubious when Janice insists on "putting this loser back in charge"; nevertheless, looking at the hopeful Judy, he confesses, "But how can he wish anything for this child but the father she needs?" (408). Recommending a bypass operation, Dr. Breit urges Rabbit, "You owe it not only to yourself but to your wife and son. And those cunning little grandchildren I've heard about" (285). Eventually, Rabbit senses that to ensure the future of his grandchildren, he must yield to Nelson.

This sacrifice entails accepting his finiteness. From the outset of the book, Rabbit feels the next generation crowding him. On the drive from the airport, Nelson sits "right behind Harry, so he can feel the kid's breath on the back of his neck" (25). Two telling images recur: taking up "space" and a "parade." The portly Rabbit feels that his stomach weighs as much "as a starving Ethiopian child" (91). Later, catching his reflection in a mirror, Rabbit "is startled by how big he is, by how much space he is taking up on the planet" (380). At the lot, he reminisces: "When he first came to the lot as Chief Sales Rep, after Fred Springer had died, he was afraid he couldn't fill the space. But now as an older man, with his head so full of memories, he fills it without even trying" (356). Nevertheless, for anyone, "filling the space" is temporary. With Janice firmly in control of the family business, she informs Rabbit that his presence at the lot will inhibit Nelson: "Let's give Nelson the space" (408).

On the drive south, paralleling the novel's opening scene on the highway, Rabbit reflects upon his "jostling for his space in the world as if he still deserves it" (442). The word "jostling" also appears in the image of a parade representing the progression of generations: "Rabbit feels as if the human race is a vast colorful jostling bristling parade in which he is limping and falling behind" (115). Earlier, recognizing his place at the head of his family, Rabbit preens: "A float of a man, in a parade of dependents" (84). Later, he recalls his childhood "house on Jackson Road, where Mom and Pop set up their friction, their heat, their comedy, their parade of days" (281). Finally, as Rabbit marches in the Fourth of July parade, he perceives that "The whole town he knew has been swallowed up, by the decades, but another has taken its place, younger, more naked, less fearful, better" (370).

Gradually, Rabbit accepts his place in life's passing parade. Rabbit cannot help contrasting the vitality of Nelson and Pru with Janice's and his own:

"Brawling, Fucking. There is something hot and disastrous about Nelson and Pru that scares the rest of them. Young couples give off this heat; they're still at the heart of the world's business, making babies. Old couples like him and Janice give off the musty smell of dead flower stalks, rotting in the vase" (101). Rabbit recognizes that his aging generation must yield to the more vital succeeding one that is "still at the heart of the world's business, making babies." As the image of the "dead flower stalks," recurrent throughout the series, indicates, this process is natural. When Rabbit prunes the forsythia in his garden, "you take out the oldest stem from the base, making the bush younger and thinner [. . .]. It doesn't do to be tenderhearted; the harder you cut back now, the more crammed with glad yellow blossoms the stubby branches become in the spring" (421).

Just as the previous generation had "made room" for Rabbit's, now it is his generation's turn to sacrifice itself: "Your life derives, and has to give" (451). At this stage, Rabbit recognizes the comic truth: "There's more to being a human being than getting your own way" (451). There comes a time for decisive action: "When you get children growing under you, you try to rise to the occasion" (139). The usually passive Rabbit rises to this occasion: "A life knows few revelations: these must be followed when they come. Rabbit sees clearly what to do. His acts take on a decisive haste" (435). This last sentence repeats almost word for word the description of his decision to flee south in *Run*. Now, however, he knows what he's doing. Through his decisiveness, Rabbit emerges as a new person. He senses this transformation immediately. Straightening up the house before leaving on his final journey, Rabbit reflects that now he is "on the far side of a decisive gulf. The he who fell asleep was somebody else, a pathetic somebody" (436).

In this novel, Rabbit discovers the idyllic "green world" in the recurring image of his granddaughter's "green eyes, greener than Pru's" (139). In *Rich*, he locates the green world in the pregnant Pru, especially in her eyes, "those staring mud-flecked greenish eyes that Judy's clearer paler eyes were distilled from" (172). Now, symbolizing the succession of generations, the promise of the green world has passed to Judy: "The child's face wears a glaze of perfection—perfect straight teeth, perfectly spaced lashes, narrow gleams in her green eyes and along the strands of her hair. Nature is trying to come up with another winner" (408). Later, in a dream, Rabbit envisions "Roy, Roy all grown up, and as tall as he" (500). In time, Roy, the new king, will emerge.

Now, however, the conflict raging between Nelson and Rabbit threatens the welfare of the Angstroms. At the airport, awaiting his son's arrival, Rabbit envisions "something more ominous and intimately his: his own death, shaped vaguely like an airplane" (3). Janice complains, "I'm tired of you and Nelson fighting your old wars through me" (249). Elsewhere, she explains to Rabbit his effect on his son: "You are to him. Psychologically dominating. You're certainly a lot taller. And were a wonderful athlete" (189). Etymologically, Nelson's name means son of a champion, and this legacy weighs on him. She elaborates, "Men have this territorial thing. You think of the lot as yours. He thinks of it as his" (227).

Symbolically, at the lot Nelson has removed from the office walls the aged photos of his father as a high school basketball star. Later, siding with her son, Janice refuses to replace Nelson at Springer Motors: "He's running the lot and it would be too unmanning to take it from him" (266). Wryly, Rabbit acknowledges, "The kid and I have something going between us. Not sure love is what you'd call it" (172). In comedy, the oedipal rivalry reverses the usual roles of father and son. One of the shrewd Jews notes: "'The way you talk about him,' Bernie said, 'he could be the father and you the son'"(71). Nelson accuses his father of being "so damned adolescent" (257). Even Rabbit recognizes this reversal of roles: "You always seemed pretty mature to me. Maybe too, early on. I didn't set such a good example of maturity" (179).

Like Peter Caldwell, Nelson takes himself too seriously. A conversation between Janice and Nelson suggests that the relationship between Rabbit and his son parallels that of George Caldwell and his son, Peter: "You were a tense child, Nelson. You took everything very seriously"; and he replies, "How else're you supposed to take it? Like a big joke, like Dad does, as if the fucking world is nothing but a love letter to yours truly?" (147). As Peter does with art, Nelson attempts to distance himself from the quotidian first with cocaine and afterwards with his new-found faith in therapy. After rehabilitation, the preachy Nelson speaks in a "steady-voiced sermon" (404); he possesses "ministerial gravity and automated calm" (417). At the same time, he still blames his parents and his wife for his problems rather than himself. Earlier, Pru rails against his "immature dependence" on his parents: "By continuing to accept the blame he's willing to assign you, you and Janice continue to infantilize him. After thirty, shouldn't we all be responsible for our own lives?" (125). The reversal of roles between father and son is evident in Rabbit's attraction to Pru: "having a wife and children soon palled for him, but he never fails to be excited by having, in the flesh, a daughter-in-law" (14). Before the sailboat adventure, Rabbit is flattered that the beach supervisor assumes Pru is his wife: "Tall and fair-skinned like he is, she might well be his" (118). Even after Pru has ended their relationship, Rabbit consoles himself with the warmth in her tone: "That level woman-to-man voice, as if he had his arms around her, her voice relaxing into their basic relation, cock to cunt, doing Nelson in" (445).

Nevertheless, in comedy youth inevitably gains the upper hand over the old. Although he feels "squeezed" when he learns that Nelson and Pru have decided to try to have another baby, Rabbit himself accepts the inevitable:

"You're not a man until you've gotten on top of your father." Rabbit acknowledges his own oedipal triumph: "In his own case, it was easier, the system had beaten Pop so far down already" (480). When the wise Stavros explains that the world's overcrowding necessarily will cause disaster, Rabbit immediately thinks of his relationship with Nelson: "Rabbit's heart dips, thinking that from Nelson's point of view he himself is a big part of the crowding. That time he screamed outside the burning house at 26 Vista Crescent, *I'll kill you*. He didn't mean it. A spark, a crack in metal. A tiny flaw. When you die you do the world a favor" (233).

The image of "crowding," recalling the opening of *Run*, suggests the theme of the natural progression of the generations that informs the entire series as well as *The Centaur*. After Rabbit's first heart attack, at the hospital Roy playfully pulls the oxygen tube from his grandfather's nose. When Nelson lashes out at the child, Rabbit intercedes, "He just wanted to do me a favor" (179). Earlier, Rabbit had articulated his feelings toward Nelson: "I love him all right, but maybe it's a him that's long gone. A little tiny kid, looking right up to you while you're letting him down—you never forget it" (172). Rabbit acknowledges his failures as a father: When a drug dealer, attempting to collect Nelson's debts, flatters Rabbit as "a very excellent father," Rabbit demurs, "Not so hot, actually" (229); when Nelson enters rehabilitation, Rabbit recognizes that "His fatherhood hasn't been good enough. They're calling in the professionals" (300). With the comic spirit that grants second chances, the aging Rabbit sees one last opportunity to avoid "letting him down."

The end of the novel, culminating with an exchange between father and son rather than husband and wife, underscores the centrality of the oedipal relationship in the series just as in *The Centaur*. At the deathbed, with Rabbit unable to speak, the petulant Nelson is "unhappy" and "complains" about his father's silence. Meanwhile, Rabbit thinks, "He feels sorry about what he did to the kid but he's doing him a favor now, though Nelson doesn't seem to know it" (511). The repeated use of the word "favor" expresses Rabbit's sense that his dying represents the older generation's stepping aside in behalf of the younger. This ending recalls the conclusion of Leo Tolstoy's "The Death of Ivan Ilych," where Ilych, another flawed human being on his deathbed, for the first time feels sorry for someone other than himself: his heartbroken son. Doing so, he finally gives his life meaning. Like Rabbit, Ivan Ilych, also unable to make himself heard, recognizes that for his family "it will be better for them when I die"(1016). Similarly, the dying Rabbit's concern is for his son rather than himself: "He wants to put the kid out of his misery. *Nelson*, he wants to say, *you have a sister*" (512).

Transcending his own plight, Rabbit seeks to console his son with the news that, after all, in Annabelle Byer, Nelson has a sister. When the frightened

Nelson wails, "Don't *die*, Dad, *don't!*" Rabbit recognizes that "the boy depends on him" (512). The Caldwell-like references to a 33-year-old as a "kid" and a "boy" suggest Nelson's lack of maturity (like the 31-year-old Peter Caldwell); moreover, just as the elder Caldwell sacrificed himself for his son and family, Rabbit intuits that Nelson also "depends on him" to sacrifice himself. Rabbit attempts to reassure him: "'Well, Nelson,' he says, 'all I can tell you is, it isn't so bad'" (512). Death is part of life; the qualifying phrase "isn't so bad" reflects Rabbit's double vision. This is "all" Rabbit can impart to his son, but it is finally "enough." With his father out of the way, Nelson now has "space."

The structure of this novel and of the series reflects the cyclic nature of life. *Rest*'s movement from Florida to Pennsylvania and back to Florida reverses *Run*'s pattern from Pennsylvania to Florida and back to Pennsylvania. The end of each chapter of *Rest* finds Rabbit in bed: first, ill with his heart attack in the hospital; next, making love with Pru; finally, dying. Rabbit's retirement to Florida suggests the circular nature of the individual's life: "the whole state babies you" (4). His experience over the years undercuts Rabbit's earlier tendency to romanticize the past at the expense of the present. Hearing of Annabelle's trials living in the city, Rabbit admits, "Brewer's a rugged town. [. . .] Always was" (293).

As he reads history, the brutality of the Revolutionary War appalls Rabbit: "He has always thought of the Revolution as a kind of gentleman's war, without any of that grim stuff" (499). Now he sees the resemblance between that celebrated war of independence and the Vietnam conflict. Reductively, Rabbit views George Washington as a comic hero, a desperate survivor with the odds against him: "But he hangs in there, patching, begging, scrambling, his only assets the fatheadedness of the British commanders, all gouty nobleman wishing they were home in their castles, and the fact that, just like in Vietnam, the natives weren't basically friendly" (484). Popular culture also undercuts nostalgia: watching an old Abbott and Costello movie, Rabbit thinks, "People yelled and snapped at one another like animals then" (498). Listening to pop music on the radio, just as he had in *Run*, Rabbit now notices that "the songs of his life were as moronic as the rock the brainless kids now feed on" (460).

The first words of the second chapter, "Sun and moon, rise and fall," herald the natural rhythm of life and recall the opening of *Run*'s second chapter: "Sun and moon, sun and moon, time goes" (127). As Rabbit ages, he rediscovers his past within the present. Driving through Brewer, Rabbit notes that "life goes on as lively as ever, though in a darker shade" (185); marching in the Fourth of July parade, he thinks, "This crowd seems a strung-out recycled version of the crowd that used to jam the old auditorium-gym" (368). The crowd's cheers celebrate Rabbit's reemergence as a local hero almost forty years since his high school glory. In the final days of his life Rabbit, in effect, revisits his youth.

With time on his hands, "He discovers some blocks back from the beachfront and the green glass hotels, old neighborhoods" (477) in the black area of Deleon. He finds himself drawn to this area because it reminds him "of the town of his childhood, Mt. Judge, in the days of the Depression and distant war, when people still sat on their front porches, and there were vacant lots and odd-shaped cornfields, and men back from work in the factories would water their lawns in the evenings, and people not long off the farm kept chickens in back-yard pens, and peddled the eggs for odd pennies" (477–78).

According to Galligan, comedy presents time and change as "cyclical and unthreatening" (34). Rabbit's lifelong journey brings him full circle: he returns to his starting point. The opening scene of *Run* depicts the 26-year-old Rabbit playing a pick-up basketball street game with some local kids; near the end of *Rest*, the 56-year-old Rabbit does so again on a playground in Deleon. In the first chapter, at the Deleon hospital, a mural depicts an Indian shooting an arrow at an explorer ("This Indian scowls with evil intent. The explorer will be killed" [157]). Here, Rabbit's opponent's "lips hint at Indian blood," his expression is "snarling," and he moves "knifingly." By the game's end, Rabbit, a Ponce Deleon-like explorer searching for his youth in this poor Florida neighborhood ("Deleon is in some way familiar" [486]), suffers a fatal "knifelike pain" (505). The emerging young generation destroys the old. Appropriately, the comic hero's last activity is play. Now the other players are Florida blacks rather than Pennsylvania whites, but the game remains the same. Rabbit's running has brought him home.

Ultimately, Rabbit's faith becomes rooted in everyday experience. As the series proceeds, Updike portrays institutional religion as less and less important in Rabbit's life. Here, the sole clergyman is the minister of the "no-brand-name" church who presides at Thelma's funeral service. His eulogy sounds perfunctory and "wrapping up" the proceedings, he "rolls on to rote assurances" (373–74). In derision, Rabbit compares the rehabilitated Nelson, with his single-vision belief in his therapeutic program, to media evangelists: "'Tell Nelson to loosen up. Just because he got over crack he doesn't have to turn into Billy Graham.' Or Jim Bakker" (446). Yet as he ages, Rabbit, without the benefit of churches and clergy, feels closer to God:

> *He'll be there.* Funny, about Harry and religion. When God didn't have a friend in the world, back there in the Sixties, he couldn't let go of Him, and now when the preachers are all praying through bullhorns he can't get it up for Him. He is like a friend you've had so long you've forgotten what you liked about Him. You'd think after that heart scare, but in a way the closer you get the less you think about it, like you're in His hand already. Like you're out on the court instead of on the bench swallowing down butterflies and trying to remember the plays. (450)

Significantly, Rabbit uses the word "Funny" to describe his faith; moreover, he chooses images from the quotidian—of friendship, sexuality, and playfulness—to express his religious feelings. The comic hero lives his faith rather than, like Nelson, pontificating or, like Jim Bakker, proclaiming it for profit. Rabbit is uneasy when Thelma patronizes him: "Believe in God, darling. It helps"; uncomfortably, "He squirms, inside, 'I don't not believe'" (206). For Rabbit, "the sound of the rain in that great beech had been the most religious experience of his life. That, and hitting a pure golf shot" (250). He speaks of a golf shot in religious terms: "the hope of perfection," "grace you could call it," and "pure" (56). Similarly, the dying Thelma finds that "her affair with Rabbit has enriched her transactions with God" (195).

Given the nature of faith, the comic hero continually wrestles with doubt: "Hard to believe God is always listening, never gets bored" (440). Reductively, Rabbit articulates his uncertainty about an afterlife in terms that echo the doubts in "Sunday Morning": "But without money around, what would they talk about?" (298). Throughout, he muses about the origin of life. Staring at his heart in the monitor during surgery, Rabbit, like Caldwell's students, confronts the mystery of evolution: "How could the flame of him ever have ignited out of such wet straw?" (270) Later, as Rabbit convalesces in the darkened bedroom of Ma Springer's old house, the light from the streetlight creates shapes out of the raindrops on the windowpanes that resemble "the origins of life in one of those educational television shows he watches: molecules collecting and collecting at random and then twitched into life by lightning" (340).

At the end of *Run*, he finds the streetlights more meaningful than the darkened church. Now, gazing at his dead mother-in-law's sewing machine, which seems to await her return, Rabbit reflects, "About as likely as that to happen as life just rising up out of molecules" (341). Near the end of his life, Rabbit proclaims his faith: "Those crazy molecules. All by themselves. Never" (437). The wonder of these humble molecules, like the primitive life that Caldwell's lecture celebrates, proves God's existence. This expression of faith, delivered as an offhand remark, employs the series' honorific epithet "crazy." When the distraught Pru reveals her fear that she and her endangered children are "trash," Rabbit quickly attempts to console her, but to himself admits, "We're all trash, really. Without God to lift us up and make us angels we're all trash" (344).

On Rabbit's return to Brewer after his first heart attack, he finds himself driving down the familiar streets of his past:

A block or two toward the mountain from Ruth's old street—Summer Street it was, though they lived there in spring, summer spelled their end—Rabbit is suddenly driving in a white tunnel, trees on both sides of the street in white blossoms, the trees young and oval in shape, and blending one into the other like clouds, the sky's high blue above tingeing the topmost blossoms as it does the daytime moon. And up top where there is most light the leaves are beginning to unfold, shiny and small and heart shaped, as he knows because he is moved enough to pull the Celica to the curb and park and get out and pull off a single leaf to study, as if it will be a clue to all this glory. Along the sidewalk in this radiant long grove shadowy people push baby carriages and stand conversing by their steps as if oblivious of the beauty suspended above them, enclosing them, already shedding a confetti of petals: they are in Heaven. (187–88)

When Rabbit, overwhelmed by this experience, asks Janice, whose opinion he now respects, why he had "never seen them before," she matter of factly replies, "You've seen, it's just you see differently now" (188). Significantly, younger couples "pushing baby carriages," like Nelson and Pru, remain "oblivious" to this beauty; it is the elderly Rabbit whom the scene transfixes. As with the rain in the trees, Rabbit perceives the transcendent within nature. He is "is moved enough to pull the Celica to the curb and park and get out and pull off a single leaf to study" (187).

The description recalls Updike's short story "Pigeon Feathers," in which a precocious young boy whose family closely resembles the Caldwells finds the evidence of God's existence in the feathers of humble pigeons: "no two alike, designs executed, it seemed, in a controlled rapture, with a joy that hung level in the air above and behind him"(105). Similarly, the "clue" of one leaf provides Rabbit with a proof from design of the universe's divine origin. This experience echoes the scene at Jungle Gardens when the sight of the colorful flamingos causes Rabbit to feel "as if in the presence of something sacred" (103). Just as Peter Caldwell makes a leap of faith with a "little lie" and assures his father that he has gained faith from him, Rabbit avers that human beings are "upheld by nothing but our mutual reassurances, our loving lies" (264). Later, Janice, informing her husband that he has taught her to have faith "in life," concludes: " 'We'll be fine,' she lies" (409). Her lie echoes Peter Caldwell's assurance to his father that, despite considerable evidence to the contrary, all will be well.

In time, Rabbit gradually comes to accept that death is a stage in life. After his first heart attack, Rabbit sees with horror that "death is not a domesticated pet of life but a beast that swallowed baby Amber and baby Becky and all those Syracuse students and returning soldiers and will swallow him, it is truly there under him, vast as a planet at night, gigantic and totally his. His death" (176). Painfully, Rabbit, recalling his Sunday-school education, attempts to comprehend the termination of his individual consciousness: "A God-made one-of-a-kind with an immortal soul breathed in. A vehicle of grace. A battlefield of good and evil. An apprentice angel" (237). With difficulty, he struggles to reconcile this image of himself with the reductive description of human beings as "disposable meat" (18). Nevertheless, as he ages, he gradually accepts mortality. Observing a crippled woman in a wheelchair, Rabbit reflects, *"Nobody knows when to quit"* (97).

The sports arena provides evidence of the irresistible march of time: "And the weekend before last, a young black girl beat Chrissie Evert in the last U.S. Open match she'll ever play. She packed it in too. There comes a time" (488). Now Rabbit fully understands the divine "word" from Ecclesiastes, sung by Babe in *Redux:* "A time to be born, a time to die." On his drive south, Rabbit, as he listens to the evocative songs of his youth on the radio, recognizes that his earlier life is irrevocably over: "Though the stars recycle themselves and remake all the heavy atoms creation needs, Harry will never be that person again" (437). Rabbit notes the equanimity with which people accept the end of their lives: "A certain dignity in the doomed one, his or her moment come round at last; a finality that isolates the ensemble like a spotlit crèche. You would think people would take it worse than they do. They don't scream, they don't accuse God. We curl into ourselves, he supposes. We become numb animals. Earthworms on the hook" (422).

The weary Rabbit ultimately recognizes that in fact death is our certain destination. The "it" that for Rabbit has always stood for the transcendent is in fact mortality. In the throes of his first heart attack, Rabbit reflects, "Once Rabbit told someone, a prying clergyman, *somewhere behind all this there's something that wants me to find it.* Whatever it is, *it* has found *him,* and is working him over" (136). This recognition, rather than terrifying Rabbit, comforts him: "Yet he feels good, down deep. There is a satisfaction in his skyey enemy's having found him. The sense of doom hovering over him these past days has condensed into reality, as clouds condense into needed rain"(139). This last clause conveys the naturalness of death. As his doctors charge, Rabbit, by refusing to diet and exercise properly, poisons himself (474). Unheroically, his fondness for forbidden junk food causes Rabbit's death. After the fatal heart attack, Dr. Morris explains to Janice, "Sometimes it's time," and adds, "He seemed to have become a wee bit morbid" (509). Like Caldwell/Chiron readying his black Buick, Rabbit prepares himself for death. As the centaur's final destination is an honored place in Zeus' heavens, that of Rabbit, descended from Swedish Angstroms, is Valhalla Village, his Florida condo named after the home of Norse warriors slain in battle. Packing for the trip to Florida, he takes both a light- and dark- colored suit: "In case there's a wedding or a funeral" (435).

Like Caldwell, Rabbit, his continual use of nitroglycerin identifying him with the pharmakos, now embodies the scapegoat. As Caldwell "prepares his lessons," naming the rivers of the dead, so does Rabbit. On his journey, Rabbit crosses the American version of the Styx and the others: "How many rivers there are! After the Potomac, the Accotink, the Pohink, the Occoquan, the Rappahannock, the Pamunkey, the Ni, the Po, the Matta, the South Anna" (443). Thinking of Pru, Rabbit recognizes that a gap now divides him from her: "She is stuck back there, she is saying, with the living" (446). Like Caldwell, Rabbit enters a cave to die, although he, suggesting an afterlife, notices that "The red cave he thought had only a front entrance and exit turns out to have a back door as well" (511).

Rabbit, by accepting his fate, experiences Caldwell-like transcendence: for the centaur, "in the upright of his body Sky and Gaia mated again"; for Rabbit, "the nature of his exertion is to mix him with earth and sky" (504). As Rabbit lies unconscious on the ground, "Adhesive dust of fine clay," the image suggesting the human fate of dust to dust, creates "a shadow, like half of a clown's mask"; this sight impels Tiger, evoking the half-equine nature of Caldwell/Chiron, to exclaim in dismay, "Pure horseshit" (506). Grotjahn notes the significance of the clown figure in comedy: "The clown is the comic figure representing the impotent and ridiculed father. He also represents the sadness of things and finally comes to stand for death in the person of the truly great tragic clown. This is the point where tragedy and comedy finally meet and symbolize human life" (273). In the opening pages of *Rabbit, Run*, Rabbit notices a lost toy, a plastic clown, consigned to the dirt of his yard. Thirty years and four books later, the stricken Rabbit himself embodies the clown left for dead on the deserted playground. Over the course of the series, the motions of grace—manifested in his concern for his family—and the external circumstances of comedy have enabled Rabbit to mature. Updike leaves his dying hero, like George Caldwell, poised between this world and the next, as described in the epigraph from Karl Barth in *The Centaur:* "He himself is the creature on the boundary between heaven and earth." Rabbit is at rest.

· 6 ·

NELSON REDUX IN
"RABBIT REMEMBERED"

"The Function of Comedy Is to Sustain Hope."
— GALLIGAN, *The Comic Vision in Literature*

"The very nature of our life is toward happiness."

W hen "Rabbit Remembered," a novella set a decade after Rabbit's death, opens, Nelson, now 42, is living a life of quiet desperation. Deserted by his wife, Pru, who has returned to Ohio with their children, Judy and Roy, Nelson works as a therapist and lives in the Brewer home of his mother, Janice, now remarried to Rabbit's long-time nemesis, Ronnie Harrison. Nelson's plight resembles that of Rabbit in *Redux*: estranged from his wife and stuck in a dead-end job. Also, like Rabbit and Janice, Nelson and Pru have never had a third child. Ironically, Pru now works for a Greek lawyer, evoking Janice's liaison with Charlie Stavros in the earlier novel. Nelson's life begins to change with the arrival of Annabelle Byer, who one early fall day in 1999 shocks Janice by appearing at her doorstep with the news that she is Rabbit's daughter, born from his affair with Ruth Leonard in *Rabbit, Run*. The jarring reminder of this painful period in her life dismays Janice, but the reality that he has a live sister excites Nelson just as the hope that he had another daughter thrilled Rabbit in *Rabbit Is Rich*. After becoming acquainted with his new sister, Nelson invites her to attend the traditional Thanksgiving dinner that includes his mother, Ronnie, and Ronnie's grown children. In the meantime, he shares with Annabelle, a nurse, his experiences at work, especially his concern for a suicidal young man named Michael DeLorenzo.

Thanksgiving, however, ends up a disaster when after an argument over politics, the coarse Ronnie, his envy of Rabbit reignited by the presence of Annabelle, insults her and she and Nelson flee the gathering. This turn of events proves liberating for Nelson just as the fortyish Rabbit's departure from the same house does for him in *Rich*. At Christmas, with Pru and the children in Akron and Annabelle visiting Las Vegas, Nelson, despite having made peace with Ronnie, spends the holiday alone in his rented room rather than celebrate with his mother and the Harrisons. His new-found autonomy is tested, however, when he hears the devastating news that Michael DeLorenzo has taken his own life.

When Pru and Roy travel to Brewer for New Year's, Nelson arranges for his wife, Annabelle, and an old childhood friend, Billy Fosnacht, to celebrate the millennium together. While getting lost in an unfamiliar part of Brewer, Nelson becomes unnerved by his sense that his father's spirit is somehow present in the car. As midnight approaches, the couples find themselves stuck in traffic and menaced by an aggressive SUV. Desperate, Nelson, in his tiny Corolla, challenges the oversized vehicle and, narrowly averting disaster, succeeds in forcing the SUV to yield. This bold action, indicative of Nelson's new independence, not only exorcises the ghost of his father but also wins Pru back. The new century finds Nelson starting a new life: reconciled with Pru, living with his family in Akron, and looking for a house and a more fulfilling job. During a phone conversation with Annabelle, he learns that she and Billy will marry and that she wants him to give her away at the ceremony. As do all of the other novels in the series, "Rabbit Remembered" concludes with a one-word sentence, with Nelson accepting, "Gladly" (359).

"Rabbit Remembered" contains farce, burlesque, and irony. Years later, Nelson recalls the travesty of Rabbit's ashes being left behind in a motel room on the family's drive home from his funeral. Nelson burlesques Billy Fosnacht "as a comical old friend. Not only are his lips fat, his nose has gotten fat; it sits there in the middle of his face like something added" (325). Everyone laughs at Roy's memory of his grandfather: "when there was any candy or nuts around you had to compete with him for them—he'd steal a candy bar right from under your nose" (339); Annabelle, however, perceives the playful irony and thanks Roy for helping make her unknown father "real" to her. The comedy, however, cannot hide grim reality. Now, in the high-tech '90s, bad news is revealed not only on television and radio but on the Internet as well, including crude e-mail jokes exchanged between Roy and Nelson: "Remember when the Kennedys used to drown only one woman at a time?"(178). As in *The Centaur* and the other *Rabbit* novels, the news not only grounds the novella in a specific period of history, but it also reflects the problematic comic world. Learning of the Kennedy plane crash, Janice despairs:

The whole late summer was soured for Janice [. . .] by the Kennedy boy's having fallen from the sky with his poor wife and sister-in-law, they must have been screaming, screaming, hitting the water like a black wall. The news analysts said it just took seconds, but what seconds they must have been, how can you keep believing in a God that would let that happen, it took you back to the baby's drowning, such an innocent, well who isn't an innocent an innocent God might argue. All those Turks in the earthquake, tens of thousands sleeping in their beds at three in the morning. (210)

As in the other novels, however, personal experiences are more meaningful than world events. After learning of his patient's suicide, the downcast Nelson puts things in perspective. In the news, the Hubble Space Telescope has been repaired and a plane has been hijacked in India, but "Michael DeLorenzo is not mentioned. He is strictly local news" (333).

Eventually, Nelson will understand his place in society sufficiently to lecture Ronnie: "We're not hotshots but we're responsible citizens" (308). Like Rabbit, Nelson's return to health begins when he visits the revivifying green world. Here the green world is located at the site of Nelson's first meeting with his half-sister: The Greenery, a health food restaurant that lately, in the spirit of comic compromise, has relaxed its standards and begun serving hamburgers and hot dogs. Here, the theme is "greenery" (255) and the waitress wears a "green uniform" and on her own brings "green tea" because "it's good for you"; in response, Nelson agrees, "Green is great" (256). Paying the check, Nelson "stares into his wallet at the edges of gray-green money as if a miracle will sprout" (258).

On the restaurant's wall is a mural until now unnoticed by Nelson depicting amid ferns and bushes a boy and a girl "wearing old-fashioned German outfits, pigtails and lederhosen, holding hands, lost" (255). As in the Florida mural depicting the killing of an explorer that prefigured Rabbit's death in *Rest*, this painting of Hansel and Gretal represents Nelson and Annabelle, a brother and sister also adrift. Together, however, they will find their way. When they part, Nelson savors the thought of Annabelle, with italics indicating the intensity of his feelings, "*My Sister. Mine*" (258), echoing the end of *Rich*, when Rabbit delights in the existence of his granddaughter, "*Mine*." The siblings' second lunch at The Greenery is less successful, reflecting the fact that the green world is not a permanent home but an interlude before returning to reality.

As in the other books, a pharmakos figure appears. Billy Fosnacht's surname recalls the reference to the pariah "Fosnacht" that Rabbit in *Run* remembers from his childhood; moreover, Billy, as a young boy, is ridiculed by Skeeter in *Redux*. Also, there is the repeated suggestion that the schizophrenic Michael DeLorenzo kills himself to avoid murdering his parents (the family continually associated with the chemicals from its dry-cleaning business). The true scape-goat, however, turns out to be Annabelle. At the Thanksgiving dinner at which she is a reluctant guest, Annabelle's courage in defending President Clinton against most of those present subjects her to ridicule and hostility. One of Ronnie's grown sons, the gay dancer Georgie, and, most strongly, Nelson support her, but they are not the targets of the Harrisons' wrath: the former "is not the scapegoat they want today"; and "Nelson isn't the scapegoat they want either" (294–95). Viciously, the bitter Ronnie attacks Annabelle, wondering "how it felt being the bastard kid of a whore and a bum" (300). In effect, his de-grading scatological comments serve to undress her in public, recalling Peter Caldwell's nightmare of his father's being "naked" and jeered at by his towns-people. For the new Nelson to be born, the old must die and, given his close-ness to Annabelle, he shares her humiliation just as Peter had felt his father's shame. The three holidays depicted parallel the three days of Peter Caldwell's resurrection: in a sense, the old Nelson dies during the debacle at Thanksgiv-ing; at Christmas, alone and distraught, he suffers hell; and finally he is re-born, fittingly, at New Year's.

At Thanksgiving, the dinner conversation exemplifies the comic discussion from which truth emerges, with Ronnie portraying the bullying alazon figure, humiliating the helpless Annabelle, and Nelson representing the eiron who stands up to him. As the plain-speaking eiron deflating the alazon, Nelson per-ceives that the true cause of Ronnie's "Buried years of righteous resentment" is his unresolved rivalry with Rabbit: "You couldn't stand it, could you. My father beating you out everytime. You, you're a loser" (301). Annabelle is left "Numb, heaped with disgrace" (302), but this ugly episode has been a revelation for Nelson ("it was clarifying. It showed me what a pipsqueak leech I tend to be" [306]), just as the aftermath of Rabbit's lovemaking with his daughter-in-law, Pru, had provided him with a revelation. Now, Nelson too knows what to do: "'Well, we're going.' Nelson tells him [Ronnie]. 'This is it, Mom'" (302). As he leaves this house once and for all, images of the green world appear fleetingly: on the television, "A football game: green-and-white uniforms deploy on a bright-green ground" while on top of the set "a heavy pale green glass egg that since his earliest childhood seemed miraculous to Nelson" (303).

Like his father in *Rich*, Nelson's departure through the front porch, which he associates with his childhood, represents his finally crossing the boundary into adulthood: "The neighbors are away for the holiday and thus miss seeing the heir leave 89 Joseph Street for good" (303). The prepositional phrase ex-presses not only permanence but the beneficial nature of Nelson's decisive-ness. From this discussion, Janice also perceives what she means to her second husband: "a kind of revenge on Harry, and the possession of this house" (304). Nevertheless, she forgives him as Nelson ultimately does as well. When Janice prods Ronnie into calling Nelson to apologize, the two men finally clear the air between them: "This is the best conversation Nelson has ever had with Ronnie. His moving out has done that in just four days" (307). In effect, Nelson resolves an oedipal rivalry with his stepfather.

Nelson's autonomy will lead to his reconciliation with Pru as well: "moving out has given him a fresh footing with not only his stepfather but his estranged wife" who "had complained for years about living with his mother and Ronnie and about his dead end job" (312). As with Rabbit, Nelson's maturation proceeds in fits and starts. Like his father, Nelson cannot help but feel a rivalry with his son: "Roy, with his stern stare and upjutting button of a penis had a touch of the alien invader, the relentless rival demanding space, food, attention" (314). At the same time Nelson is haunted by his father, who appears in his dreams as a Sisyphean golfer, "Discouraged. But dogged" (278). Until Nelson matures, Rabbit's spirit cannot rest in peace. On his own, Nelson struggles with loneliness, the frustrations of his job, and his inadequate income. Michael DeLorenzo's suicide causes Nelson to despair as Rabbit does in *Rest:* "Nelson tastes the iron at the core of even green planets. No fresh start, no mercy" (344).

Organized religion offers no consolation. The only churchgoing mentioned is Ronnie's faithful attendance at "that no-name fundamentalist church" (304). As Rabbit learned, Nelson must find meaning in everyday life. Just as the older Rabbit began to behave like George Caldwell, Nelson begins to resemble his father: Janice "had been thinking of how much like Harry Nelson was" (298). Annabelle's appearance motivates Nelson to progress from the aesthetic to the ethical sphere of existence. He has the uncanny feeling that "she's something my father left me to take care of" (308). Nelson's fatherly e-mails to Roy and his dedication to his patients reveal his growing sense of responsibility.

True to comic tradition, Nelson's maturation proves liberating. Making the decision to strike out on his own bolsters his confidence. His recognition that prudence becomes irrelevant in the comic world is evident in his behavior during the climactic scene on millennium eve. Recalling the episode in *Rich* when he jars his father out of his rut by crashing cars on the Springer lot "comically fast," Nelson here risks a collision with a huge SUV driven by another bully, "Some brat of the local rich" who attempts to barge through an intersection "against all decency and order" (352). This scene in effect presents a vehicular version of an alazon/eiron confrontation. Nelson's boldness reflects the comic hero's willingness to cross the boundary between rationality and irrationality when necessary. His daring, as already noted, succeeds in winning Pru back and eventually results in Nelson's reuniting with his family. Reflecting the location of the transcendent within the mundane, "Christian-rock music thumps away in the vast illumined excavation on their right" (353). Earlier, he crossed another boundary when he cruelly forced Annabelle to admit that as a young girl she had been molested by her stepfather. Like Rabbit's lovemaking with Pru, Nelson's outrageous behavior here proves beneficial because revealing the truth helps lead to Annabelle and Billy's marriage since she now doesn't "have anything to hide from him" (358).

On that night, Nelson unconsciously retraces Rabbit's steps. Nelson's frustration in losing his way in Brewer while listening to Annabelle and Billy snuggling in the back seat recalls Rabbit's panicky failed drive south in *Run*, which left him lost in a lover's lane. As Nelson meanders through Brewer, he passes a number of locations significant in Rabbit's life: Kroll's Department Store, where Rabbit and Janice first met; Verity Press, where Rabbit worked and was laid off; Jimbo's Friendly Lounge, where Rabbit began his own return to health; Springer Motors, where Rabbit became prosperous; and even the Chinese restaurant that, unknown to Nelson, was the scene of Rabbit's first date with Annabelle's mother, Ruth Leonard. That all of these places no longer exist, except in memory, underscores the comic theme of the inevitable succession of generations. Symbolically, passing the deserted site of Springer Motors, "Nelson sees the ghosts of his father and himself and Charlie Stavros" (349). After the confrontation with the SUV, Nelson exorcises his father's ghost: "Nelson shivers as if a contentious spirit is leaving him" (353). Finally, Nelson's oedipal struggle with his father is over.

Fittingly for comedy, the novella—and thus the series—concludes with a happy ending: one marriage planned and another restored. Paradoxically, the boorish Ronnie provides a comic mantra with the quote from the book he gives Nelson at Christmas: "The very nature of our life is toward happiness" (357). With the mystery of Annabelle's identity finally resolved, Rabbit's fondest wishes are fulfilled: he has another daughter and Nelson has matured. Nelson, back with his family, is awed by his daughter's beauty as Rabbit had been in *Rich*. When Nelson hears of Annabelle's wedding plans, after some initial skepticism, he can only rejoice in his half-sister's happiness: "Happiness for her is already rising in him" (358). Symbolizing Nelson's maturation, Annabelle asks him to fill the role of his father and give her away at the wedding. Nelson's acceptance of this responsibility—the final word in the series, "Gladly"—expresses the joyful spirit of comedy. With Nelson's maturation from the aesthetic to the ethical sphere of existence, Updike concludes the series by uniting the two central figures of *The Centaur* and the *Rabbit* novels: the feckless rabbit has evolved into the responsible horse.

· CONCLUSION ·

WHAT UPDIKE'S COMEDY
HAS TO SAY

"Only Goodness Lives. But It Does Live."

—THE CENTAUR

"Accept the place the divine providence has found for you, the society of your contemporaries, the connection of events. Great men have always done so, and confided themselves childlike to the genius of their age, betraying their perception that the absolutely trustworthy was seated at their heart, working through their hands, predominating in all their being. And we are now men, and must accept in the highest mind the same transcendent destiny; and not minors and invalids in a protected corner, not cowards fleeing before a revolution, but guides, redeemers and benefactors, obeying the Almighty effort and advancing on Chaos and the Dark."

—EMERSON, "SELF-RELIANCE"

In his fiction, Updike heeds Emerson's exhortation to the American democrat. Both men recognize the contradictory nature of life; at the same time, they write from a religious perspective that seeks to make sense of human existence. By accepting their place in society ("the society of your contemporaries"), human beings conform to the wishes of "divine providence." From the everyday experience of "working through their hands," they discover the transcendent "predominating in all their being." Refusing to distance themselves from the turmoil of life ("not minors and invalids in a protected corner, not cowards fleeing before a revolution"), they fulfill their roles as "guides, redeemers, and benefactors." In particular, the use of the word "redeemers" implies that average men and women reenact a Christ-like sacrifice when they live for others. With faith ("confided") that is "childlike," they perceive an order that connects all life and overcomes the "Chaos and the Dark."

For each writer, the divine ("obeying the Almighty effort") manifests itself within a cyclic quotidian. In "Self-Reliance," "As soon as the man is at one with God, he will not beg. He then will see prayer in all action" (518). In *The Centaur*, "All joy belongs to the Lord" (220); In *Rabbit, Run*, "God rules reality" (140). Essentially, the twentieth century America of Updike's fiction does not differ from the one portrayed in Emerson's nineteenth century essay. True to the comic point of view, Emerson declares: "Society never advances." He elaborates: "It undergoes continual changes; it is barbarous, it is civilized, it is christianized, it is rich, it is scientific: but this change is not amelioration" (519). Instead, it is always the individual who must change, develop, and mature. Emerson emphasizes, "This one fact the world hates; that the soul *becomes*." Evolving, Updike's everyday heroes struggle through trial and error to find their way.

For Updike, the good person lives a comic morality. Human beings mature, or gain Kierkegaard's ethical sphere, by fulfilling their societal and generational responsibilities. Just as a joke establishes a relationship between apparently disparate elements, comedy discovers beneath the surface chaos a congruity where life becomes meaningful. In *Rabbit Redux*, Rabbit explains, "Confusion is just a local view of things working out in general" (405). By understanding his true place in time and the world, the comic hero recognizes the hollowness of selfishness. George Caldwell lives what Peter Caldwell struggles to assimilate and what Rabbit and eventually Nelson learn: through self-sacrifice, individuals attain what Emerson terms man's "transcendent destiny." Updike's linking of goodness with life in *The Centaur* is fitting: "Only goodness lives" (220). In Updike's comedy, human beings live fully when they lead good lives.

BIBLIOGRAPHY

Published Works by John Updike

The Afterlife. New York: Knopf, 1994.
"A Soft Spring Night in Shillington." *Self-Consciousness: Memoirs*. New York: Knopf, 1989.
Assorted Prose. New York: Knopf, 1965.
Bech: A Book. New York: Knopf, 1970.
Bech at Bay: A Quasi-Novel. New York: Knopf, 1998.
Bech Is Back. New York: Knopf, 1982.
Brazil. New York: Knopf, 1994.
Buchanan Dying. New York: Knopf, 1974.
The Carpentered Hen and Other Tame Creatures. New York: Harper & Brothers, 1958.
The Centaur. New York: Fawcett Crest, 1988.
Collected Poems 1953–1993. New York: Knopf, 1993.
Couples. New York: Knopf, 1968.
The Early Stories: 1953–1975. New York: Knopf, 2003.
Gertrude and Claudius. New York: Knopf, 2000.
Hugging the Shore. New York: Knopf, 1983.
In the Beauty of the Lilies. New York: Knopf, 1996.
Just Looking: Essays on Art. New York: Knopf, 1989.
Licks of Love. New York: Knopf, 2000.
Marry Me: A Romance. New York: Knopf, 1976.
Memories of the Ford Administration. New York: Knopf, 1992.
Midpoint and Other Poems. New York: Knopf, 1969.
A Month of Sundays. New York: Knopf, 1975.
More Matter: Essays and Criticism. New York: Knopf, 1999.
Museums and Women and Other Stories. New York: Knopf, 1972.
The Music School: Short Stories. New York: Knopf, 1966.
Odd Jobs: Essays and Criticism. New York: Knopf, 1991.
Of the Farm. New York: Knopf, 1965.
"One Big Interview." *Picked-Up Pieces*. New York: Knopf, 1975: 493–519.

Olinger Stories: A Selection. New York: Vintage, 1964.

Picked-Up Pieces: New York: Knopf, 1975.

"Pigeon Feathers." *Pigeon Feathers and Other Stories.* New York: Fawcett Crest, 1959: 84–105.

The Poorhouse Fair. New York: Knopf, 1959.

Problems and Other Stories. New York: Knopf, 1979.

Rabbit Angstrom: A Tetralogy. New York: Knopf, 1995.

Rabbit at Rest. New York: Knopf, 1990.

Rabbit Is Rich. New York: Knopf, 1981.

Rabbit Redux. New York: Knopf, 1971.

"Rabbit Remembered." *Licks of Love.* New York: Knopf, 2000: 177–359.

Rabbit, Run. New York: Fawcett Crest. 1993.

Roger's Version. New York: Knopf, 1986.

S. New York: Knopf, 1988.

The Same Door: Short Stories. New York: Knopf, 1959.

Seek My Face. New York: Knopf, 2002.

Self-Consciousness: Memoirs. New York: Knopf, 1989.

Too Far to Go. New York: Fawcett Crest, 1979.

Toward the End of Time. New York: Knopf, 1997.

Trust Me: Short Stories. New York: Knopf, 1987.

"Ungreat Lives." *Odd Jobs: Essays and Criticism.* New York: Knopf, 1991: 649–56.

"Why Rabbit Had to Go." *New York Times Book Review* 5 Aug. 1990: 1, 24–25.

The Witches of Eastwick. New York: Knopf, 1984.

Secondary Sources

Ahearn, Kerry. "Family and Adultery: Images and Ideas in Updike's Rabbit Novels." *Twentieth Century Literature* 34 Spring 1988: 62–83.

Apollodorus. *The Library.* Vols. I and II. Trans. Sir James George Frazer. Cambridge, MA.: Harvard University Press, 1954.

Auden, W.H. "Dingley Dell & The Fleet." *The Dyer's Hand and Other Essays.* New York: Random House, 1962: 407–28.

——. "Don Juan." *The Dyer's Hand and Other Essays.* New York: Random House, 1962: 386–406.

——. *The Dyer's Hand and Other Essays.* New York: Random House, 1962.

——. "The Globe." *The Dyer's Hand and Other Essays.* New York: Random House, 1962: 171–81.

Baker, Nicholson. *U and I: A True Story.* New York: Vintage Books, 1992.

Barber, C.L. "The Saturnalian Pattern in Shakespeare's Comedy." *Comedy: Meaning and Form.* Ed. Robert W. Corrigan. San Francisco: Chandler Publishing Company, 1965: 363–77.

Bergson, Henri. "Laughter." *Comedy.* Ed. Wylie Sypher. Garden City, NY: Doubleday & Company, Inc., 1956: 61–190.

Bloom, Harold, ed. *John Updike*. Modern Critical Views. New York: Chelsea House Publishers, 1987.

Boswell, Marshall. *John Updike's Rabbit Tetralogy: Mastered Irony in Motion*. Columbia, MO: University of Missouri Press, 2001.

Brenner, Gerry. "*Rabbit, Run:* John Updike's Criticism of the 'Return to Nature.'" *Twentieth Century Literature* 12 April 1966: 3–14.

Broer, Lawrence R., ed. *Rabbit Tales: Poetry and Politics in John Updike's Rabbit Novels*. Tuscaloosa, AL: University of Alabama Press, 1998.

Browning, Robert. "Pippa Passes." *Poetical Works 1833–1864*. Ed. Ian Jack. London: Oxford University Press, 1970.

Burchard, Rachel C. *John Updike: Yea Sayings*. Carbondale and Edwardsville, IL: Southern Illinois University Press, 1971.

Burke, Kenneth. *Attitudes Toward History*. Boston: Beacon Press, 1937.

Clinton-Baddeley, V.C. *The Burlesque Tradition in the English Theatre after 1660*. London: Methuen and Co., 1952.

Cornford, F.M. *The Origin of Attic Comedy*. Gloucester, MA: Cambridge University Press, 1968.

Corrigan, Robert W. "Aristophanic Comedy: The Conscience of a Conservative." *Comedy: Meaning and Form*. Ed. Robert W. Corrigan. San Francisco: Chandler Publishing Company, 1965: 353–62.

——. "Comedy and the Comic Spirit." *Comedy: Meaning and Form*. Ed. Robert W. Corrigan. San Francisco: Chandler Publishing Company, 1965: 1–11.

——, ed. *Comedy: Meaning and Form*. San Francisco: Chandler Publishing Company, 1965.

Detweiler, Robert. *John Updike*. New York: Twayne Publishers, Inc., 1972.

Donaldson, Ian. *The World Upside Down: Comedy from Jonson to Fielding*. Oxford: Clarendon University Press, 1970.

Duprey, Richard. "Whatever Happened to Comedy?" *Comedy: Meaning and Form*. Ed. Robert W. Corrigan. San Francisco: Chandler Publishing Company, 1965: 243–49.

Emerson, Ralph Waldo. "Self-Reliance." *Major Writers of America I*. Ed. Perry Miller. New York: Harcourt, Brace, & World, Inc., 1962: 510–21.

Feibleman, James. *In Praise of Comedy*. New York: Russell and Russell, 1962.

Freud, Sigmund. *Jokes and Their Relation to the Unconscious*. New York: Norton, 1966.

Frye, Northrop. *The Anatomy of Criticism*. Princeton, NJ: Princeton University Press, 1957.

——. *T.S. Eliot: An Introduction*. Chicago: The University of Chicago Press, 1963.

Fuchs, Daniel. *The Comic Spirit of Wallace Stevens*. Durham, NC: Duke University Press, 1963.

Gado, Frank. *Conversations with John Updike*. Schenectady, NY: Union College Press, 1971.

Galligan, Edward L. *The Comic Vision in Literature*. Athens, GA: University of Georgia Press, 1984.

Galloway, David D. *The Absurd Hero in American Fiction: Updike, Styron, Bellow, and Salinger*. Austin: University of Texas Press, 1966.

Graves, Robert. *Greek Myths* Vol.I. Baltimore: Penguin Books, 1955.

Greiner, Donald J. *John Updike's Novels.* Athens, Ohio: Ohio University Press, 1984.

Grotjahn, Martin. "Beyond Laughter: A Summing Up." *Comedy: Meaning and Form.* Ed. Robert W. Corrigan. San Francisco: Chandler Publishing Company, 1965: 270–75.

Gurewitch, Morton. *Comedy: The Irrational View.* Ithaca, NY: University Press, 1975.

Guyol, Hazel. "The Lord Loves A Cheerful Corpse." *English Journal* 55 1966: 863–66.

Halperin, John, ed. *The Theory of the Novel: New Essays.* Oxford: Oxford University Press, 1974

Hamilton, Alice and Kenneth. *The Elements of John Updike.* Grand Rapids, MI: Eerdmans Publishing Company, 1970.

Howard, Jane. "Can a Nice Novelist Finish First?" *Life* Nov. 4, 1966: 74–82.

Hunt, George. *John Updike and the Three Great Secret Things: Sex, Religion, and Art.* Grand Rapids, MI: Eerdmans Publishing Company, 1980.

James, William. "The Varieties of Religious Experience." *Writings 1902–1910.* New York: The Library of America, 1987: 1–469.

Kern, Edith. *The Absolute Comic.* New York: Columbia University Press, 1980.

Kierkegaard, Soren. *Concluding Unscientific Postscript.* Trans. David F. Swenson. Princeton, NJ: Princeton University Press, 1941.

Koestler, Arthur. *The Act of Creation.* New York: Dell Publishing Company, 1947.

Langer, Susanne K. "The Comic Rhythm." *Comedy: Meaning and Form.* Ed. Robert W. Corrigan. San Francisco: Chandler Publishing Company, 1965: 119–40.

Lucian. *The Works of Lucian,* Vol. II. Trans. A.M. Harmon. Cambridge, MA: Harvard University Press, 1915.

Lynch, William F. *Christ and Apollo.* New York: Sheed and Ward, Inc., 1960.

Macnaughton, William R., ed. *Critical Essays on John Updike.* Boston: G.K. Hall and Company, 1982.

Markle, Joyce. *Fighters and Lovers.* New York: New York University Press, 1973.

Martin, Robert Bernard. "Notes Toward A Comic Fiction." *The Theory of the Novel: New Essays.* Ed. John Halperin. Oxford: Oxford University Press, 1974: 71–90.

Marx, Leo. "Pastoral Ideals and City Troubles." *Journal of General Education* XX 1969: 251–71.

McCollom, William G. *The Divine Average: A View of Comedy.* Cleveland, OH: The Press of Case Western Reserve University, 1971.

McFadden, George. *Discovering the Comic.* Princeton, NJ: Princeton University Press, 1982.

Meeker, Joseph. *The Comedy of Survival.* New York: Charles Scribner's and Sons, 1972.

Meredith, George. "An Essay on Comedy." *Comedy.* Ed. Wylie Sypher. Garden City, NY: Doubleday & Company, Inc., 1956: 3–57.

Newman, Judie. *John Updike.* New York: St. Martin's Press, 1988.

Oates, Joyce Carol. "Updike's American Comedies." *Modern Fiction Studies* 21, 1975: 459–72.

O'Connell, Mary. *Updike and the Patriarchal Dilemma: Masculinity in the Rabbit Novels.* Carbondale, IL: Southern Illinois Press, 1996.

Polhemus, Robert W. *Comic Faith.* Chicago: Chicago University Press, 1980.

Potts, L.J. "The Subject Matter of Comedy." *Comedy: Meaning and Form.* Ed. Robert W. Corrigan. San Francisco: Chandler Publishing Company, 1965: 198–213.

Preminger, Alex , ed. *Princeton Encyclopedia of Poetry and Poetics.* Princeton, NJ: Princeton University Press, 1974.

Pritchard, William H. *John Updike: America's Man of Letters.* South Royalton, VT: Steerforth Press, 2000.

Richardson, Joan. *Wallace Stevens: The Early Years 1879–1923.* New York: Beech Tree Books, William Morrow, 1986.

——. *Wallace Stevens: The Later Years 1923–1955.* New York: Beech Tree Books, William Morrow, 1988.

Ristoff, Dilvo I. *John Updike's Rabbit at Rest: Appropriating History.* Modern American Literature Series, Vol. 18. New York: Peter Lang, 1998.

——. *Updike's America: The Presence of Contemporary American History in John Updike's Rabbit Trilogy.* American University Studies, Ser. 24: American Literature, Vol. 2. New York: Peter Lang, 1988.

Samuels, George J. *John Updike.* Minneapolis: University of Minnesota Press, 1969.

Santayana, George. "The Comic Mask and Carnival." *Comedy: Meaning and Form.* Ed. Robert W. Corrigan. San Francisco: Chandler Publishing Company 1965: 73–80.

Schiff, James A. *John Updike Revisited.* New York: Twayne Publishers, 1998.

——. "The Pocket Nothing Else Will Fill: Updike's Domestic God." *John Updike and Religion.* Ed. James Yerkes. Grand Rapids, MI: W.B. Eerdmans 1999: 50–63.

Scott, Nathan A. Jr. "The Bias of Comedy and the Narrow Escape into Faith." *Comedy: Meaning and Form.* Ed. Robert W. Corrigan. San Francisco: Chandler Publishing Company, 1965: 81–115.

Searles, George J. *The Fiction of Philip Roth and John Updike.* Carbondale, IL: Southern Illinois University Press, 1985.

Shakespeare, William. *As You Like It. The Complete Works of Shakespeare.* Ed. George Lyman Kittredge. Boston: Ginn and Company, 1936.

Stevens, Wallace. *The Collected Poems of Wallace Stevens.* New York: Alfred A. Knopf, 1964.

Sypher, Wylie. *Comedy.* Garden City, NY: Doubleday & Co., Inc., 1956.

——. "The Meanings of Comedy." *Comedy.* Ed. Wylie Sypher. Garden City, NY: Doubleday & Co., Inc., 1956: 193–258.

Taylor, Larry E. *Pastoral and Anti-Pastoral Elements in John Updike's Fiction.* Carbondale, IL: Southern Illinois University Press, 1971.

Thorburn, David and Howard Eiland, eds. *John Updike: A Collection of Critical Essays.* Englewood Cliffs, NJ: Prentice-Hall, 1979.

Tolstoy, Leo. "The Death of Ivan Ilych." *Literature: The Human Experience.* Ed. Richard Abcarian and Marvin Klotz. Shorter 8th ed. Boston: Bedford/St. Martin's, 2004: 976–1016.

Uphaus, Suzanne Henning. *John Updike*. New York: Frederick Unger Publishing Company, 1980.

Vargo, Edward P. *Rainstorms and Fire*. Port Washington, NY: Kennikat Press, 1973.

Wood, Ralph C. *The Comedy of Redemption: Christian Faith and Comic Vision in Four American Novelists*. Notre Dame, IN: University of Notre Dame Press, 1988.

Yerkes, James, ed. *John Updike and Religion*. Grand Rapids, MI: W.B. Eerdmans, 1999.

INDEX

**MODERN
AMERICAN
LITERATURE**
New Approaches

Yoshinobu Hakutani, *General Editor*

The books in this series deal with many of the major writers known as American realists, modernists, and post-modernists from 1880 to the present. This category of writers will also include less known ethnic and minority writers, a majority of whom are African American, some are Native American, Mexican American, Japanese American, Chinese American, and others. The series might also include studies on well-known contemporary writers, such as James Dickey, Allen Ginsberg, Gary Snyder, John Barth, John Updike, and Joyce Carol Oates. In general, the series will reflect new critical approaches such as deconstructionism, new historicism, psychoanalytical criticism, gender criticism/feminism, and cultural criticism.

For additional information about this series or for the submission of manuscripts, please contact:

Peter Lang Publishing
P.O. Box 1246
Bel Air, MD 21014-1246

To order other books in this series, please contact our Customer Service Department at:

800-770-LANG (within the U.S.)
(212) 647-7706 (outside the U.S.)
(212) 647-7707 FAX

Or browse online by series at:

www.peterlangusa.com